THE NEW
EVOLVED CHAKRAS

EXTRA-ORDINARY ASCENSION CHAKRAS FOR **THE NEW ERA**

VITAL SUBTLE BODY ANATOMY

INCLUDES:

NEW EARTHING CHAKRAS

NEW PSYCHIC CHAKRAS AND ANATOMY

NEW SIGNAL-SURVIVAL CHAKRAS

ADVANCED SOUL BODY ANATOMY

NADIS AND THE NEW GRIDDING SYSTEMS

NEW CHAKRA BALANCING FOR THE NEW ERA

AUTHOR: MYRA SRI

Healing Knowhow Publishing

www.myrasri.com

Copyright and Legal Notice

This Book is and the unique information contained herein is Copyright © 2014 and Beyond: Myra Sri (the 'Author'). All rights reserved worldwide.

Reproduction or translation of any part of this work beyond that permitted by section 107 or 108 of the 1976 United States Copyright Act without permission of the copyright owner is unlawful. Requests for permission or further information should be addressed to the Author. No part of this eBook may be translated or reproduced or transmitted in any form or by any means, electronic or mechanical, including photocopying, recording, or by an information storage and retrieval system without the express permission of the Author.

This publication is designed to provide accurate and Authoritative information in regard to the subject matter covered, based on the Author's experience, research, practice and understandings. The Author and publisher do not recommend anything contrary to common sense. If professional medical or nutritional advice or other expert assistance is required, the services of a competent professional person should be sought.

First Published as an electronic book in Australia 2016
First Printing, **August 2016**
Published by Healing Knowhow Publishing,
P.O. Box 126, Toukley, NSW 2263, Australia

National Library of Australia Cataloguing-in-Publication entry:

Sri, Myra, author

Title: The new evolved chakras : new earthing chakras, new psychic chakras and anatomy, new signal-survival chakras, advanced soul body anatomy / Myra Sri.

ISBN: 9780992392468 (paperback)

Notes: Includes bibliographical references.
Subjects: Chakras.
 Energy medicine.
 Mind and body.
 Mental healing.
 Spiritual healing.

Dewey Number: 131:

Acknowledgements

Thank you to my clients, students and colleagues for your encouragement to share my knowledge with a wider audience.

Thank you, Leonie, for your support, honest feedback and amazing confirmations in ways that were so different to mine.

***

Books By The Same Author

Energy Healing Secrets Series

Secrets Beyond Aromatherapy

Secrets Behind Energy Fields

Secret Truths to Health and Well-Being

The New Crystal Codes – Align to the New Incoming Energies

Guided Meditations at www.myrasri.com/new-healing-store

Amazon Series Reviews:

"Thrilled with the content of this book and I have read almost every aromatherapy book there is"

"I wonder why this book is not used as a textbook"

"Thanks to this eBook, I am teaching myself to rise above the conflict at work… these life skills are priceless!"

"This is an excellent, practical, down to earth book that is filled with simple techniques to get in touch with yourself, your own energy, what is affecting it and then how to do something about it."

"I found this book very informative and the techniques were simple and easy to follow. I would recommend it to anyone who does energy work."

CONTENTS

BOOK OVERVIEW 13

INTRODUCTION 15
   New Era Energy Healing Technology 17
   New Era Frequencies 17
   Ancient Egyptian, Atlantean, Mayan and Vedic Secrets - Upgrades 21
      Choosing to Avoid Confusion 23
      Priority Priority 26
   Quantum Science Meets Esoteric 28
   Soul Journey 29
   Different Chakras – Different Souls? 32
      Soul Streams or StarSeeds 32
   StarSeed Issues 34

IN THE BEGINNING 37
   The Background Story 37

THE CHAKRA SYSTEMS 39
   What are Chakras? 39
   The Physical 'In-Body' Chakras 40
   The 'Out-of-Body' Chakras 41
   Front and Back Chakras 41
   The Current Basic Chakra Systems 43
      The Main Chakra System 43
      Minor Chakra Systems 43
      Higher Chakra Systems 43
   The New Chakra Systems 44
   Differing Chakra Systems 44

WORKING WITH THE NEW CHAKRAS 45

BALANCING TECHNIQUES AND TOOLS 47
   Preparation 47
   Soul Registration 47
   Important Balancing Techniques 47

THE CURRENT CHAKRA SYSTEMS 55
MAIN CHAKRA SYSTEM 57
   MAIN CHAKRAS MODEL 57
      BASE CHAKRA 58
      SACRAL CHAKRA 58
      SOLAR PLEXUS CHAKRA 58
      HEART CHAKRA 59
      THE THROAT CHAKRA 59

THIRD EYE CHAKRA (BROW) 59
CROWN CHAKRA 60

MINOR CHAKRA SYSTEMS 61
    Minor Chakras Or Sub-Major Chakras 61
    Joints Chakras 62
  THE MINOR CHAKRAS 66

HIGHER OR UPPER CHAKRAS 69
    Higher Chakras List 70
    Higher Chakra Attributes and Functions 71
      Soul Star Chakra   - 8th 71
      Causal Chakra   - 9th 72
      Universal Gateway   - 10th 72
      Cosmic Connection   - 11th 72
      Divine Threshold – 12th 73

HARA SYSTEM 75
    Earth Star 77
    Tan Tien 77
    Core Star 77
    Soul Seat 78
    Soul Star Chakra 78
    Hara Line 79
  DYSFUNCTIONS IN HARA SYSTEM 81
    Dysfunction in The Soul Star 81
    Dysfunction in The Soul Seat 81
    Dysfunction in The Core Star 82
    Dysfunction in The Tan Tien 82
    Dysfunction in The Earth Star 83
    Dysfunction in The Hara Line and Its Points 83

AURA, HARA AND RECALIBRATION ANATOMY 85
  Shock or Trauma Issues in Chakras 86

NEW EVOLVED CHAKRAS AND ANCHORING ANATOMY 87
  EXISTING MODELS 88
    New Developing Anatomy 89

THE NEW EARTHING CHAKRAS **and ANATOMY** 91
  Section Agenda: 91
  Current Earthing System 92
    Stage 1 92
    Stage 2 94
  First Things First 96
    Preparation to Work with the New Evolved Earthing System 96

THE NEW EARTHING CHAKRAS and EARTHING CHAKRA MATRIX 99
   Working with the New Evolved Earthing Chakra Modules and Their Light Frequencies 99
   Healing the Earthing Chakras 101
      Initial Activation 102
      Healing a previously balanced Chakra 103
   Order to the System. 104

1 – 5: THE RECALIBRATION 105
      Keywords 105
      Working with The Recalibration 105
   Development of the First Five Earthing Chakras 107
      Sequence of the Formation and Development of the First Five Earthing Chakras: 107
   Module 1 – Earthing Chakras 111
   Anatomy of 'The RECALIBRATION' Earthing Chakras 1-5 112
   Recalibrations Chart – Connections 113
   Earthing Chakra Nadis or Cord 114
   First Earthing Chakra 116
      Keywords 116
      Chakra Clues 116
      Connections 116
      Key Chakra Codes Statements 117
   Second Earthing Chakra 118
      Keywords 118
      Chakra Clues 119
      Connections 119
      Key Chakra Codes Statements 119
   Third Earthing Chakra 121
      Keywords: 121
      Chakra Clues 122
      Connections: 122
      Key Chakra Codes Statements 122
   Fourth Earthing Chakra 123
      Keywords 124
      Chakra Clues 124
      Connections 124
      Key Chakra Codes Statements 124
   Fifth Earthing Chakra 126
      Keywords 127
      Chakra Clues 127
      Connections 128
      Key Chakra Codes Statements 128
First Module: Anchoring 129
   Perform the Calibration Anchoring 130
      Calibration Statements 130
      Connections 130
      Key Chakra Codes Statements 130

1 - 8: THE PLATFORM 133

The Platform Chart - Connections	134
6 – 8: THE PLATFORM - Overview	135
Keywords:	135
Working with The Platform	135
Healing the Platform Chakras	137
6TH Earthing Chakra	137
7th Earthing Chakra	138
8th Earthing Chakra	138
Sixth Earthing Chakra	140
Keywords	141
Chakra Clues	141
Connections	143
Key Chakra Codes Statements	143
Seventh Earthing Chakra	144
Keywords	144
Chakra Clues	145
Connections	145
Key Chakra Codes Statements	145
Eighth Earthing Chakra	147
Keywords	148
Chakra Clues	148
Iron Suplementation	149
Connections	149
Key Chakra Codes Statements	150
Healing the Eighth Chakra	150
Establishing the Platform:	152
Anchoring 'The Platform' Earthing Chakras 1-8	153
Key Code Statements	153
Notes on The Platform	154
Transducer Benefits	154
Compromised Earth Healers	154
Connections	155
Soul Choices	155
9 – 11: THE HIGHER FUNCTION	157
THE HIGHER FUNCTIONS: CHART	158
The Higher Function – 9th – 11th Overview	159
Ninth Earthing Chakra	160
Keywords / Main Purpose	160
Chakra Clues	160
Connections	161
Key Chakra Codes Statements	161
Tenth Earthing Chakra	164
Keywords / Main Purpose	164
Chakra Clues	164
Connections	165
Key Chakra Codes Statements	165

Eleventh Earthing Chakra 167
    Keywords / Main Purpose 168
    Initial Action of 11th Earthing Chakra 168
    Connections 168
    Chakra Clues 168
    Key Chakra Codes Statements 169
    11th And 12th Chakras now Established 171

12: THE FUTURE 173
Stargate; 'Future' 174
Twelfth Earthing Chakra 175
    Keywords / Main Purpose 176
    Connections 177
    Chakra Clues 177
    Connections 177
    Key Chakra Codes Statements 177
The New Earthing Chakras Assembly to Twelfth Earthing 179
The Higher and Earthing Chakras 180
A Word on our Earth / Gaia 181

THE NEW PSYCHIC CHAKRAS and ANATOMY 183
Section Agenda: 183
The New Evolved Psychic Anatomy 184
Sensitive Trap 185
Shifts and Changes 188
    Navigating With New Tools 189
    Old School Psychic Structure Information 190
The New Evolved Psychic Anatomy 191
    Spiritual and Psychic 192
    Psychic Anatomy 194
    The New Psychic Chakras and its Subtle Body Anatomy 195
    Psychic Body And Its Purpose 196
    For LightWorkers or Just For 'Psychics'? 198
Psychic Body Basics 200
    Current Psychic Anatomy Understandings 200
Psychic Body Foundation – Middle Pillar / Core 203
Psychic Body Anatomy – The Head 205
    The Antennae, 'Psychic Horns' or Horn Antennae 207
    Transpersonal Chakra 210
    Third Eye-s Chakra 212
    Eye Chakras 213
    Ear Chakras 214
    Ear Filters 214
    Nose and Mouth Chakras 216
    Nose Chakra 216
    Mouth Chakra 217
    Throat Chakra 217

- Shoulder Transducer Chakras 217
- Master Chakras 218
  - Psychic Head Chakras 218
  - Crown Psychic Function 220
  - Psychic Centres In The Brain 220
  - Spatial Chakras 221
- Psychic Chakras in the Body 222
  - The Throat Connection Point 223
  - Back of the Neck Connection Point 224
  - Core Star Connection Point, Front and Rear 225
  - The Navel Connection Point 225
- Gateway Chakras 226
  - Shoulder Transducers Chakras 228
  - Spatial Chakras 229
  - Mid-Shins Chakra 230
- Psychic Body Chakra Links 231
- SUMMARY - Psychic Body Chakra List 234
- Healing the PSYCHIC Chakras 236
  - Balance and Calibrate the Psychic Body 236
- Psychic Body Connections; Astral and Soul Bodies 238
- Some Considerations; 240

THE NEW SIGNAL CHAKRAS and ANATOMY 243
- Signal / Survival Chakra System Overview 243
- Survival Chakras 244
  - Shock and Survival 244
  - Dealing with Survival, Shock and 'In-Crisis' Frequencies 245
  - Repeat Shock 246
  - Shock Alerts, Signals and Alarms 246
  - Tribal and Culture Resonances 247
  - Recognition and Anchoring of Being and Anatomy 247
- Healing the Signal Chakras 248
  - Use Compatible Energy 248
  - Using The Signal Information To Rebalance. 249
  - Forms and Types of Shock 249
  - Shock Keywords 250
  - Resonances of Shock 252
  - Meridians 253
  - Shock Law 254
- Affirmations 254
- Healing Procedure 255
  - Identify Shock 255
    - Shock Indication – The Test 256
    - Shoulder 'Shock Tap' Position 257
  - Colour Frequencies 257
  - SKELETAL REGISTRY - Shock Points 258
    - Front of Body 258

Process, Purpose and Intention 260
    Order sequence 260
    Energise And Reconnect.. 260
    Reconnection... 260
    Shock 'Skeletal' Positions and Levels 262
Colour Frequency Chart 264
    Skeletal Registry Colours 264
    Positions plus Overall Keyword or Tone 265
    Colour, Keywords and Meanings Behind 'Shock'... 265
    Front Or Back 266
Hand Position Combinations Sequences 267
    Initial Sweep 267
    Shock Balance Positions 267
    Sequence 1.. 268
    Secondary Balance Positions... 269
    Other Positions.. 269
    Final Position 269
    Sequence 2 270
    Other Balance Support 271
The Crown Point 271
Sensory and Recognition Survival System 272
    Face Aspects... 272
    Sensory Chakras Positions / Keywords:... 274
    Other Balance Support 274
    Sensory Considerations... 274
    Secondary Signal / Survival Chakras 276
    Secondary Chakra Considerations 277
Signal Chakras Quick Reference Charts... 278
    Front 278
    Back.. 279
    Sensory Aspects 280
    Affirmation Ideas.. 281

THE NEW ADVANCED SOUL BODY ANATOMY 283
    Soul Registration 285

NADIS AND THEIR FUNCTIONS.. 287
    What Are Nadis?... 287
    Human Nadis 289
    Chakra Nadis 289
    Auric Nadis 290
    The Aura 292
    Planetary Nadis.. 293
    Universal Nadis 293
    Galactic Nadis... 294

GRIDDING SYSTEMS 295
- Brain Gridding System 297
- Heart Gridding System 298
- Link (Chakra) Gridding System 301
- Family Organism Gridding System 302
  - Families: or Types of Families 302
- Planet/ary Gridding System 303
- New Galactic Gridding System 305

EXTRA-ORDINARY CHAKRAS 306
- Link Chakra 306
- Relational Chakras 307

PREPARING TO WORK WITH THE NEW CHAKRAS 309
- Light Channels, Filters, Blocks 310
- Clearing Blocks and Filters 314
  - Blocks; 314
  - Implants; 315
  - Filters; 315

AFFIRMATIONS: 316
- Soul Healing Registration 316
- General Affirmation Ideas 316
- General Earthing Chakra Statements 316
- Psychic Affirmations 316
- Shock Affirmations 317
- Signal Affirmations 317

SUMMARY – Evolution or Enlightenment 318
- Spiritual Power, Not Force 319

PUTTING IT ALL TOGETHER 321

FAQ's 323
- I heard that there are many more Chakras above the head – how come? 323
- Will there be a further increase in the number of Higher Chakras? 324

GLOSSARY 326

Further Information 329
- About the Author 330
  - Energy Healing Secrets Series 333

Book Overview

THE NEW ERA

- INTRODUCTION and BACKGROUND

CURRENT CHAKRA SYSTEMS

- MAIN (MAJOR) CHAKRA SYSTEM
- MINOR CHAKRA SYSTEMS
- HIGHER CHAKRA SYSTEMS
- HARA SYSTEM

NEW EVOLVED CHAKRAS AND ANCHORING ANATOMY

- THE NEW EARTHING CHAKRAS and ANATOMY
- THE NEW PSYCHIC CHAKRAS and ANATOMY
- THE NEW SIGNAL CHAKRAS and ANATOMY
- ADVANCED SOUL BODY ANATOMY
- NADIS
- GRIDDING SYSTEMS
- EXTRA-ORDINARY CHAKRAS

F.A.Q's

GLOSSARY

FURTHER INFORMATION

INTRODUCTION

If you have found this book, then it may well be that you are ready to begin a journey like no other. One that will take you into a new knowing of yourself and of your energetic and subtle body anatomy.

For some time, we have been undergoing major changes in response to not only where we find our self in time and in space, but also in our own personal Soul evolution and journey. Some of us may feel that we have experienced certain things before, a kind of déjà vu experience, whilst others may also feel that inner resonance with some of the dramas being played out on a familial level, communally, socially, nationally and globally. Add to this mix our extension of consciousness to other worlds or realities and the possibilities of other cosmic families, and we have come a long way from the hunter-gatherer and his generally localised concerns of merely feeding his family and community to a very different awareness of multi-functioning and multi-level activities and thoughts.

It became apparent to me personally after the turn of the century that something momentous was happening in our energetic systems. Searching and researching, I began to receive answers to the questions I had as to these etheric changes and impacts that I was perceiving. New information began to accumulate over the following years and as I documented all of the things I was discovering, a different picture emerged as to our human Chakra systems.

In short, etherically and energetically, the existing Chakras and the Chakra systems were being added to, upgraded if you like. It also became clearer that through the advent of the current New Era Energy frequencies, both Galactic and Earth driven, we were developing and Evolving *new* Chakras and *new* energy systems.

Besides our current Chakras, it appeared that included in these 'new' Chakras were actually other Chakras that were already pre-existent, but that had been suppressed, inaccessible, interjected or disconnected. The stories as to how these deactivations in certain evolved beings had taken place are too numerous to document here, and cover many spans of times, species, experiences, incarnations and planets.

Whatever our personal incarnational history, we are now in the time of reactivating and reconnecting these ancient Chakras and of establishing the new Chakra systems, as they are essential to our full spiritual development and etheric evolution.

The focus of this book is on these re-emerging Ancient Chakras and the extra and extra-ordinary New Evolving Chakras. The time is right for this information to be revealed.

Many people today are undergoing huge changes, and as their destiny unfolds and their Soul evolves, their subtle body anatomy can now develop and mature. This then leads to more unfolding and developing, until the correct energy crescendo is reached for their lift to another level or dimension, in whatever form that may take

NEW ERA ENERGY HEALING TECHNOLOGY

For some time we have been becoming more and more aware of the Higher Chakras that exist above the head. These beautiful Light transformers have been further evolving and aiding in the alignment of the higher energies and supporting those Souls who are following a spiritual journey. Alongside these, other Chakras have also been evolving, though at a slightly slower rate. However, it would seem that with the advent of the new century and coinciding with the advent of the new millennium, the Earthing Chakra system came of age. Their purpose is to not only anchor and balance the Higher Chakras, but also to provide a greater assimilation of the varying energies that challenge us as we move from purely 3D energies and anchor 4D energies. And for some this also means their greater ability to safely anchor 5D energies and beyond.

NEW ERA FREQUENCIES

What do I mean when I use the term 'The New Era Energies' or 'New Era Frequencies'? This means simply that I am referring to the new currently existing and further new incoming frequencies that have been impacting our planet and human consciousness for some time now, and more particularly since the turn of the century – there is not a precise date to their arrival, simply a gradual shift that became more obvious and manifest. As with all new things, there is a time 'before' or a pre-existence of a state, then a time of actualising when something is taking form but has not yet fully formed, then there is the time of reality or concretisation in matter of what was intended or inevitably happening. Or in this case – a concretisation and crystallisation in Etheric Matter.

In nature and by observation, we are instructed as to the action of waves... there usually tends to be waves preceding the sea tide that moves toward and forward in an ever increasing persistence to eventually create the high tide... so in energetic tides there is a correspondence that is energetically experienced as a state of becoming in gradual increments before the result of the full tide energy frequencies - and these frequencies or energy waves bathe one's senses energetically and so can be felt, yet not fully understood until the final picture, if you like, becomes clearer and the full tide of these energies has arrived and established itself. So it has been with the new incoming energies.

It is said that the planet herself exists with her own energy shifts – for a season of time she operates on an In-breath, and for another period of time she resorts to an Out-breath. As she moves, she breathes, and as she breathes the great Cosmos also breathes...

You may have heard of this description of shifts and changes in the Planet herself, which would also contribute to some of the energetic shifts we feel as one type of planetary frequency meets another celestial frequency.

In ancient cultures there have been many comparable predictions of ages and of times or eras. Many theories circulate about calendars, beginnings and endings, and there are some excellent records or translations of existing ancient writings that provide some light on our true human history and our possible futures.

According to the ancient Vedic Scriptures, the Planet has been completing her difficult journey through the Kali Yuga which lasts for around 26,000 years. Our Planet travels ever onwards around the Sun – Sol, and in her journeying orbits in a spiral dance with the other family members of our Solar System.

Whilst she engages in this dance, she is also continually moving, together with her family, in a spiral dance with other Galaxies. So this Solar Family is rotating and turning, dancing its rotary dance whilst also moving with the Galaxies of the Milky Way around even larger Star and Cosmic Systems.

All of this circular motion takes place around another central body commonly called the Great Central Sun. At the same time as these travelling revolutions are taking place, huge amounts of space are being covered that have not been occupied previously, for Planet Earth never revisits the exact same place and position in Space as she did before – her spiral wiggles prevent her from a simple orbit and well-worn orbital tracks – so each moment of each day we are embracing and experiencing a new place and space in the Celestial Ethers, even though the view from our window still embraces our familiar planets and stars – our Solar System is travelling as a celestial tribe in Space.

This brings new Space Winds, and 'fresh' vibrations. And in some cases, really ancient vibrations – for who knows who or what occupied that exact same place in Space long before we did? And our view and connection with the other Galaxies and Cosmic bodies may also be in a different relationship, as these too contain their own orbits. Each planet, each heavenly body, because of its composition and unique orbit and action, can leave trails and traces as they too move through the heavens.

This creates unique vibrations and etheric traces which are similar to being in a huge ocean with a variety of flotillas of various sailing vehicles – some leave oil behind, some leave detritus, some leave a clean wake, some leave the sound of dancing and celebration, some leave a sense of doom and fear. Planetary masses have their own unique frequencies and vibrations and can leave 'ghosts' of these energies and frequencies which we can then experience as our reality in their wake and these traces of energies meet and impact on each other.

Even though it takes 26,000 for this long journey, at the end of it we will not be in exactly the same place as we were before we started, though we may well be in the same relational aspects with our neighbours as we were before. We will all have moved.

Like a large wide spiral staircase, the lower spiral does not meet up in a similar position at the end of its spiral, nor on the same floor, but progresses to the next floor, then the next, and so on. So does our spiral dance lead us to different levels.

This movement impacts on everything on our planet. And on us as its inhabitants. And especially on those who are aware, conscious and sensitive to it. This is so even though the rest of the inhabitants will necessarily also be dragged along as well, whether they feel or notice the passing celestial and cosmic vibrations or not.

These shifts and progressions have caused evolutions within our own energy bodies, with ancient memories being triggered for many in some part our consciousness. These triggers can cause an evolution, or an opportunity for growth and release. Or release and growth. Or it may trigger unresolved issues that are relived, and that need to be addressed.

Shifts in human consciousness through these energetic activities and activations provide us with a new opportunity for the better. Though as well it can also provide for further resistance by those still not ready to progress.

Alongside all of these energies and shifts of energies, the actual energetic results of these impacts further creates new waves that get added to or that further multiply energetic movement, almost like cross-waves from many boats in a now turbulent harbour which was once relatively smooth.

This is not to say that our Earth's passage through space and time has ever been smooth, but that it is now somewhat different, and in some ways possibly more complicated.

However, this is not the subject here, simply some background to what is occurring or recurring that impacts the human state, our energetic experiences, our consciousness ultimately, and probably our future – depending on how we all choose to handle it.

Ancient Egyptian, Atlantean, Mayan and Vedic Secrets - Upgrades to the Current Chakra Systems

Along with all of this action, this movement, this awakening or shaking of humanity on many levels, along with all of this, we have - like raw seeds in hard cold ground - been growing and developing and re-activating new Chakras and anatomy to further support our journey, our evolution and our experience.

The beauty of all of this change and potential, even though one may have to initially look for it, is that for many Souls their energy bodies are undergoing a re-membering, as well as an evolution. For those of us who have been around at certain times in Earth history or in Cosmic history previously, we will be re-connecting some of the dots again, as bits of ancient knowing or anatomy re-emerge for acknowledgement and assimilation. We are growing as well as re-discovering.

During the discovery process and subsequent mapping of the New Earthing Chakras, I received impressions from Ancient Times. It became apparent that in times past, some of this current subtle body anatomy and evolution activity was foreseen and indeed in some Higher Souls, already activated. Because a lot of ancient knowledge has been misdirected, lost, destroyed or hidden, it is hard to trace exactly what was known and understood by whom. Or indeed when. It is my suspicion that some of us have been in this situation before; possibly in a previous incarnation or journey on a previous Planet similar to Earth, yet in circumstances that prevented full evolution and that was somewhat prematurely arrested ... And we are again presented with the opportunity to fulfill obligations, resolve past residual karma and finally pass Initiation into Ascension. There are of course, other explanations of where we each currently find ourself, and other stories to be told, and indeed that have been told.

Throughout ancient human history, pockets of consciousness have been aware of some of these things (I hesitate at this point to suggest that all parts came together completely at any one time for this would have probably made a huge difference in human consciousness – which is currently not apparent) but certainly the mystery schools and the esoteric schools of the initiates may well have known of some of the secrets and energetic techniques and anatomy that are emerging in current times and that are more readily available for those on a serious journey to seek and to find.

In the journeying with these new Chakras, I came to realize that there were bits from different eras, different cultures, overlaps of knowledge and understanding and it was a task to find exactly which bit went with which ancient system.

The advanced Mystery Temples and Schools of the Initiates had many secrets, skills and techniques that were passed down through the ages. But there is no guarantee anywhere that these still exist in their original fullness, integrity and completeness – cultures have been destroyed, floods and disasters have changed the course of nations and histories, wars have made their marks, and dictators and greedy empires have wrought havoc with what would possibly have been our spiritual inheritance.

In part, because we are in a new Space-Place in the Cosmos, the effect of the Chakras will be interpreted in a new way anyway, so we would be better benefitted if we focus on the Chakra anatomy and the functions rather than on the actual nth degree of their history. Suffice it to say that I had experiences of Ancient Egypt together with symbols, messages, hieroglyphics as well as seeing the Ancient Guardians whilst some of this information was emerging – I was re-membering. Also during these explorations confirmation came through regarding the Atlantean rememberings and the culmination of the Long Count Mayan Calendar seemed to cement some of the information and understandings.

Let me reiterate, at the risk of sounding contradictory, that I feel that for many this is mostly new and evolved Chakra information, whilst for those Souls who have long journeyed, it is a time of re-discovering, re-membering and re-activation.

If for some, our anatomy had simply 'fallen asleep' or never been correctly activated, then we would be hard put to be aware of it anyway. However if this was already revealed to a select few back in ancient times, and I myself was having flash-backs about this as well, then I cannot deny origins that are other than of today.

To put it in a different context, the anatomy was enhanced and available for a select few, possibly of a particular StarSeed or Genetic group back then.

As with many secrets, knowledge has been hidden, or lost.

It is also possible that the consciousness of man has been affected in such a way that he could not remember what was rightfully his in the first place. Was this overlay of 'forgetting' caused by the emergence of the worst of man's proclivities and lusts and power-fits? Was there some agenda or power behind certain human individuals that was intent on robbing or preventing mankind from connecting with his true and right potential and possibility?

In some ways, we have been given a fresh sheet as it were, to achieve and evolve; but within each of us, old ancient memories may stir and ancient resonances again rear to be reconciled or resolved. This is an extremely significant time in the history of humanity and of consciousness… And for some it will be completion time of their earlier Egyptian trainings. For others, their arrested Atlantean and Lemurian progressions can be completed. And the students and initiates of the Temples of Mithra and the early Mayan spiritual postulates can complete their esoteric and spiritual upgrades.

The New Evolving Chakras will therefore comprise some of the ancient systems, though apart from the Earthing Chakras and some of the Psychic Chakras I cannot for sure say exactly which came first. For as I mentioned before, these new systems were revealed to me over a period of time starting in 2001 when I first became aware that what we knew was not all that there was, and the Chakras began to make themselves known to me. What I do know is that we are in a time where we can re-member, re-connect, activate, initiate and utilize this advanced energetic anatomy and evolved vibrational structuring.

And benefit from them!

Choosing to Avoid Confusion

There are many Higher Chakra and Extra Chakra models out there, and I have recognised some of these as Arcturian, Sirian, Pleiadian etc.

For the purposes of this book, I outline the **Human** Evolved Chakra systems and relevant current Human Chakras. Some of these have their root and basis from Mayan, Ancient Egyptian, and other long-forgotten times, but much of these are all part of the *Human* Chakra system. The actual advanced and evolved Chakras are part of *Humanity's* evolution, advancement, maturation and essential technology in this current age.

If one is familiar with other Chakra systems, or has found some of their Chakras or their identification names as part of the issue they are faced with, then by all means, deal with them using the information you have to hand.

But after this, it is wise to ensure that the client's energy systems are reinstalled or correctly equipped with the correct *Human* Chakra anatomy. To do otherwise may quite possibly cause them to continue to be trapped by debilitating, limiting or long-past etheric equipment and energy systems that will not support them so well as a human at this time on this Planet.

An energetic system that was once legitimately one's StarSeed heritage may well not now be sufficient to currently equip one with correct function for this life-time as a Human. I have come across many who make claims of their past cosmic Origins, but if truth be told, most of us possess similar stories. Does it really matter? Do I need to re-iterate my own personal Soul history credentials; for what difference would that make to the knowledge of the correct current evolved *Human* Chakra system, really? Are we here to establish another civilisation on the Planet, or to assist in Humanity's evolution on this Planet in its own right?

Others have already outlined or attempted to chart the Higher Chakras that reside above the Crown Chakra, and there are a variety of models to choose from. Even though there is an overview of the system I use included in this book, there is no need to go into greater depth here as there are already many books currently available on individual systems.

The important points and functions of these Chakras of the Higher System that I think are most relevant to the Human Chakra system are summarised. These Chakras are an essential component for the correct activating and anchoring of the newer evolved Chakras. Using another Chakra model or system, no matter the species of origin or their perceived accuracy, will not necessarily guarantee correct human energy anatomy alignment and functionality.

When facilitating with Chakra Systems of another species or from other origins and installing them or maintaining them in current human esoteric anatomy, confusion may remain for the Soul who does not know how to align or harmonise both systems within their being.

It takes an advanced Soul to be able to use or apply correct application of another system in a way that allows the intellect, capacity and energetic intelligence to note and correct any differences for continued or enhanced Human functionality.

When a client presents in a session with issues related to other Chakra systems, a good question may be – where to start?

How does one decide what Chakra or system to work with first? Or indeed, what *issue* to work with first? Is there a choice?

I trust that I have already answered the first part of this question but to ensure that there is no misunderstanding, I will address the question again.

'How does one decide what Chakra or system to work with first?'

If one is seeking to complete this life time's Soul journey as a Human (no matter their Soul Source), it is my opinion that one must ultimately return to the Human Chakra system model. Having worked with, and used personally, various other systems myself, it has been my own personal discoveries of the systems I outline in this book that have equipped me better to ride my journey as a StarSeed in human form. If I am driving a Ford, it is best to use a Ford manual and spare parts. If I am driving a Rolls-Royce, it is best to utilise a Rolls-Royce manual. No matter the qualification or status of the driver, each make or model of vehicle is individual and this must be acknowledged. If an upgrade has occurred, and new modifications been acquired, then it is best to utilise the appropriate manual dedicated for the vehicle in question. And our physical vehicle is a **Human** one.

In answer to the latter question – '...*What issue to work with first?*' I always work with the priorities of a given situation. These priorities are often set by the client's current state, not just their desires... it is no use me fixing their money situation if they are in pain and unable to think pain-free. Mostly the issues are related... the client is usually paying you for a particular outcome so considering *all* aspects preventing this are best included in one's approach.

Testing or agreeing on what the main priority for the session is and working towards that gives a context for the priority issues to be identified. Recognising that not *all* issues can be cleared with *all* clients on *all* occasions in just the one session frees one up to focus on creating safely and effectively the largest shift and change that is possible for them right now in their ongoing experience or toward their desired life outcome.

PRIORITY PRIORITY

In practical terms in my own practice, when I am faced with a physical issue (or indeed any issue), I have organised a form of protocol that I apply which identifies the Priority Issue of what the client requires.

Bear in mind that there can be several priorities that need looking at to get the best long term results, so my actual mindset is in noting the various priority issues, but then questioning further and seeking for the ultimate initial *Priority* - the *current* top level *Priority* of *all* of the available priorities; the *Priority priority* - that will achieve the most results, the safest results and the best results.

Some priorities can change if they are the symptoms of another priority issue. (For example the memory or overlay of another Chakra or etheric body system that is overriding the client - which needs to be cleared to get to a more authentic list of priorities personal to the client.) Finding the priorities that are causing the most debilitating problems will not only reduce the *number* of priorities, with the associated symptoms and the most momentum toward a *healing* state, it will also demonstrate to the body that it can change for the better in an elegant and speedier way; this can also encourage a different mindset and physical experience that supports a deeper changed perception and healing for the client, on all levels, from the *past* state.

The *Priority* priority can be on any level. For example, it may be *physical*; to support any upcoming positive energy changes and adjustments – it may be *emotional*; finding balance to make energetic 'space' to allow for further energetic challenges that would have swamped the available emotional resources of the client – it may be *energetic*; supporting the Chakras to a balance before creating changes rather than create further upset in an already compromised situation – it may be *spiritual*; cleansing out what is damaging or compromising the clients own inner connection within themselves.

Finding what the body and being requires for the most elegant results means being open to what their immediate and top level Priority is.

On the physical level for many, this can mean that their hydration is *the* top *Priority* priority that requires attention, and correcting and enhancing this will bring into alignment all of the other digestive and associated physical processes dependent on correct fluid balance and availability in the body.

Which also means that the brain begins to function better, being dependent on electrical information which is processed through the body via the electrolytes, hormones and other substances maintained by water or fluid in the body. And then we proceed to the next Priority priority… Which may well be the desired outcome the client wishes to achieve. Physical functionality is necessary to hold any energetic change… if a vehicle is *kaput* and its driveability is compromised it matters not what goodies and valuables one has on board, nor the status of the person driving.

Optimising the body's ability to hold and support change and may be dependent on Nutrition, which can only work if the processes and mechanisms set to manage this work.

For instance, putting fuel in a car only works if the starting motor, engine, delivery system, gears and accompanying driving apparatus are in some kind of working order.

How does this model of hydration or the Priority priority apply here?

If one has an issue that is not emanating from or found in the Main or Major Chakras, nor in the Higher Chakras, or that has compromised the optimum or possible functionality of the physical vehicle, then no matter what you do, you will not get the best results.

The layer you are dealing with may well not be the causation or causal layer.

And add to this that if you are not working directly on the client's own personal energy system, but instead on someone else's overlay on them, then you will only get temporary relief and not long lasting results. Nor, whilst it may provide some relief, will the work fully benefit the client.

So, to apply this on a personal level and not just in a clinical or healing situation, if you personally have somehow been triggered with a past life memory or experience, and this has energetically recalled or 'thrown-up' a past life with different energetic anatomy - or you have appropriated an incorrect Chakra system - and you do not know not only *how* to recognise it, but also how to *deal* with it, then being aware of the various possibilities and then seeking your personal current 'Priority priority' will lead to a much more accurate, profound, elegant and beneficial healing result.

Quantum Science Meets Esoteric

Science has also been getting up to steam with their relatively recent discoveries of Quantum Physics and the 'God Particle' or whatever referencing label they currently give to their findings of the secrets of the unmanifest and of consciousness potential - and space laboratories are plotting the celestial maps and discovering the actions of dark matter and dark energy in outer space and of how this impacts on the physical heavenly bodies.

Alongside this, we have made further more public headway proving the hidden frequencies surrounding the human body as well as those resonating throughout it. Behind the scenes, experiments have been going on for many years that have yielded the ability for the military and other policing groups to track the human body without visual sight or ordinary sound... Pushing beyond the basic narrow band of visible colour in the light spectrum, the technologists are now publicly beginning to agree with the vibrational energy expert and the psychic seer and Aura reader. At last.

This lift or shifting process through to a now possible and available increased consciousness together with more freely available information means that there is better access and opportunity for awareness.

The church or indeed any form of traditional religion can no longer completely override the free flow of information with their dictum to rely on blind 'faith' alone, and we are being encouraged to think for ourselves as the undeniable is being acknowledged in the public and internet arenas as well as the media presentations of the Hubble discoveries and other exploratory 'eyes' and discoveries as open and common entertainment.

This means that there is more potential for freedom of thinking and the exercising and exploration of man's own consciousness, and this too is assisting in the possibility of planetary evolution, with many beginning to prepare for greater access to the incoming Light energies and frequencies already being released in anticipation of the new Galactic In-Breath in these current and upcoming times.

SOUL JOURNEY

Many have experienced the trials and tribulations of being a more aware or evolved Soul than some of those Souls around them, and of one who is currently or recently incarnated in a human body at this moment in the Planetary and Galactic cycles. Often for these Souls, the current and associated energetic increase in intensity has made even more inner searching necessary.

The variety of incarnational choices, missions and existing genetic streams, together with contract and contact fulfilments available in this generation and age has made some of the earlier models and explanations of the esoteric, theosophical, and energetic systems of subtle body anatomy seem almost obsolete. With many StarSeeds and even original creator Souls being present right now, their needs have not necessarily always been met with the normal handed-down or current operating human systems, methods, laws, lores, resonances and resources.

The descriptions and locations of the new Chakras give a general positioning that so far has applied to most of the advanced Souls that I have worked with or with whom I have explored their evolved anatomy. Any slight differences, if you find that any exist, are mainly due to the inherent characteristics of different StarSeeds or Star lines, different genetic lines and tribes, and different Soul Groups who have resonated to slightly differing systems. And that are still running these.

Interestingly enough, in the early days of this work I found that an anatomy can be aligned to be absolutely spot-on (and fully and correctly functioning) for a client, and yet later these same Souls have been affected energetically by a differing energy system – this may be from someone close to them affecting them or involved with them in some way, or because they have been exploring other models or streams - and this has sometimes created a change in the presenting anatomy we next work on that is now over-riding or over-laying their own that creates an inhibiting difference. Discovering another Chakra system from some past existence may be fun and exciting, but it can pull them out of alignment with their Human Mission and also be somewhat confusing and make navigating in a human vehicle that much more disorienting.

These have had to be addressed to find that underneath all of their StarSeed reflections there exists the same potential evolved Human Chakra systems. And any seeming problems are solved once we, or they themself, have cleared any other party's energy overlay from their own, and they are back to their own true human energetic anatomy. This then means we can actually work on enhancing and balancing *their* anatomy, and not someone else's.

Overlays or memory triggers that can disfigure the Chakras described in this book can emanate from beings or Souls that have had past incarnational experiences as a Reptile, or any another species that is considered to be somewhat alien to some Starseeds or to Humans, or those who are capable of evolving to a higher consciousness.

One thing I have learned that may help understanding at this juncture, is that not all Souls are equal. That is, that they are not all on the same path, do not all have the same mission and purpose to accomplish this life time, do not necessarily have all of the same ethical codings within that render human laws or commandments unnecessary, and that they do not necessarily possess or desire even the same positive or co-operative outcome. Reptile Soul natures in particular find it very hard to change to an expansive, generous, kindly or gracious disposition, and if one has been first incarnated as a Reptile life form, they can find it extremely different and very challenging to rise to a higher frequency. This is not to say that it is impossible, simply more challenging and difficult. And those that make it have worked hard indeed.

Those Souls that have been first born as a Star Seed or some other higher species, and have later experienced being born into a Reptile stream as part of their learning experience, may more easily overcome this resonance in their nature. Having said that, other Reptiles that they have had past lives with can trigger an archetypal experience of whatever went down in that life time, and possibly cause one to relive the drama, karma, memory, trauma or pain of it. This memory can also cause (sometimes temporary, sometimes not) an overlay on their Chakra systems, and subsequently clearing the Chakras, or re-aligning them back can resolve the issue more easily for them.

A Reptile Chakra that has been triggered through a past memory or through meeting a past associate from that time can really muddy up one's energy systems and may even create depression, anger or sense of disaster in one's human life. Clearing the unwanted Chakra and realigning to one's new Human Chakra system allows re-connection back to one's own purpose for this human life and experience again.

That is why the systems faithfully described in this book are very comprehensive. You will find all the new Human energy systems laid out here.

We are now at a stage where true individuality and one's own Soul Journey now dictates and requires its correct Human esoteric and energetic structure be in alignment.

Soul Dreaming – Myra Sri

Different Chakras – Different Souls?

Soul Streams or StarSeeds

Over the years I have discovered that not everyone has the exact same Chakras in the exact same positions. And some have Chakras that other people don't.

In many healing circles, there has been observation that the Eastern Emotional body is different to the Western body in attributes and also that it is more closely layered to the physical body. This may possibly be accounted for by the fact that many of eastern culture, philosophy or teachings have a different attitude to life – this can include emotional matters and reincarnation - than most westerners, and possibly process Emotion differently whilst others think differently. This also, of course, depends upon the Tone and the Values of the Soul housed within the physical body together with its individual genetic and ancestral pre-dispositions.

When we consider the basic acceptance of the possibility of (or even a firm belief in) the common eastern acceptance of reincarnation, this can impact on how we subsequently view life, our place in life, our purpose here, and therefore how we deal and interact with our emotions and life, as well as how we interact with others.

Add to this the possibility that many of us are already aware on some inner level that we have been here before, or at the very least, have experienced different consciousnesses or different bodies at some time or another.

This possibility can also apply to different Soul Streams – that is, similar Souls belonging to unique streams or groups. Sometimes a physical body and its etheric form will be more set or imbued with a particular Chakra template than others in the same group if they have experienced multiple incarnations with a particular type of energy body or Model.

Though Soul Streams or groups may echo a certain energetic system or components that resonate with a particular strain or line of Souls from a particular Star System, they are not necessarily mutually exclusive, and therefore, even Souls from the same Soul Stream or Group can have a more or less different Chakra make-up to some degree.

Having said all of this however, there is still a generalised system that is the basis for the current human incarnation and experience, and the basic Earthing

Chakra system seems to be consistent with most incarnational types, StarSeeds and Human Seeds.

What is meant by the term *Human Seeds* is referring generally to those who have had their first incarnation as a Human Being on this planet (or another of Gaia's past Earth incarnations) and this then becomes the major canvas of their experiences, the filters through which they process their journey and experiences. This does not necessarily discount any other layers of other experiences in other places or spaces that overlay this.

If a StarSeed has had a predominance of lives on Planet Earth as a Human, they may well also find that they may possess much of the resonances, knowings and energetic systems of the Human Seeds or the human energetic anatomy. In other words, they have driven an earth body before as well as a Star body – this is a bit like being able to drive a manual as well as an automatic, though one might not necessarily wish to be in the version of vehicle they may find themself in. It is also interesting to note that Human Seeds often tend to feel more comfortable on Planet Earth, simply because of this fact, whereas StarSeeds can register discomforts and alienations of sorts on occasion, often wishing that they were somewhere else that feels more like 'home' on a deep inner level.

A StarSeed may also be dealing with a past life memory or a genetic imprint or an inherited resonance that responds to one particular Chakra model, even though their true Chakra and energetic system model is different.

Even though I have had existences in Sirius and Pleiades, I can recognise others from those systems, and I am aware that on occasion I have displayed more Siriun (though some may prefer the term 'Sirian') or Pleiadian than Human Chakra issues, and that learning how to align myself to where I currently find myself living (Planet Earth!) as a Human has been essential for the continued health and harmony of the human body I find myself in. Working through issues arising in my Siriun makeup or constitution that were still unresolved allowed me to leave that system behind and to look at my Human Energy system makeup. However, knowing what I now know, were I to have known and gone directly to my Human energy systems and re-instituted that correctly, maybe I could have bypassed some of my past Sirius history.

Maybe.

However, one thing I have learned quite clearly is that driving a particular vehicle and disregarding the requirements of the workings of that vehicle, no matter the breadth and width and travel of knowledge of the driver of the vehicle, does not necessarily gain the best mileage (so to speak) from it. It may help to some degree, but a gear box for one type of vehicle can be totally different from another's, and no amount of trying to make it so may well not necessarily make it work or go better.

If one considers the new Evolved Chakras as an essential upgrade to the Human Energy Systems and gets these right, can only aid the human experience and vehicle correctly.

Having knowledge of these new Chakras may be really valuable for the energetic worker or healer who wants to create true Soul balance in their client. Particularly if you are working with a Human Seed Soul who is struggling with the new energy frequencies, or a StarSeed whose Chakra systems are out of whack due to sharing, surrogating (to some degree) or absorbing the Planet's energetic struggles for freedom and respect.

I would encourage every Light-Bringer and energy worker not to automatically discount previous knowledge of other Chakra systems that they have worked with and that relate to a client at a given point in time. These can also be valuable tools in the understanding of a Soul's journey. To further learn as much as one can about the new Chakra systems can serve their client's highest interests for better alignment for their human vehicle. There is not necessarily a 'wrong' system, and the focus is on finding the 'appropriate' system that best suits the client in their present moment.

StarSeed Issues

Much has already been written about various StarSeeds already incarnated. Various perceptions have told of 7 major groups or inter-planetary incarnations or origins, whilst other sources quote 12 groups. It is accepted that not everyone is able to know everything, and also that certain StarSeeds or 'Root' races may have been annihilated over time, which could account for these apparent discrepancies.

My own take on this would be that there may be as many as 13 StarSeed races currently incarnated, however, when I have tuned in etherically, I have seen a much broader span of extra-terrestrial overlays, and estimate 25 or possibly more different types. However, my sense of this is that in some beings, the incarnation overlay may be somewhat stronger, more familiar, or more identified with than their original StarSeed etheric body. This may cause an apparent inconsistency. Another interesting observation is that even in one Star or Planetary population, there may be several Tribes. Consider Planet Earth, with our multi-racial inhabitants, with many different skin colors and facial bone structures, cultures and languages, yet all housed on the same earthly spaceship, and all members of the Human Race.

Using the term of StarSeed can simply mean coming from the Stars or originating from another Galaxy, Star System, Cosmic location or Cosmic consciousness.

Some StarSeed origins can include, though not be limited to, Beings or Souls from the following Star Systems:

- Lyra (Vega etc)
- Sirius (several races)
- Orion (several races)
- Pleiades
- Arcturus
- Andromeda
- Mars
- And more...

Besides these StarSeeds, we must also mention some of the other Species from the Cosmos, those who are not necessarily seeking Light.

In fact, some of us, even those of the original Angelic lines, may have experienced incarnations on the Lesser evolved Planets. There are many reasons for this, and sometimes in order to change a lower consciousness, those of a Higher Consciousness may choose to volunteer to incarnate into it to assist to raise the vibrational frequency potential – this is usually in order to facilitate the necessary shift and improvement in energy and evolution for the entire species or group. This can also create later problems for these same volunteers when these historic resonances are later triggered by a similar situation, or a similar species encounter.

Some ultra-sensitives may find themselves reliving or acting out this old energy until they have recognised it and realigned their energy bodies and Chakras accordingly and appropriately. And some have even been caught up in a replay of these experiences until they have realised or discovered their origin and cleared the responsible or associated energetic anchor and resonance.

This is also where the new Chakra Systems can help, for the Signal Chakras may house some of these old or ancient energy frequencies, and balancing these can 'free the load', whilst further balancing of the associated Earthing or Psychic Chakras can assist in claiming further stability and more optimal use of the incoming energies toward a higher Soul expression.

The Signal Chakras are invaluable in helping to locate old, historic and long buried shock and trauma, and releasing this locked-in energy can free up the being and their energy systems as well as reduce the resonances that may continue to attract or create similar problems.

IN THE BEGINNING...

THE BACKGROUND STORY

The information in this book has taken nearly fifteen years to compile and has been shared with healers and practitioners over the last ten years. I am now thrilled to present it to the world at large.

With the advent of the new incoming energies over the last 20 – 30 years, the subsequent shift from the old, the old ways, and the old energies has also naturally caused an acceleration regarding the Planetary agenda to get us 'up-to-speed' energetically and spiritually speaking.

The discoveries of the new Earthing Chakras and The New Chakra Systems came as a revelation in answer to some of my own personal questions and searches on healing in these current times.

Many are now familiar with the current Main Chakra System, which is comprised of the seven Chakras. Some are also already aware of the minor chakras held in the body, as well as the new Higher or Upper Chakras, which are located above the Crown of the head. These are important for our spiritual development and evolution. But these are not the only Chakras, nor yet the only *new* Chakras.

There are several New Chakra Systems that have been revealed to me; the new Earthing Chakras, the Psychic Body Chakras, and the Signal or Survival Chakra System. These systems include not only their specific Chakras but also their associated Subtle Body Anatomy and relevant energetic connections. These are separate to, and just as powerful as the Main Seven Chakra System and the Higher or Upper Spiritual Chakra Systems.

I had earlier discovered that when I participated in various spiritual exercises, I had the ability to be more grounded (or under-the-ground-earth connected) than many others doing the same exercises. I came to realise that this was a skill I possessed. I was not aware of this when I first consciously started my own spiritual journey from mainstream religions, dogma or understandings, and it only became apparent over time. Then as I journeyed, and as I sought answers, past life accumulated information and experience also emerged and began to inform me of this earth-ing skill or ability. Maybe this is what led to my working with these energies in this way.

Being a Sensitive has meant that I experienced the world a little differently to some others. Originally I saw myself as the label that had been placed upon me by others who knew very little of these things, and the label was 'Oversensitive'... During my childhood I had to learn to be polite to the rude and the deceitful, or I would embarrass my parents – and get a cuff on the head later – and I had had to learn to distrust what I experienced in favour of my parents insistence that 'It's all in your imagination'! It took many years for me to realise where and how I had been 'dumbed-down' in an energetic and inner knowing sense. After a traumatic experience where I lost all that I had through another's deceptiveness and cunning, I was so pushed and challenged by this incidence that it seemed to crack through something, and I began to listen to my intuition-ings. This was because I could *hear* them now. The veil of illusion had cracked, the spell placed on me and on my energetic anatomy split, and I began a new phase of my life and my knowing. This thrust me into becoming aware of where I had been compromised energetically, for the answers no longer lay in the Main Chakras. Realising where my own psychic anatomy had been compromised, and where stored shock in my body had compromised my abilities was the beginning of enormous changes for me.

Many people today are also undergoing huge challenges and changes, and as their destiny unfolds and their Soul evolves, their subtle body anatomy develops and matures. This then leads to further unfolding and developing, until the correct energy crescendo is reached for the lift to another level or dimension, in whatever form that may take.

So to Light-Bringers and Light Seekers everywhere, Blessings as you enhance your energetic systems and Light Bodies.

What has been talked about, dreamed about, and longed for by ethical and gentle Souls has now arrived. And with it our anatomic technology is poised to allow for the new in whatever form or forms it may take. We have evolved, and will continue to evolve – but like the new iPhone, iPad and other 3D technological advancements, our equipment to function energetically in these changing times is now updated and upgraded. And available!

So let's start learning how to use it!

THE CHAKRA SYSTEMS

Our current Chakra System for most people consists of the Main or Major Chakras residing or originating in the body and sometimes referred to as In-Body Chakras. Let us look at what a Chakra is.

What are Chakras?

The word Chakra in Sanskrit means; Circle, wheel (of light), psychic centre in humans.

Chakras are generally considered as points of energy and have been known to most ancient and Eastern cultures as well as South American cultures (such as the Mayans) for thousands of years. The ancients such as the Hindus knew about them, comprehensively mapped them and worked with them. There are also similarities with the Chakra system in connection with the ancient Hebrew Kabala.

Chakras are actually portals of energy, the spectrums of which vary as they may have simple or complex duties, depending on the individual's own make-up and life purpose. Some of them can be 'mirrored' within the layers of the etheric bodies too. They may also act as gatekeepers to other issues; past, parallel or present issues; and it can become important to keep any blockages connected to these clear, as issues may repeat themselves, creating dis-ease, and eventually disease. Cleansing, clearing and balancing chakras are one of the fundamental keys of inner and outer healing.

Chakras generally exist on the etheric level within the body, that is that they are generally invisible to the naked eye, though they emanate from within the physical body. This is true of the Main or common Chakras. Some people can feel the energy of these chakras when they place their hands in the proximity of one, such as a sense of warmth, or slight resistance like a cushion of air, or the faintest ripple of movement, or slight tingling. Some people can actually see them, though these are generally in the minority at present. Others can somehow sense them, as they feel an inner confirmation registering within.

Chakras can also be connected to a kind of 'grid', one which is specific to the particular system it is part of. This holographic grid of chakras may be thought of as circuitry. And certain key Chakras can be anchoring points for where certain grids cross-over or connect with. There may sometimes appear to be an overlap, which can occur on different levels or dimensions within the body or the etheric aspects of the being. Chakras of your present self may communicate to your past, parallel or present Self at any given time.

The Physical 'In-Body' Chakras

The Main Chakras are responsible for keeping certain energy flows balanced in the body. They are linked together through a central energy channel approximately parallel to the spine that goes through the body from the top of the head or Crown Chakra ending at the urino-genital area, commonly called the Base or Root Chakra. Some believe it is connected to the spinal column, or the flow of spinal fluidum or the nerves travelling through the spine. I see it as a superimposition that is not so physically fixed, though it tends to relate to the travel of nerve messages and sensing abilities within these. There is an interesting mirror correlation with the physical Nervous System.

Currently all Chakras within the main physical 3rd Dimensional body are also mirrored or reflected in 4th Dimension and have their corresponding physical nervous system component as mentioned. This means that though Chakras function through the 4th Dimension and other Dimensions not immediately visible in the physical or in this everyday 3rd Dimension, they reside in etheric space near groups of Ganglionic nerves that exist within the physical body.

Chakras act as doors or transducers of energy, translating energetic messages into the physical. Interweaving as they do with these nerve centers, when balanced they make for a smooth flow and ease of movement, not just in the physical, but also through life and its journeying. Blockages in these energy centers generally always pre-curse illness or dis-ease or dysfunction of some kind.

Chakras have either electrical functions, or magnetic functions or a combination of electro-magnetic functions – which means that they can receive energetic messages (magnetic) or impulses, or send them (electrical), or do both (electro-magnetic).

In-Body Chakras also include the Minor Chakras at the joints, organs and glands. The New Signal or Survival Chakras – so-called on their initial discovery because they are key or Signal points which indicate quickly when the body is in Survival Mode. They can also be key balancing Chakras to locate shock and trauma in the body at deep levels.

The 'Out-of-Body' Chakras

Those Chakras not actually located etherically in the physical body still function similarly to those within the body. Similar to the In-Body Chakras, they receive information, or send it, or do both.

These new Chakras include the Upper or Higher Chakras, the Earthing Chakras, and the Psychic Body Chakras.

For some advanced Souls they may well automatically become activated, which can in itself bring about a crisis or a memory replay for one to deal with. Balancing and working with the new Chakras in a conscious way can avoid this and make the transitions required an easier experience.

Left to themselves, it is possible that these new Chakras can organise and sort themselves out, though the length of this time could actually be a matter of many more years, depending on the level or degree of awareness housed within the Chakras, one's Soul aptitude, their genetic loading or inheritance and their chosen journey.

For those individuals that are working on themselves energetically, these Chakras are important to enhance their evolution and stability as well as their ability to anchor the different dimensions properly during these energetically active and stimulating times.

When one knows what and where these new Chakras are, it increases and speeds up their ability to process energy and issues as well as to increase their awareness and evolution. The information and potential inherent with these new Chakras can bring fresh revelations and also enable one to clear issues to new levels of clarity and self-actualization.

Front and Back Chakras

The front can generally be seen as Output of Connection, the back as Input. But this is not a hard and fast rule.

Generally speaking, the front Chakras deal with what is present in your life; that which you are facing. Back Chakras have been connected with what is behind you, what is 'back' in the past, that which you have not yet faced, or the karma or lesson you have not yet faced.

Front Chakra Issues:

- That which lies in front of us
- That which we are currently dealing with
- What has now emerged for us to address directly
- That which has been projected on to us and may not even be ours
- Past issues being re-presented in a new guise

Some issues regarding the **Back Chakras** or Back of the Chakras are:

- The Past – this lifetime
- Denied or repressed issues
- Lessons still not fully absorbed
- Ancient history
- Others issues
- Others cords or agendas
- Projections or perpetuations by others
- Past Life issues

Side Chakras are often connected to relating and relationships, whether with another or with what surrounds us and our place and space within our environment and life.

Every Chakra healing you experience shifts an aspect of yourself, and once integrated, will then allow the next imbalance to surface for more healing of the being. As we clear the old, we awaken the newness and possibilities within which begin to emerge for our growth and enhancement.

Any of the Chakras can receive connectors or energy lines, and can also send these to another. Those connectors that do not wish to relinquish contact or are involved or in depth and wish to retain connection tend to have hooks on them. These hooks and connections need to be released and removed and the area cleared and cleaned up. (See the '*Secrets Behind Energy Fields*' book for some ideas on personal and spiritual clearings.

THE CURRENT BASIC CHAKRA SYSTEMS

In order to clarify this new Chakra situation, and to be able to utilise and balance it to the best advantage, it is wise to have some knowledge of the existing Chakra system, as these are the basic energetic foundations for human experience and necessary for the human experience and health.

Here is an overview of the current and commonly accepted Chakra working model and systems.

The CURRENT CHAKRA SYSTEMS

- Main (Major) Chakra System
- Minor Chakra Systems
- Higher Chakra Systems

THE MAIN CHAKRA SYSTEM

The Main or Major Chakra System are located or originate within the body and this consists of seven Chakras:

- Base (or Root) Chakra
- Sacral Chakra
- Solar Plexus Chakra
- Heart Chakra
- Throat Chakra
- Third Eye Chakra
- Crown Chakra

More information is given for these later.

MINOR CHAKRA SYSTEMS

A subset of smaller Chakras also exists within the body, which tends to govern individual organs, glands, joints and nervous system junctions. More information on these is found further on.

HIGHER CHAKRA SYSTEMS

This is a series of Chakras that sit outside of the body, all but one being vertically aligned above the head, and tending to proceed or to be activated in order from the Crown Chakra upwards.

The New Chakra Systems

The New Evolved Chakra Systems are:

- The New Earthing Chakras
- The Psychic Body Chakras
- The Signal / Survival Chakra System
- The Advanced Soul Body

Each of these separate energetic systems have their own Subtle Body Anatomy and relevant energetic connections.

These are separate to the Main 7 Chakra System and the Higher Spiritual Chakra Systems, though they can require an energetic connection between certain Chakras or parts of the subtle body systems to fully benefit. Though these have been documented in manual form and taught in experiential workshops since 2009, further revelations, updates, connections and understandings have furthered their benefits, and are presented here.

Differing Chakra Systems

As has been mentioned, the Higher or Upper Chakras have been documented by others, though there appears to be several models of this particular Out-of-Body Chakra system, depending on the perception, work, history and experience of the practitioner who has documented or written about them. Some authors may even claim (some already have) that their writing is definitive and that their model of Chakras or Light Bodies is the *only* accurate one.

I disagree. I strongly incline to the possibility that there are various systems or models, and that there are indeed accuracies in each model. But as mentioned previously, they may also differ to the *Human* Main Chakras in that they may well be from other times and places or species, and they may have somewhat different uses or functions *other than human* depending on the person and their journey. And history. It is also my view that some practitioners and healers are currently working with some of the Human New Evolved Chakras - they may be discovering these for themselves, even though they do not yet have an atlas for them, or a name for them. Nor do they yet have a clear chart or map. Until now.

WORKING WITH THE NEW CHAKRAS

In each section of the New Chakras, there are recommended procedures for healing and balancing the Chakras. There is also a section on **Balancing Techniques and Tools**, which follows shortly.

To work effectively with the new evolved subtle body energy systems, and with their related Nadis, one needs to have clear channels to intake and utilise the available positive Solar, Light, Pranic and other appropriate healing energies necessary.

As part of preparation of your healing and alignment process, it will greatly assist your success to clear your light channels and to ensure appropriate connection to your true Divine Source.

Using this same process with your client can also enhance your client's energy systems for a greater intake of energy and connectedness – if they are willing to do the exercise and if it is appropriate for them at this stage in their awareness and development. Another benefit of this alignment process is that any previously unseen or unacknowledged parasitic, controlling or dark energy is arrested and removed. This benefits not only the healing process but other aspects of one's human experience.

There are usually two different energetic types of light channels in the head and whichever one uses or possess is frequently simply dependent on the Soul's own journey, growth and experience. There is no right or wrong, simply *different*, and the two channel methods are illustrated shortly. The process of clearing the Light Channels is covered in the Chapter on *Preparing to Work with the New Chakras*.

There may also be filters along the channels, which are part of their protective and supporting mechanism. These filters need to be consciously cleansed and instructions are also given for this.

After your preparations and processes, after your healing session, it is recommended that one ensures that the healing has been registered with the Soul Star above the head as covered in the next chapter.

However, before embarking upon in-depth work with the New Evolved Chakras, or even before working with any of the illustrations – which are prone to activate or trigger issues visually – it is beneficial to read the **Balancing Techniques** section first.

This then prepares one for supporting any process that commences personally through reading the information or sighting the images. I would suggest you do this before reading any section on new Chakras that you are not yet familiar with.

Not all Chakras are equal, and there can be differences in how one handles one particular Chakra compared to another. The focus in this book is on balancing the New Evolved Chakras and systems in ways that I have personally discovered. (These are the Earthing Chakras, the Psychic Chakras, the Signal Chakras and the Advanced Soul Body and Extra-Ordinary Chakras.)

Most Recalibrations occur when addressing and balancing the individual Chakra, but it can also encompass a whole section of Chakras, such as the first five Earthing Chakras, which is actually a recalibration that I consider essential for the Human anatomy and function at this point in humanity's progress.

Most of the new Chakras tend to begin to recalibrate once they are recognised, and they are supported. Recalibration simply means that their ability is activated and that their frequency interface is aligned and correctly and appropriately reset in harmony with the available higher frequencies.

Working with the contact or Connection Points is generally the key with the Psychic and Signal Chakras. Though the Affirmations can be very powerful in activating any issues, residual or inhibiting, with any Chakra.

As these new Chakras are for enhanced Soul journeying and Evolution, I have included a couple of reminders in relevant places to ensure that each healing includes or addresses the Soul for ultimate (final) registering of the healing process.

As mentioned, for more balancing and healing information, refer to each Chakra section for further individual approaches and specific Affirmations.

There are also sections *on Affirmations* and a *Glossary* near the back of the book

BALANCING TECHNIQUES AND TOOLS

Recommended healing tools are listed here, but the energy worker can use whatever is accurately indicated for the client and the situation. These are simply the tools that I tend to use the most or that I feel are the most effective to work with by others who haven't done my workshops yet.

These suggestions should be used with the **more specific Healing information** and any other balancing procedures that accompany their relevant Chakra sections. They are listed generally in the order of awareness, effect and usage.

PREPARATION

As outlined, clear the inner Light Channel in the Head.

Using the exercise in the Psychic Chakras section, prepare the Core Channel. *The Psychic Body Toner helps to clear the Central Core Channel. Or you may choose to use the Hara Line and Hara body information to create a clear channel this way.*

SOUL REGISTRATION

A primary consideration is that *at the end of all healings*, or major junctures in healing, is this:

All healings should be locked-in or registered at the Soul level; This now involves the Soul Body in the healing process; this ensures that the essence of the client's *total-ity* of being has *acknowledged* the positive changes and *registers* them in order to *integrate* the healing; and to further align and support the Soul's ongoing journey. This is usually done via the Soul Star Chakra, which is the Soul's Individuation point. A suggested procedure is shown in the new Advanced Soul Body section.

IMPORTANT BALANCING TECHNIQUES

The techniques and tools following are listed in order of use or awareness when approaching a session;

Preparation – Clear your energy channels (Light Channels, Central Core) first if you are working with or on someone. Clear your energy channels if you are doing any work on yourself.

Imagination – Using the Third Eye, Intuition, Imagination, psychic abilities etc, ascertain which Chakra and what is required based on the information provided.

Words - The function and structure of each Earthing Chakra is described to enable personal, energetic and spiritual understanding and activation.

Pendulum or **Kinesiology** Testing – Test for which Chakra or module is imbalanced or requiring assistance, then test the individual Chakra information provided to ascertain where the imbalance is, using the Keys to assist in full revelation and activation.

Issues and Layers – These can be long term or recent. One or several. They may exist at different levels or dimensions. If you have the skills, access these (*safely*!) for complete resolution.

Keys and Keywords – Words have power, and the exact word can hit the exact vibration, or trigger what is *not* of the exact vibration, allowing the issue or memory to reveal itself.

Affirmations / Statements - Using the ***Key Chakra Code Statements*** (especially with the Earthing Chakras) will provide the trigger vibration for hidden issues for these. When spoken aloud, the statements assist the existing vibrationary frequencies and resonances to reveal and further activate any issues and energies that are other than the truth and veracity of the statement. Those that have worked with balancing the energies of Affirmations will more quickly understand the potency of this tool. If the correct frequency is not triggered, the Shadows of the issue may remain – unresolved or uncleared.

Mindfulness - Focussing on the position of the particular Chakra and exploring its possible colour and function mindfully will also assist in the energetic balance and one's true connection to the Chakra itself. One may even find that identifying the Chakra, its function, colour and shape and its imbalance, and focussing through the ***Key Chakra Code Statements*** can very quickly begin the balancing process. Occasionally I have had to do very little for some Chakras to bring them not only into alignment, but into full function quickly.

However, other Chakras may be arrested, depleted, damaged, inhibited or blocked, and may require some exploration and time-space-history tracking to remove any past impeding resonance, trauma or residue.

Order - During the Earthing Chakra workshops, we explore each Chakra in its correct order through guided meditation, mending the issues as we go.

All the client and student reports from these explorations and healings have been amazing testimonials to the power of these Chakras and of the consciousness that threads through them. After each Chakra has been fully balanced, activated and aligned, and its stage or module (in order) is functioning according to its purpose, then if an individual Chakra indicates it has a newly revealed or activated issue or has been misaligned at a later date, it is easier and safer to address only that Chakra and its module.

This means that one doesn't necessarily first have to balance every previous single Chakra prior. It then becomes a simple matter to connect the modules without having to address each individual Chakra. This means that having done the alignment process correctly in the first place, one only needs to address where the 'link in the chain' has slipped or misaligned. A Chakra that was balanced and is now not balanced could simply mean that a Connection point has been disconnected or that some past issue has emerged or been triggered and requires resolution and clearing.

Checking down through the Chakras is recommended to ensure accuracy, as each module or stage is built on the one before. But if, say, the first stage (Recalibration) shows that all are balanced, one can then proceed to the next stage and so on until one finds which stage or module is unbalanced. Then trace it to the actual Chakra or Chakras within that module that are the cause of the imbalance.

Once that Chakra has been rebalanced and aligned, ensure that its relevant module or stage is also rebalanced and functioning correctly again before proceeding or diagnosing further. Finally, ensure that each module is complete and aligned with its Connection points.

Major Junction Points / Major Earthing Chakras – The Fifth, Eighth and Twelfth Earthing Chakras are Major Junction and Power Points in the Earthing Chakra system, and these may be used as a quick check point to see if the module is balanced and working; if the Fifth indicates as fine and balanced, but the Eighth is not, then one may safely assume that the Platform module is where the imbalance is located. In this case, simply check the Sixth and the

Seventh before checking the Eighth to ascertain which in this module requires attention. If it is the Sixth or Seventh, after correcting, recheck for any impact on the Eighth to ensure that all Chakras in this module are aligned again. Then check its relevant Connection Points as listed.

Images – Visual imagery and symbology can be very powerful in healing. When a cohesive picture is presented to the eyes, the cerebral cortex in the brain is activated. Because there can also be a spiritual and energetic connection, depending on the image, the Soul itself can become involved. Those that are open and ready can begin the process of activation with the correct visual triggers and representations.

Beyond the normal conscious and mental process, symbology and pictures bypass the intellectual and mental belief systems and constructs, which allows access to the Higher Intellect. This is where the pictures can register – given the tone of the spiritual and Soul connectedness in the individual – and the higher processes can begin. The eyes, being Psychic receptors and projectors that we further explore in the Psychic Body section, can also be connected to the Inner Eye; and this Inner Eye can be a powerful healing tool when used correctly. For oneself as well as for others.

Ego Monitor – If the Ego arises and thinks it can fix something by simply looking at it, thereby not in actuality creating any real change or rebalance, one can be forgiven for temporarily being misled and listening to its persuasive arguments. When one has an independent checking system that is built on self honesty, impartiality, non-investment and neutrality, one is able to ascertain more accurately whether or not a 'change' action has taken place or not, and to check the status of a Chakra correctly.

Using a double-checking system to confirm or otherwise can assist in managing and monitoring results, and the Ego can tend to be less insistent about the results. My recommendation can be using kinesiology testing, pendulum testing or another form of confirmation – all of these of course assume there is no overriding dishonesty within the being. See *Neutrality*.

Neutrality – The most powerful and real healings are done in the presence of acceptance and allowance; that means they are performed or facilitated in a state of accepting and allowing the Chakra to be in whatever state and condition it is in at the time. Rather than placing a judgment based on previous experience or other healings, one is better able to be open to the particular issues of this Chakra with this person at this time.

This is the beginning point.

From here, using the information given and any other insights that present themselves, stay open and in neutrality progress with all of the tools at your disposal until there is no more action or attention required for the Chakra, and its module.

Essences – Certain Chakras really benefit from the use of essences, and Essential Oils can figure largely here as energy support for certain processes. There are many essences that assist with these new Chakras and Systems, and they can include Shell essences, flower essences, gem essences, stellar essences, AuraSoma and other forms of vibrational, herbal or mineral essences.

Aromatherapy – Essential Oils have great power to heal and balance when used correctly: the right oil with the right intention and the right time and in the right way. See my book *'Secrets Beyond Aromatherapy'* for more on this. Essential Oils have unseen etheric colours which have their own individual sequential colour codes. Aligned with these colour infusions which works on the energy bodies and Chakras, their 'note' or perfume works on the limbic system, nervous system, the Psychic Body and other Chakras.

Colour – Colour holds powerful energetic frequencies of Light, and using the right colour in the right place in the right way can powerfully change errant, incorrect or disturbed frequencies. Essential Oils Etheric colours can span known and seen colours through to other unseen spectrums. Learning the right way to draw colour into the body allows the colour frequency to penetrate beyond the surface of the body, and into matter.

Sound – Notes, music, the right mantra, the right statement, words, affirmations, cymbals, drums, singing bowls, bells – the list is exhaustive. Sound frequency penetrates through matter, sometimes going places where colour cannot go, unless it's drawn in energetically. Sound frequency assists in clearing or in resonating back into alignment again. strong powerful sound can clear negative frequencies, but should only be used if it accurately indicated on an individual level and doesn't disturb other senses of the body and being.

Meditation – Meditating upon a specific Chakra or, once one is advanced in knowing the Chakras and their best supports, then guided meditation on its Chakra system, can be very powerful and beneficial. Using some of the other techniques mentioned here are of great help. Guided Meditations are available at the Healing Store: http://www.myrasri.com/new-healing-store.

Energy Healing Application – Depending on the sensitivity of the client and upon their own self-healing awareness and capabilities, vibrational essences such as gem, herb, flower, colour, sound and word can create changes very quickly. Advanced clients can move quickly and effectively through an issue. There are some occasions though, where they may require some further energetic support. I would rather energy healing application be considered last rather than as first application, so that the least possible amount of energy of the healer is associated or applied with the healing process.

Healing Energy must go through a channel, and unless that channel is scrupulously clear, energetically, intentionally and egoically, it will become contaminated. I know from my own experience with some 'healers' that many think they are clear channels, but they can well leave a residue behind or a hook or connection, or some ego thought, that as a Sensitive, then gets processed through me. This is not nice, not pleasant, not appropriate, not ethical, and also not smart. Learning how to master the energy we work with is essential. Not just in calling oneself a 'Master' because we have certain credentials, but in mastering ***our own*** energy! It is a responsibility of every energy worker to contain and maintain their own energy systems in a way that brings no harm to another. So when possible, avoid direct application of healing energy.

However, there are occasions when the client needs the human touch, or they need that extra boost of a higher frequency that will rebalance or shift the issue. This then is the time to do so.

The Signal-Survival Chakras often need the energetic physical human touch in order to hold a steady frequency that is *not-of-shock*, to assist in releasing the *of-shock* frequencies.

The Psychic Chakras can be retuned or cleared by the hand of the client themself if they choose to do so and the Chakra is reachable.

I personally work with the **Earthing Chakras** easily and quickly and without negative effect either way. But I have mastered using energy without letting my ego get in the way.

One thing to learn as well is this – not only can a client absorb energy from a healer during a session but the healer or facilitator can also absorb energy directly from a client (I speak from experience here).

For in the moment of being fully present for the client, one's boundaries can be compromised.

I have seen many kinesiologists and energy practitioners become very sick through this and have even been personally challenged.

The Toxicity Clearing Guided Meditation is specifically designed for this problem. It is available at http://www.myrasri.com/new-healing-store. You may have other tools, but please do ensure that your energies are totally separated from your client's at the end of each session.

THE CURRENT CHAKRA SYSTEMS

In order to better understand where and how the new evolved systems fit in, let's explore the existing systems.

This provides a foundation of sorts on which to build.

And for those not yet fully au fait with the current existing systems, this may well also provide some basis of understanding for better diagnosis in energy and healing work.

MAIN CHAKRA SYSTEM

The Main or Major Chakras are:

MAIN CHAKRAS MODEL

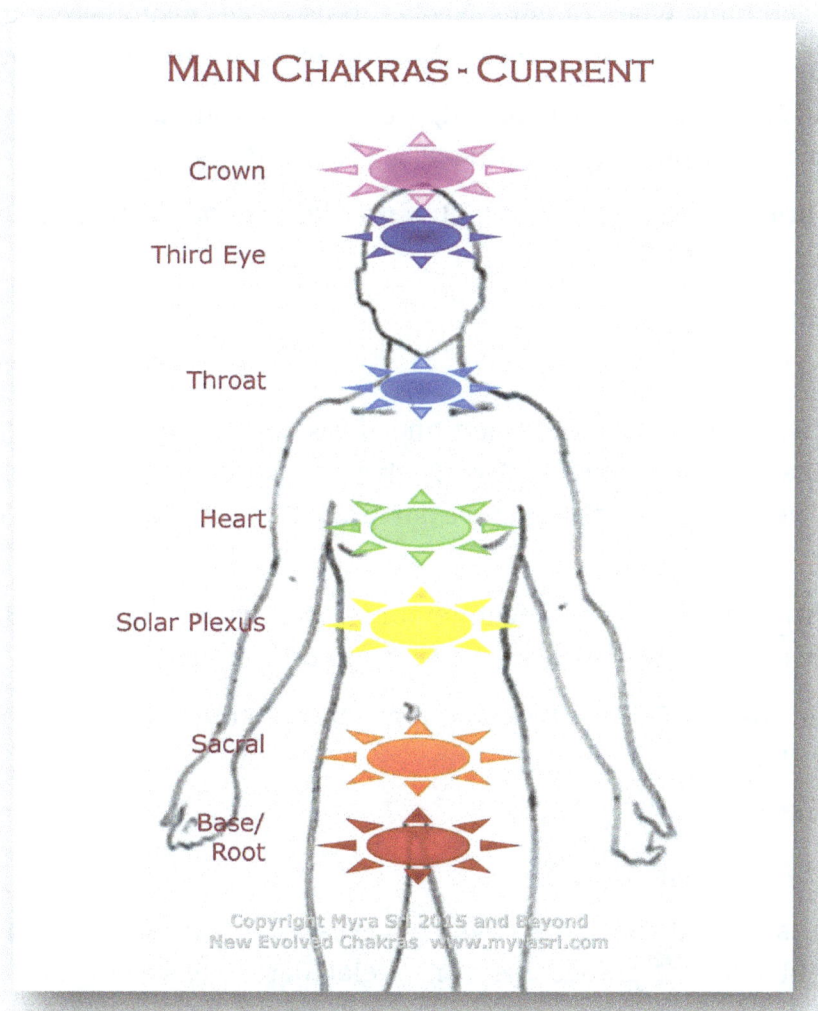

The Main Chakras mainly exist in 3D (the physical realm) though they also interface with 4D and the energetic bodies.

Here follow brief descriptions of the Main Chakras, and their locations in-the-body.

BASE CHAKRA

The Root or Base Chakra is located at the base of spine, and is responsible for our ability to respond physically. Its energy can govern the Upper Brain, Right eye, Adrenals, Spinal column, and Kidneys. Connecting correctly with Mother Earth, it assists with life-force energy which helps to rebuild the physical parts of the body and mind when flowing freely. It also governs understanding of the physical body. It is the energy centre through which we feel the Flight or Fight.

If UNDERACTIVE we can lack confidence, feel ungrounded, weak, unlovable, and may have a fear of being abandoned.

If ACTIVE and BALANCED - we feel centered, grounded, healthy, unlimited physical energy, fully alive..

COLOUR RED

SACRAL CHAKRA

Located between the lower abdomen and the small of back, halfway between base of spine and your navel, this Chakra is associated with feelings, and emotions. The energy of this centre governs Gonads, Reproductive system, Kidney, Spleen.

If UNDERACTIVE – we may feel lethargy, repression, Kidney and Spleen disorders, sexual energy disorders, guilt, frigid or impotent.

ACTIVE and BALANCED - friendly, optimistic, creative, imaginative, and emotionally stable.

COLOUR ORANGE

SOLAR PLEXUS CHAKRA

This Chakra is located above the navel, governs the Pancreas, areas of Stomach, Liver, Gall Bladder. Nervous system. Related to one's Will, and ability to initiate and direct action, it also is the clearing house for emotional sensitivities and issues of personal power

If UNDERACTIVE - depressed, lacking in confidence. Worry about what others think, afraid of being alone, confused.

ACTIVE and BALANCED - Out going, cheerful, respectful of oneself. respectful of others, strong sense of personal power, spontaneous, relaxed.

COLOUR YELLOW

HEART CHAKRA

Located between the shoulder blades behind your heart, this centre develops intuition, growth and love, associated with compassion, understanding and love, promotes your interconnection with self and your relationships with others.

UNDERACTIVE - feel sorry for self, paranoid, indecisive, afraid of getting hurt, afraid of letting go, afraid of being abandoned.

ACTIVE and BALANCED - compassionate, humanitarian, sees the good in everyone, friendly and outgoing, active in the community. Choose to give and receive love.

COLOUR GREEN Relates to the Thymus gland.

THE THROAT CHAKRA

This Chakra is located just below your larynx or voice box at the base of the skull, it is your centre of truth; the colour of its energy is electric or silvery blue. Associated with the communication. Relates to the Thyroid, Bronchial and vocal apparatus, Lungs, Alimentary canal.

UNDERACTIVE - scared and timid., holds back, quiet, inconsistent, unreliable, weak, cannot express their thoughts.

BALANCED - contented, centred, can live in the moment, perfect sense of timing, good speaker, spiritual teaching. Choose to speak freely and openly.

COLOUR BLUE

THIRD EYE CHAKRA (BROW)

Located in your skull between your eyebrows, promotes spiritual growth. Associated with Pituitary gland, Lower brain, Left eye, ears, nose, nervous system, it is the eye of personality, connection with our spiritual centre, assists with future planning and cognition. Imagination.

UNDERACTIVE - non-assertive, undisciplined, oversensitive to the feelings of others, afraid of success.

BALANCED - charismatic, access to the source of all knowledge, can receive guidance, not attached to material things, no fear of death, telepathy, astral travel, past lives connection, master of self. I choose to see clearly.

COLOUR INDIGO

CROWN CHAKRA

The Crown is located inside the top of your head, allows cosmic energy to flow in and out, associated with the spiritual world, connection with God and the Universal energy, covers upper brain and right eye and petals face down toward the Pineal gland as well as upward.

UNDERACTIVE - No spark of joy, catatonic, unable to make decisions.

BALANCED - Open to the divine, miracle worker, can transcend the laws of nature, possible immortal. I allow, I surrender, The Divine Will is my Will.

COLOUR VIOLET/WHITE

MINOR CHAKRA SYSTEMS

The Minor Chakras are many and varied. It has been claimed that there are Chakras at *every* joint and at *every* valve in the human body. I do not dispute this, and for those who work energetically on the human body this is handy to know and will no doubt enhance their own work.

The same applies to the Organs of the human body, as well as the Glands, in that each possesses its own Chakra and energetic system.

However, for an attempt at simplicity for greater effectiveness, when one is aware of an imbalance in an area, be it a joint, bone, organ or a gland then one can work energetically and mindfully to create balance there.

The Sub-Major Chakras (or Minor Chakras) that have an impact on the health and well-being of the body the most are listed here.

Minor Chakras Or Sub-Major Chakras

The body has many minor chakras, related to joints, organs, glands (adrenals, parotids, salivary, gall bladder etc), senses, nervous system junctions, and has been numbered in the hundreds.

Usually if the major system is 'out' or has an imbalance, you can guarantee that a minor is out somewhere.

Here are some **Minor** or **Sub-Major Chakras** interesting aspects:

1. Feet - Path, direction, freedom
2. Ankles - Mobility, timing, stability, adaptability
3. Knees - Flexibility, past life restrictions, causes, agendas
4. Hips - Stability, strength, self centering
5. Womb - Creativity, fulfillment
6. Lungs - Taking in, infill with life
7. Liver - Storehouse, pleasure
8. Pancreas - Life's sweetness, joy, pleasure
9. Spleen - Trust, sincerity, acceptance, resistance
10. Hands - Giving/receiving, caress, hold onto, gripping, healing
11. Elbows - Spatial awareness, time-present, maneuvering

12. Shoulder - Self responsibility, burdens
13. Thymus - Be-ing, perfect as is, adequate
14. Back of Throat - Psychic Protection Point – 4 ½ Point
15. Jaw - Passion for life, taking in, speaking out
16. Mouth - Words, language, laughter, agony, taste, assimilation
17. Base of Head - (Atlas/Axis point) Amygdala, DNA / emotion transducer
18. Back of Third Eye - Download point – Causal
19. And more

JOINTS CHAKRAS

Here is a simplified overview of key words on the joint Chakras. These are generally concerned with recent events and issues. There is an expanded list on certain key joints that are part of the Signal / Survival Chakras; this new system indicates and registers deep level shock in the body.

JOINTS	Flexibility
Shoulders	Expectations / Demands
Neck	Communication and Flexibility in outlook
Knees	Bend, Flow with Life
Thighs/Legs	Move forward with Life
Fingers	Handle /Grasp life's experiences easily
Arms	Approachable and Welcoming

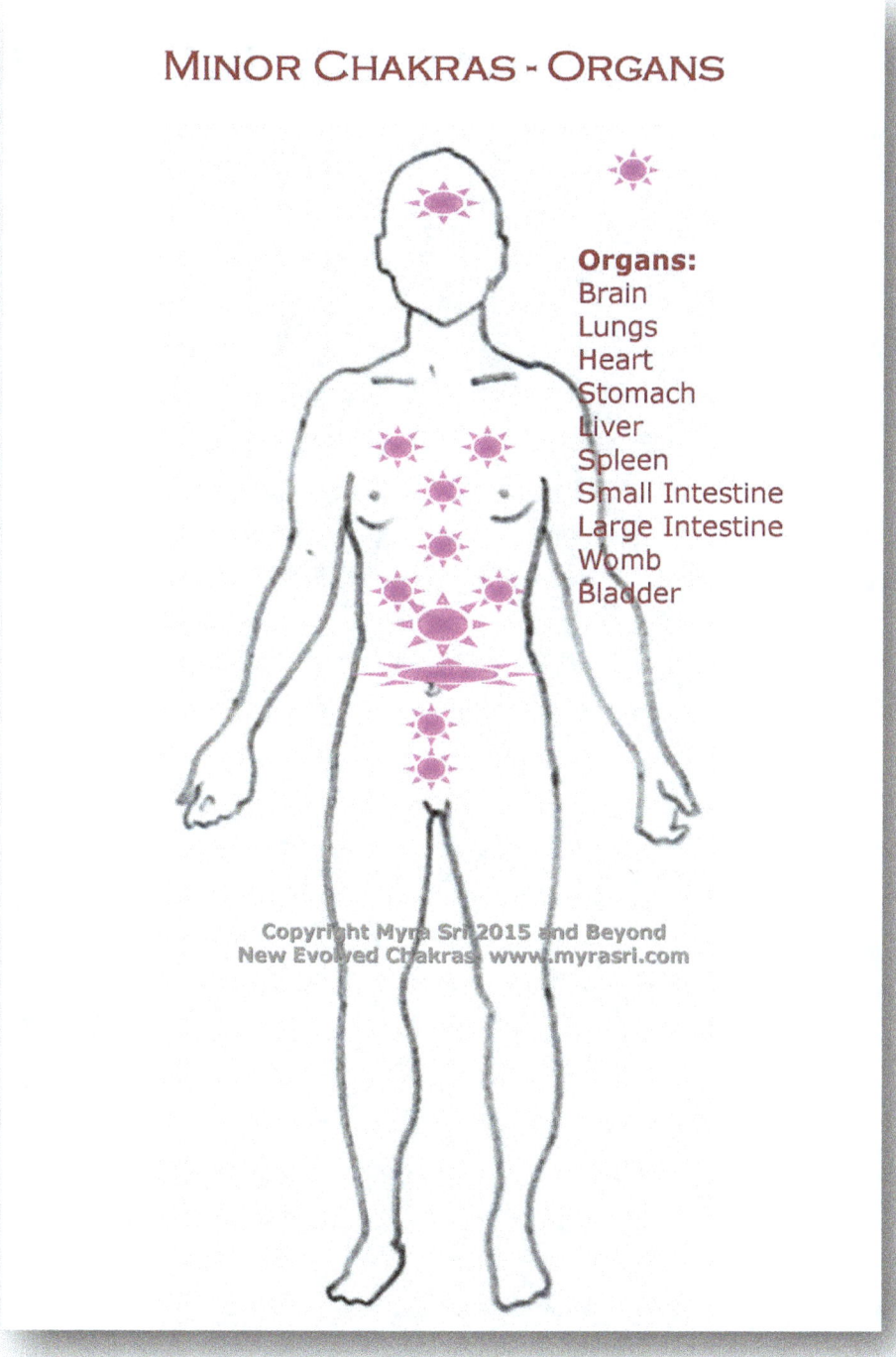

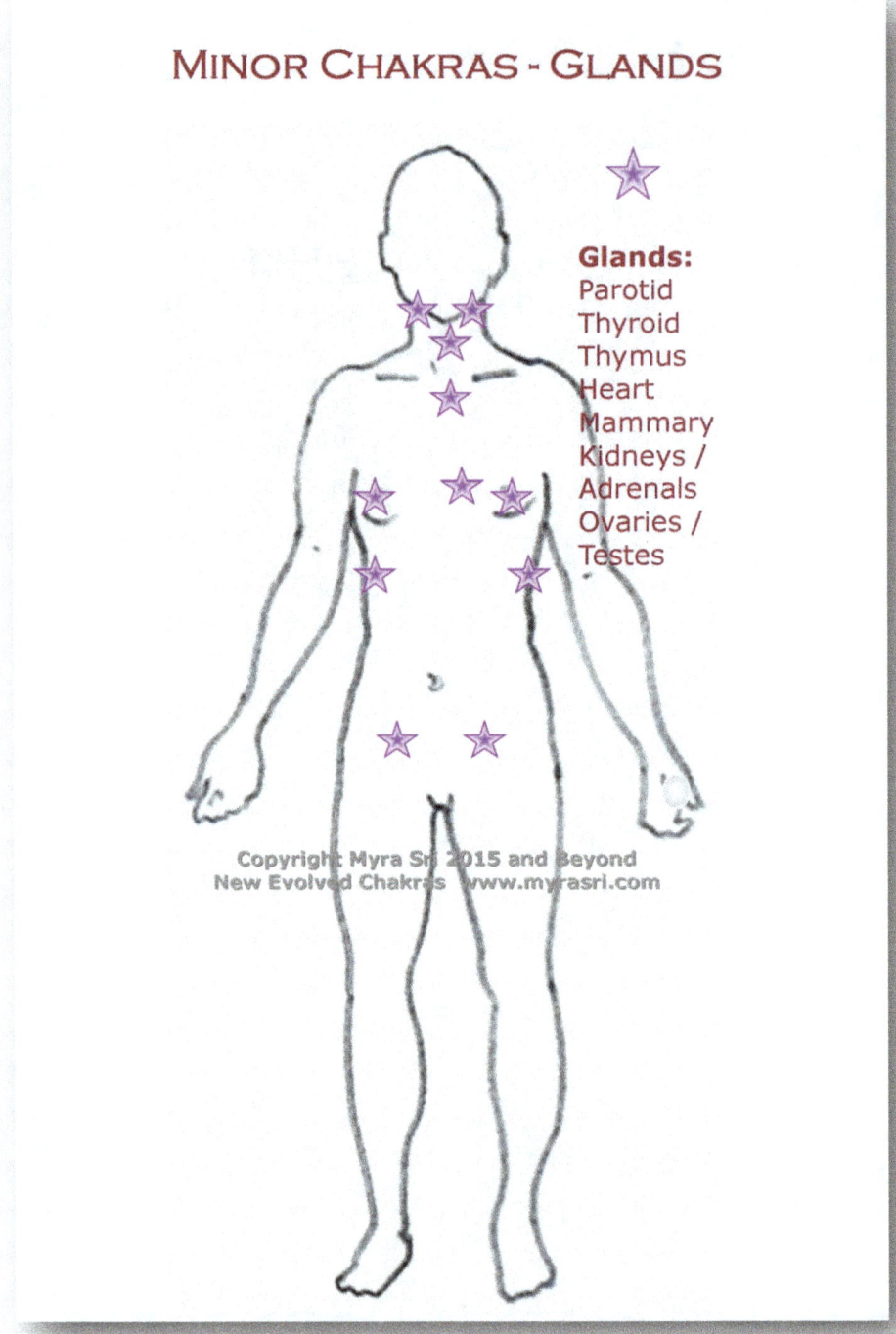

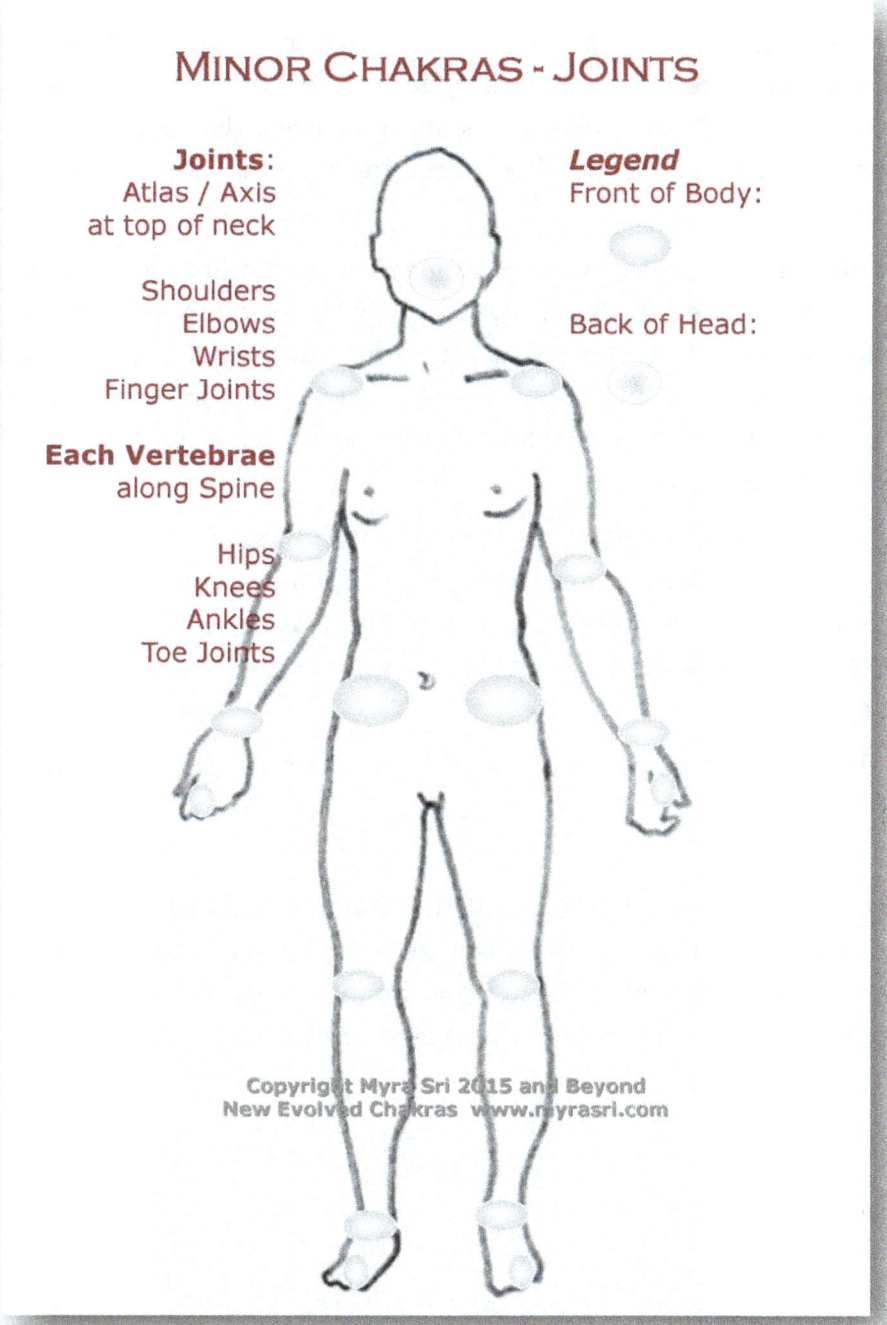

THE MINOR CHAKRAS

As you can see, there are a number of Chakras or energy centres within the body that comprise the Minor Chakra system. We can even go deeper into the body Chakra system, but for all intents and purposes, the main control centres that govern energy within the body and its systems are covered by those illustrated here.

Putting it all together gives us quite an interesting picture; some Chakras may appear to superimpose others. They don't, as they occupy different energetic levels. Making the assumption that only one thing exists at one location in energetic work may be incorrect, whilst working on 3D level and with 3D matter this may well be true. A chair cannot occupy the exact some space as a car at the exact same time. Yet!

When we are working with glands, organs, meridians and body systems, and we are also working with a comprehensive Chakra system, and we are able to identify exactly which of these we are actually dealing with then we can make real progress in changing the energetic dynamics of the presenting issue or experience.

Working with specific points may also reveal that more than one issue may be located in a similar position, though one can be at a deeper physical or energetic level.

The following illustration shows all of the Minor Chakras together. This may assist those who wish to use the chart as a 'scanning guide' for those times when they scan the body using their hand or their intuitive knowing, and wish to identify the possible Chakra at a given spot on the body.

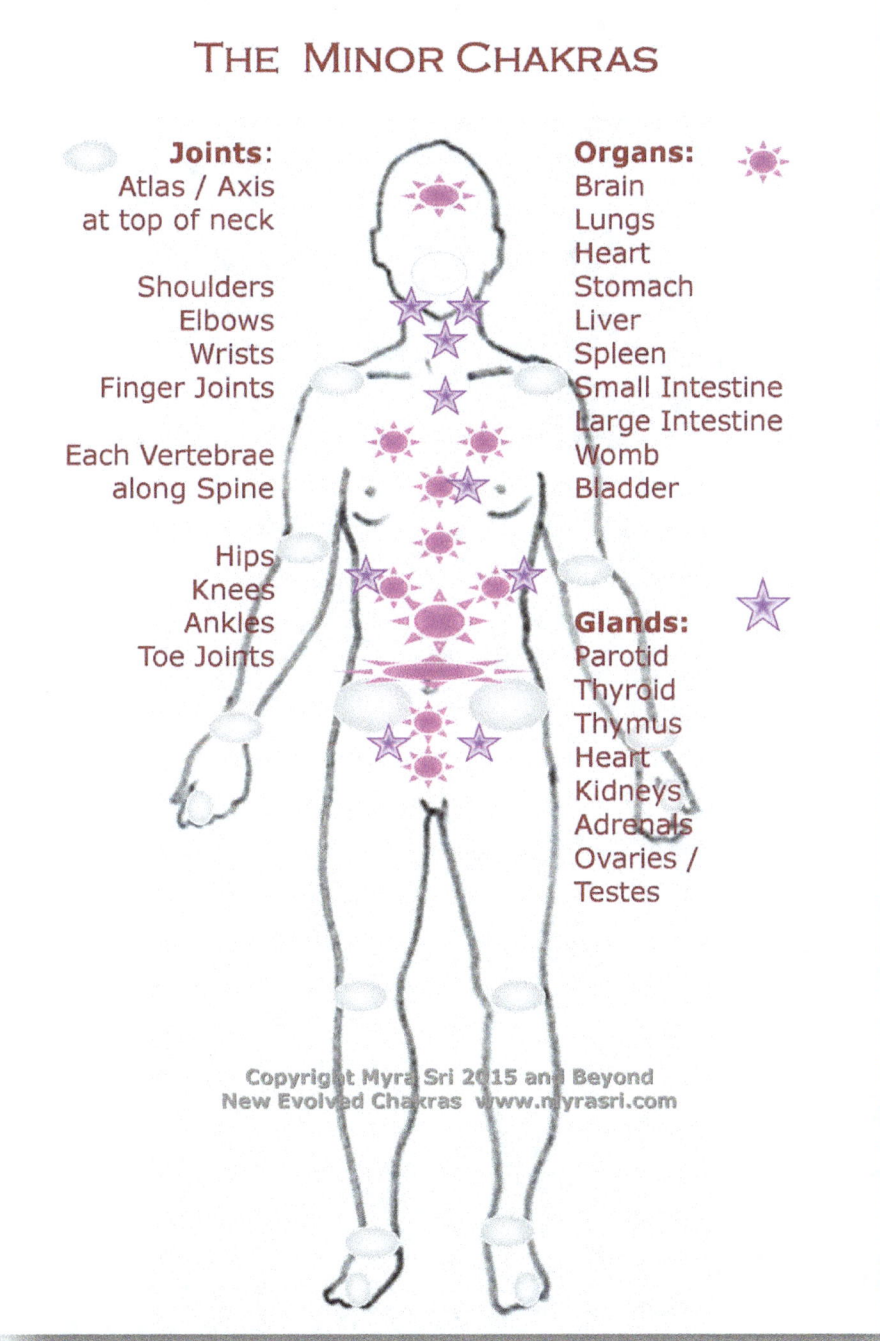

HIGHER OR UPPER CHAKRAS

As mentioned earlier, there appears to be a variety of Higher Chakra models to work with from a range of sources. Some people may resonate to one or more of these models, depending possibly on the issues they are working on. If I had the space and the time, I would list all of the models and their appropriate StarSeed group connections. But that I feel is another book.

The focus of this book is on those Chakras not previously presented before. And with that in mind and also because I like simplicity and order, I am giving the Chakra model I work with here. They are numbered here for ease of placement and reference from the topmost Chakra down.

Then their details are listed in order of alignment and evolution from the Crown Chakra upwards.

Divine Threshold	12th
Cosmic Connection	11th
Universal Gateway	10th
Causal Chakra	9th
Soul Star Chakra	8th
Crown Chakra	7th

There is a need to have some sort of list, as when we get to the Earthing Anchor Chakras, it is important that some of them are connected or anchored to, and and Echo within, these Higher Chakras.

These Higher Chakras are really 4D and 5D Chakras. They do not exist along the same vibrational level as the Main 3D-4D Chakras that are related to the Nervous System, physical body and basically the Human functioning.

Higher Chakras List

Here is my list of the Higher Chakras.

In order from the Crown upwards:

Crown Chakra	7th	Higher Chakra Bridge	
Soul Star Chakra	8th	Soul I.D. Point	
Causal Chakra	9th	Back of the Head	
Universal Gateway	10th	Above the Head	
Cosmic Connection	11th		
Divine Threshold	12th		

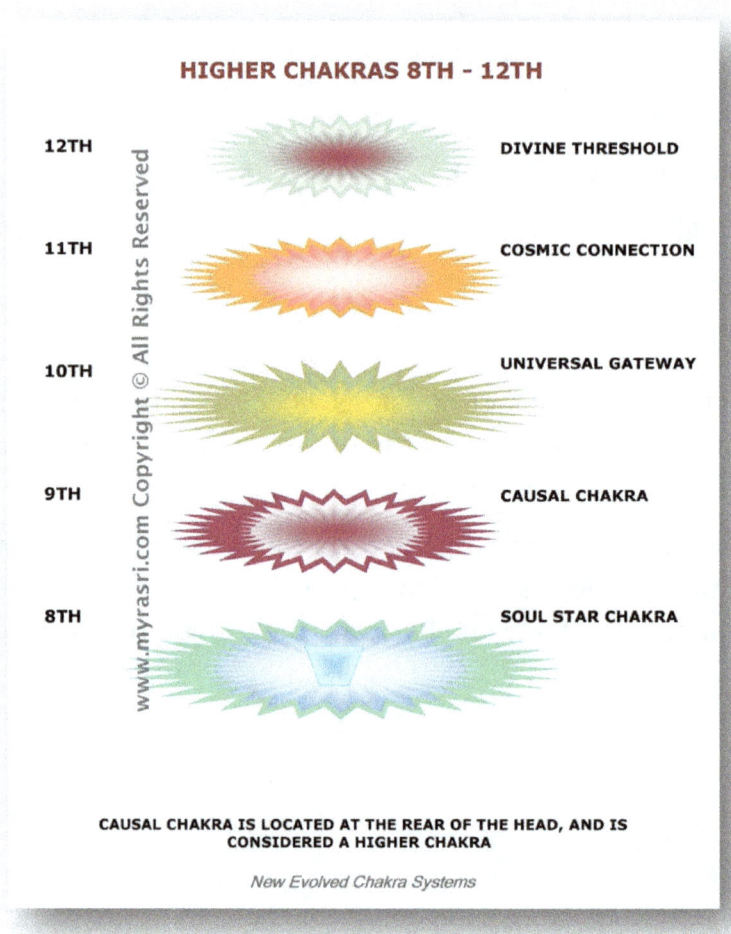

HIGHER CHAKRA ATTRIBUTES AND FUNCTIONS

Below is a list of keywords, functions and attributes connected with these Chakras. They are developed and matured in order of their number, and aligned and activated as one evolves. Each Chakra, once activated, supports the progress and maturation over time of the next Upper Chakra.

Not everyone has all of these operational, and not everyone is required to do so, though more and more people are moving into the possibility of developing these Upper Chakras.

SOUL STAR CHAKRA   - 8TH

Located approximately 15-30cms above the head (6-12"). This is a major Connection Point for the Soul Body anatomy. **Colour** is often White Sparkling or Pearl Light or can be Pale-Pale Blue or Turquoise.

BANK OF EQUITABLE LICENSE

Soul Identity and Individuation

Personality Choice This LifeTime

Spirit and Matter Union

Soul and Spirit Connection

Sacred Mission

Life Purpose

Light Body Codings Activated

Access Flow Of Divine Inspiration

Physical Body Houses the Light Body

Becoming Who You Truly Are

Soul DNA, Codings and Data

Soul Family Connections

Wanting To Escape Home

Major Anchor Point For Healings – Must Be Locked-In Here

CAUSAL CHAKRA - 9ᵀᴴ

Positioned approximately 10-15cm out from the back of the head, may be parallel to or slightly higher than the location of the stepped stairway Light Channel. This can be quite active in Sensitives and Intuitives.

Colour: Often Magenta, Gold, Platinum.

>Download Point For Inspiration, Data
>
>Open Mind
>
>Connects Soul and Mind

UNIVERSAL GATEWAY - 10ᵀᴴ

Located at about 40-60cms above the Crown of the head (1 ½ to 2 feet). Its orbit tends toa slightly slower one than the 9th.

Colours: White Light, Palish-Pale Ultra-Violet, Pale Olive Green.

>Doorway To Universality Of Being
>
>Universal Flow Of Oneness
>
>Spiritual DNA and Codings
>
>Spiritual Blueprint And Records
>
>Awareness As Creator
>
>Akashic Records / Book Of Life
>
>Full God Consciousness
>
>Connect To 5th and 8th Earthing Chakras
>
>Infinite knowledge
>
>Security Process To Annul Incoming Interference Or Instruction (Including Alchemical)

COSMIC CONNECTION - 11ᵀᴴ

Location: You will generally find this Chakra can be anywhere around 1 metre upwards from the Crown.

Colour and structure possibilities; Gold, Copper, Pearl Essence, Indigo.

>Integration; Limited and Unlimited, Spiritual and Physical,

- Consciousness and Experience, Immortality and Self
- Beyond the RAS (Reticular Activation System)
- Beyond Time-Space Collective Consciousness
- Stellar Gateway
- Soul Group and Higher Soul Mission
- Connect To 12th Earthing Chakra

DIVINE THRESHOLD — 12TH

Located approximately from 1.1 metres to 1.5 metres (around 3-4 feet).

Magenta and Turquoise often figure here, as do the vibrations and geometric structures of Platinum and Osmium.

Colour: Magentas, Pale Rose Pink Luminescent Platinum.

- Truth of Being / Real Self
- Gifts of The Infinite
- Beyond Illusion
- Indefinitive and Unfathomable
- Ultimate Connection of / to Divine Source, The Unknown, The Infinite, Life Force / Creator
- Connect To 5th, 8th and 12th Earthing Chakras
- Totality of Being

HARA SYSTEM

The Hara System is a valuable anatomical basis for much of the subtle body anatomy. It supports the Soul Body and its evolution. Barbara Ann Brennan first published her map for this in 1993 in her book 'Light Emerging' where she gives her account of working with the Hara System.

It has evolved somewhat since then in that the Soul Body anatomy has experienced upgrades. The Hara System itself though is still basically the same. It is mostly a 4D system and assists with aligning us to our purpose and intention for this lifetime as well as enabling us to connect with our Soul Group.

This is the basis for the Soul Body – which now interacts through several dimensions – and this sits separate to but interacts with other Chakra Systems.

Ensuring that this Subtle Body System is connected, repaired or balanced has been invaluable in healing work both personally as well as for connecting others back to who they truly are. Many of my sessions with clients includes a check to see if their Hara line is viable, connected and in functional condition.

The Hara System is based on the Hara (or Tan Tien) situated just below the navel. Naming these from the ground up, the components are:

- Earth Star – Grounding (now further supported by the Earthing Chakras)
- Tan Tien – Power Centre
- Core Star – Centre of Being
- Soul Seat – Current and Past Experiences
- Soul Star – Identity or Individuation Point

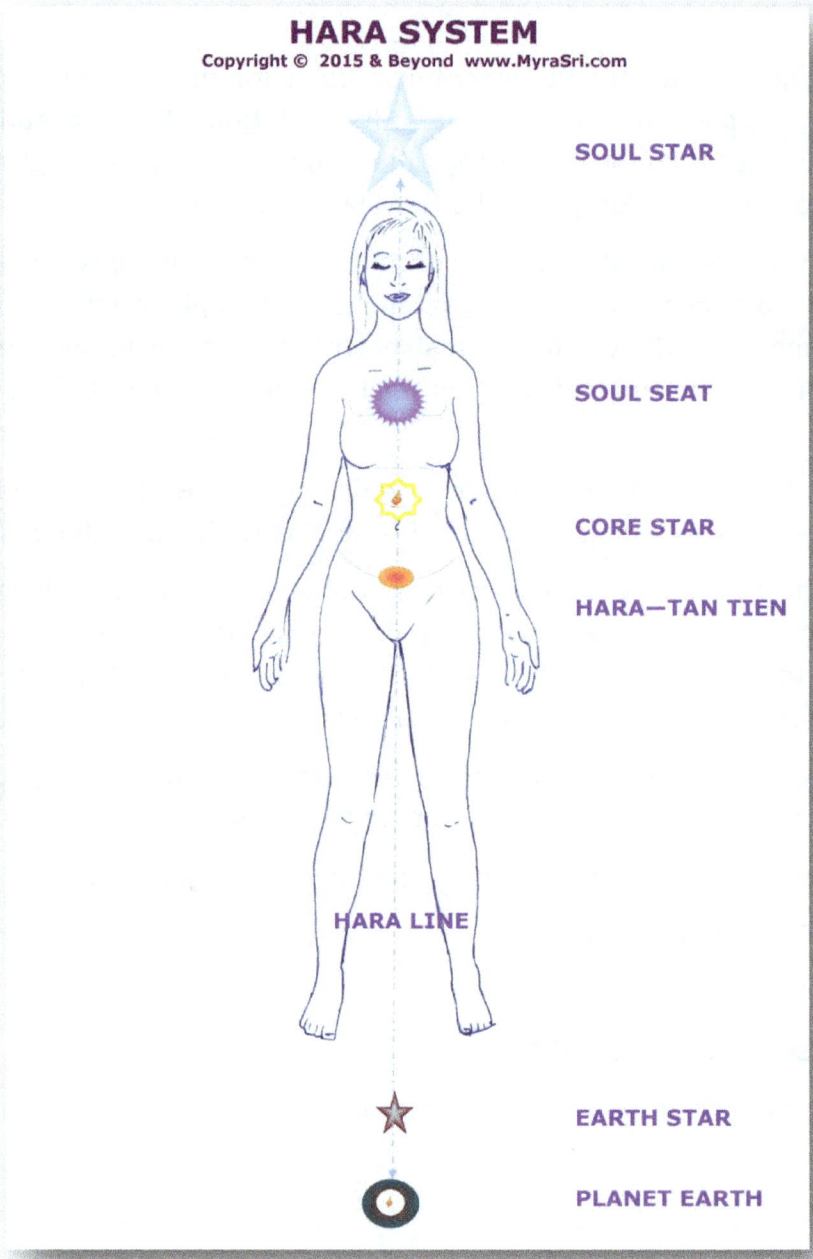

Earth Star

Positioned approximately six inches or fifteen centimetres below the feet, and placed centrally between the feet, this helps to ground this subtle body energy system.

Connection between this and the other components of this system is vital for health and well-being.

The Earth Star is the precursor to the newly evolved Earthing Chakra system.

Tan Tien

This vital energy point is situated approximately one to two inches or three to five centimetres below the belly button and the same distance within the body. Even if there is a large area of fat on the body at this position, the Tan Tien can still be contacted at this point.

This area is often used when working with Martial Arts. It can be damaged or disconnected by trauma and is important for recovery of vital energy. Repair and rebalance can allow the being to bring again into its life that which it requires for health, action and support.

Once activated, it will support and allow energy and vitality back into the lower body, and allow one's innate power to circulate. It can also assist to align with one's purpose and own internal power source. It benefits hormonal balance and brings fresh energy into the lower abdomen and limbs.

Core Star

This Chakra is *the* inner core of energy that supports the being. It is related to the Core of our Being, our *Essence* and our existence.

This can become clouded, overlaid, stagnant or its light output exhausted. It can become disconnected from, or prevented from transmitting to, the other vital energy aspects of the Hara system itself. Rebalancing, reconnecting and reigniting this point can allow the being to not only revitalise itself and other Hara Line points but also to self heal and self transform.

It sits approximately half way between the navel and the heart, and is not to be confused with the Solar Plexus Chakra.

SOUL SEAT

Located in the upper chest, approximately half way between the heart and the throat, the Soul Seat tends to harbour all of the deep feelings of the Soul, the deep records from its past and present experiences.

When one suffers a shock, one often holds their hand to this area to comfort it or to assist in 'holding it together'. It is also the passport record to all notable lifetime experiences.

SOUL STAR CHAKRA

Located above the Crown Chakra, this is often referred to as the **Soul I.D. Point** or may be known as the **Individuation Point**.

This is because this is the point at which the Soul takes on its new personality for its current lifetime; the persona it will wear for its current Soul journey. Through this, the Soul can grow and evolve, as it can choose a different persona to incarnate with for each lifetime. Expression of personality may change, but the Soul essence potential itself doesn't, though the Soul uses varying personalities and expressions to develop and evolve.

Within the Soul Star is an access point that the Hara Line, or **Soul Nadi Line** as it now becomes at this point, needs to pass through cleanly to reach its true Soul origin or Source point.

It is like a funnel that allows shifts and frequency adjustments through to the different dimensions of Soul to Soul Source. If there are any negative or potent entities around, steps must be taken to protect any further journeying from this point until it is safe to do so. This is very important for the health of not only the Soul but its current incarnation.

Within this Chakra is the chosen destiny for this lifetime. The chosen goals and challenges for progression are known here. However, there is occasion when another (person or entity) has inserted their own preferred chosen destiny for this Soul, one which they desire for this Soul to do for them. It may be a boss, a bullying sibling, even a parent, but is usually one who wishes to control or override the Soul's own choices, often thinking that they know best. They do not. Nobody has the right to override or dictate to another Soul what they should do in their life or lifetime.

These insertions are called *Destiny Lines* and **must** be removed for the Soul to experience its own autonomy and function.

For healing to take full effect, it is important to perform a registration of the healing with the Soul Body usually via the Soul Star Chakra. There is more on this in the section on *Working with the New Chakras*.

Hara Line

The Hara Line is a pale bluish-whitish thread or Nadi Column connection that connects all of these core components of the Soul Body. It does not necessarily end at the Soul Star Chakra / Soul I.D. Point, but can also connect to the Cosmos.

Its destination through the Crown or Soul Star is to – with protection and guidance - reach its own Soul Source.

This must be undertaken carefully, as in today's erratic cosmic environment there may be debris or negative consciousnesses on the way to its true source. This can impact on the Soul and its Hara line, and was an issue that I had to deal with personally. Interference on this vital and important connection line can debilitate the Soul on its journey, and may even prevent the Soul feeling the support from its own 'home' source of origin that is often essential to well-being and progress.

The Hara Line connects all of the above Soul connection points in the body, and emerges through the Earth Star to engage with the Planet. Now, with the advent and discovery of the new Earthing Chakras, we have a whole new formula for anchoring and enhancing the evolved Soul's journey.

In a carefully guided meditation, some Soul's may well possibly experience a looping in the Hara Line, where it runs clearly and correctly through the body's Hara System and Soul Chakras, through to the heart of the Planet, looping out to its origin of Source in the Cosmos and then back again down through the Soul Star and into the Crown. This can indicate an evolving or evolved journeyer.

Simply connecting the Hara Line to the Upper Chakras and the Earth Star may now no longer be sufficient to move one through to their next level, their next plateau… The evolution of the Earth Star to a fully developed Earthing Chakra system is now here, and the various subtle energy bodies may well need alignment or activation to gain further 'grip' or traction on their evolution or ascension process.

Due care should be taken when working with this anatomy of the Hara system, as this is the basis for the Soul body itself. Ensure that one is equipped to deal with any problems that may be encountered along the way; some issues may not be easily recognised to the unaware or untrained eye.

Let's have a look at the Hara System anatomy dysfunctions.

DYSFUNCTIONS IN HARA SYSTEM

Here we explore the various possibilities of mis-alignment or dysfunction. The dysfunctions are listed in order from above the head downwards.

However, the following six points are recommended as the best order in which to clear, rebalance and heal the Hara System:

1. Check the connectedness and positioning of the **Hara Line**, for this is the connector between all of the aspects of the system and needs to be centred, central and unbroken for correct alignment
2. Attend to the **Tan Tien** first, as this is the physical power center and important for the body to house and maintain the new functionality of the restored Hara system
3. Anchor into the **Earth Star** (and the Earthing Chakras if known).
4. Cleanse and heal the **Soul Seat**, then connect Tan Tien and anchor to it.
5. Clear and align the **Soul Star** (I.D. Point) and connect as previously.
6. Attend to the **Core Star**, and upwell energy into all of these points.

DYSFUNCTION IN THE SOUL STAR

Distorted in form or clogged up; Cynicism about life, 'no God', loss of personal experience with God. Inability to come to grips with why they are here. Confusion about life purpose and destiny, and a sense of feeling lost.

TO HEAL: Clear and reconnect. *Destiny Lines*: Remove other people's intents or designated 'purpose' or 'destiny' that has been superimposed on the Soul's own purpose.

Issues or childhood memories may re-surface regarding connection with god / God or trusting their Divine Source.

DYSFUNCTION IN THE SOUL SEAT

Disfigured by shrouding; dark cloud of energy; blocks to feeling what one wants now or in future: 'give up', 'don't care', 'life is boring/meaningless', deep sadness. May have taken on the projections of other's blaming or even their personal (and denied) shame.

TO HEAL: Clear any clouds of dark energy: enhance light input and reception in the Soul Seat. Reconnect to Soul Star (I.D. Point), Core Star and Tan Tien, then anchor into Earth Star and Earthing Chakras. Check that the connection with the Link Chakra (see chapter on Link Chakra) is in place.

There may be one of two initial reactions: an immediate new lease of life, and embarking on a creation according to the Soul longing; or initial mourning for all one has wanted to do but felt time lost, then after a mourning period find new meaning.

Sometimes losing a loved one causes this. Allow the mourning period, then re-ignite plans or recreate new plans.

DYSFUNCTION IN THE CORE STAR

The Core Star is concerned with transmitting the essence of who we truly are, not only throughout the Hara system anatomy and associated energy bodies and connections of the being, but is also concerned with the expression of the Soul creatively, spiritually, practically and energetically.

Dysfunction can be caused through major trauma, negative energy attack or intent, the emergence of a serious past life issue or a karmic memory of gravity. This can disconnect the Core Star from the rest of the Hara System, or cause it to shrink, 'blow-out' energetically or turn in on itself. It has also been known (though rarely) for another Soul to hook into another's Core Star whilst seeking their energy or control over them.

TO HEAL; clear any clouding and shrouding issues, clear any negative attachments, hooks, drains or impediments, and resolve past or karmic issues. Then activate, infill, upwell and broadcast the flux of energy into the entire body and Hara System, energy systems, being, and finally the surrounding auric egg and subtle bodies or energy fields.

DYSFUNCTION IN THE TAN TIEN

Displaced – lower back pains:

- Too far forward – lower part of pelvis tipped backward – trying to jump ahead of the self
- Too far back – lower pelvis tilted forward – 'holding back' from life task
- It may lean to one side of the body
- May be ripped or torn through trauma or attack
- It may be misshapen, damaged, shrunken or blown open: body and psyche can be badly shaken (hysterical or physically weak; leg problems). Dysfunction here can affect hormonal balance.

TO HEAL: Repair it, re-position it correctly along the Hara Line, re-connect it to the earth through the Hara Line and recharge it. Light physical exercise is recommended to re-inforce and bring conscious awareness to the body again.

Dysfunction in The Earth Star

The Earth Star is located below the feet and dysfunction here impedes its ability to keep one grounded and able to function in a 3D world. Because this is the access point to earth energies and earth support, problems here can cause dizziness, clumsiness, unable to manifest ideas or creativity and faulty electromagnetic field interpretation.

TO HEAL: Repair, restore the triangular connection to the Soles of both Feet (Sole Chakras) and the Hara Line. Some may require linking or connecting in to their Tan Tien and/or some other Hara point. Anchor the Earth Star then check for connection to the first five Earthing Chakras. The 5th Earthing Chakra is a major anchor point and energy transducer and is important to the well-being and progression of the more evolved spiritual and subtle body anatomy.

Dysfunction in The Hara Line and Its Points

Many people are misaligned most of the time. Martial arts may help to improve or maintain connection to earth energy and the alignment of Hara Line.

- Tan Tien off to the right of center; causes aggression
- Laser line of Hara Line not connected correctly to the earth; no grounding to support energy to be used positively; dangerous person that can be irrationally aggressive without power; difficulty in relating to others
- Tan Tien not connected to Soul Seat, physical existence not connected to spiritual longing designed to lead one through life, so cannot know or feel why here, or what to accomplish
- Breaks along this line can cause disconnection or a sense of being 'lost'

TO HEAL: Check first that the facilitator or healer's Hara Line is fully connected, straight and grounded then ask for help and assistance, focus on aligning the Hara Line and reconnecting it and where necessary check how many sessions are required to 'fix' or retrain the Hara Line.

Allows for more centering in one's own energy and communication between all points along the Hara Line.

AURA, HARA AND RECALIBRATION ANATOMY

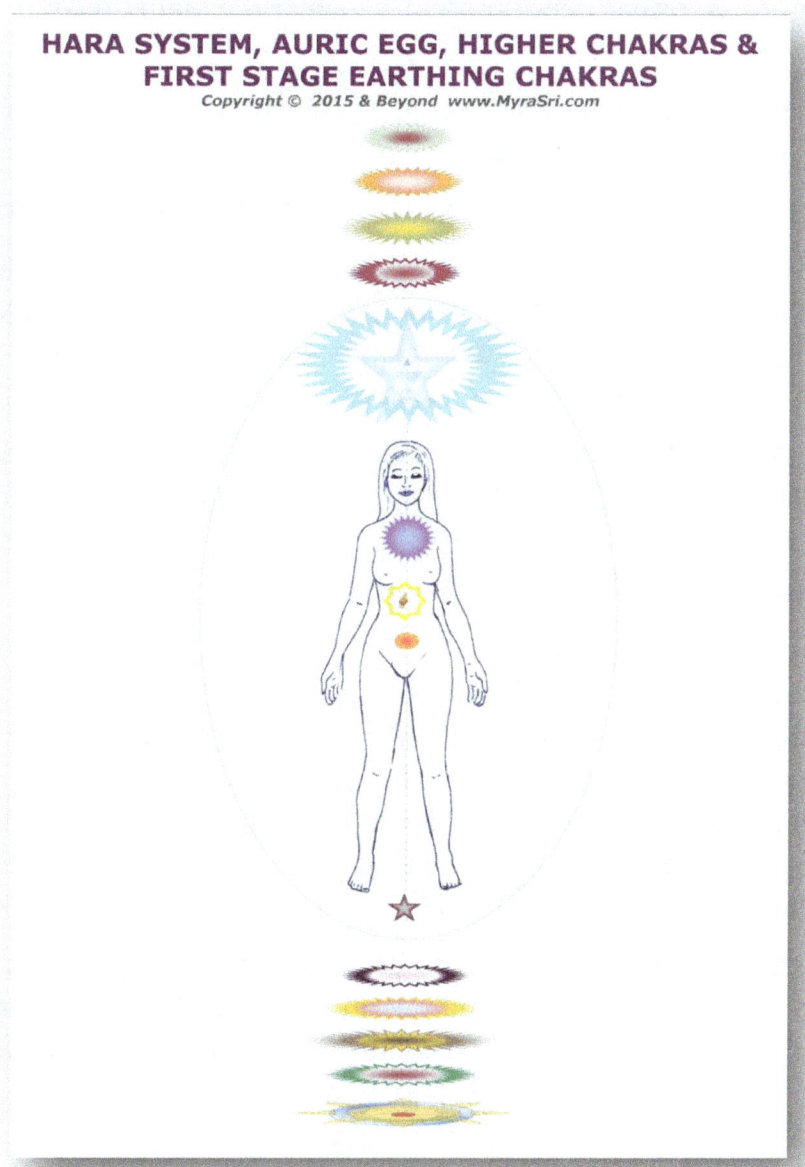

Combining the Hara System, **which forms the basis for the Advanced *Soul Body*,** with the Upper Chakras and the Recalibration set of five Earthing Chakras gives us this picture. For more on the Aura, see the *Nadis* Section.

SHOCK OR TRAUMA ISSUES IN CHAKRAS

As an energy practitioner or kinesiologist, one may find that Shock or Held or Residual Trauma is (or has been) present in one of the Main Chakras. Or in any of the Chakras.

This includes the Earthing Chakras, particularly the Fourth, Fifth, Sixth, Seventh or Eighth Earthing Chakras.

It may also register in the Signal Chakras and Master Psychic Centres in the Brain.

When one discovers Shock on *any* energetic level or in *any* Chakra, it is worthwhile in checking *all* associated Chakras *and* systems where Shock can be registered in order to clear it from all centres and systems.

In this way, and in clearing up all remaining resonances, one makes a more thorough healing and resolution; this then creates a solid foundation on which to build one's way forward.

Suggested priority areas to check for Shock include;

- Main Chakras
- Soul Seat, Tan Tien, Hara Line
- Fourth, Fifth, Sixth, Seventh or Eighth Earthing Chakras
- Master Psychic Centres in the Brain / Head
- Skeletal Registry in the Signal Chakras
- The Nervous System, Glandular System
- Etheric and Auric Energy Fields

If you have the knowledge and skills to do so, when working with trauma and shock of any kind, scan the body and energy fields in these above areas for a thorough and complete tracking and excavating of these disruptive energies.

NEW EVOLVED CHAKRAS AND ANCHORING ANATOMY

The new subtle body anatomy has been sectioned into several very clear and distinct energy bodies. There will be some inter-connectedness, some inter-communication, some inter-relatedness, simply because of the nature of energetic structures in the one place.

- THE NEW EARTHING CHAKRAS and ANATOMY
- THE NEW PSYCHIC CHAKRAS and ANATOMY
- THE NEW SIGNAL CHAKRAS and ANATOMY
- ADVANCED SOUL BODY ANATOMY
- NADIS AND THEIR FUNCTIONS
- GRIDDING SYSTEMS

EXISTING MODELS

There has not been much information available until now on these new emerging and evolved Chakras and their systems.

When working with the new information on the Chakras, in part I was relieved to have it all confirmed to me by psychics, clairvoyants and other visionary energy workers. There is always a danger that one gets an idea, then sets out to prove it, becoming invested in the idea more and more regardless of whether it is actually real or not. I did not want to fall into this trap. And so I trod very gingerly even when I felt so sure that what was revealing itself was very real to me. It also needed to be real to others and to those who were already energetically working with advanced subtle body anatomy. As a practitioner myself, I had been noting the differences in some client's individual and personal energetic anatomy, and each time I discovered a new point, a new Chakra, a new Connection. At times I could see as well as feel these new Chakras, and was so impressed when their function became obvious and the consequent shift in energy and attitude simply confirmed what was becoming more and more apparent to me.

When my discoveries were continually and consistently being confirmed by those who could 'see' more clairvoyantly than I could, and that not only what I experienced or worked with in client sessions was also being confirmed by others, I felt more confident in presenting this to my students, and finally to the world at large.

As part of presenting these findings, I did some further research to see what others thought were relevant in regard to these new energetic and subtle body structures. As mentioned, I found very little that had been published that would support my own conclusions, but the continual confirmation and subsequent changes for clients was enough to confirm and reconfirm authentically and factually the accuracy of these new discoveries.

Eventually, I did find a smidgen, a hint, of information which in a way reflected to a small degree some of my discoveries of this new energetic anatomy. This was in a totally different model and referencing system which fundamentally had no real bearing on my own discoveries. What *is* important is the confirmation of the growth beyond the main Chakras and the development of other energy bodies for the evolved, the advanced and the true journeyer.

NEW DEVELOPING ANATOMY

With the advent of the new energies over the last 20 – 30 years, the shift from the old, the old ways does seem to coincide with the beginning of what became known as The Great Harmonic Convergence which culminated around 1987; though there have since been several waves of energies unique to the Planetary positioning and the influences of other planets in our Galaxy.

The Convergence seemed to herald a change in frequency and an opportunity for spiritual consciousness in humanity to change. There have also been changes in the Schumann Resonance cycles which have experienced an increase in Hertz over the last 30 years or so. As previously discussed, our position in Galactic Space has also contributed to some of the changes in energies Planet Earth and her citizens or rather, inhabitants, have been experiencing. All of these new energies combined have and are resulting in an acceleration in the Planetary agenda to get us 'up-to-speed' energetically and spiritually speaking.

What has been talked about, dreamed about, and longed for by ethical and gentle Souls is now arriving. And with it our anatomic technology is poised to allow for the new in whatever form or forms it may take. We have evolved, and will continue to evolve – but like the new iPhone, iPad and other 3D technological advancements, our equipment to function energetically in these changing times is now updated and upgraded. And available!

So let's start learning how to use it!

THE NEW EARTHING CHAKRAS and ANATOMY

Section Agenda:

~ Background Information to the Discoveries of the New Evolved Earthing Chakra System.

~ Current Grounding and Earthing System

~ Preparation to Work with the New Evolved Earthing System

~ Working with the New Evolved Earthing Chakra Modules and Their Light Frequencies -

- 1 – 5:   THE RECALIBRATION
- 6 – 8:   THE PLATFORM
- 9 – 11: THE HIGHER FUNCTION
- 12+:   THE FUTURE

~ Summary Charts of each Section or Module

Current Earthing System

We have previously had a look at the earlier recognised Earthing anatomy in the Hara System. This formed a good basis for energy work and subtle body anatomy education. It is my experience that this has served us well and that for the spiritual seeker it is now superseded.

As time speeds up, and we progress and further develop our technology and understanding about the brain, anatomy and genetic processes, we also further refine current energetic information technology and processing. We are simultaneously developing more evolved and evolving subtle body anatomy.

Let's look at the Earth Star and its current recognised earthing system.

This is the basis on which I began my journey into the Earthing Chakras.

Stage 1

In this diagram the Earth Star is connected and aligned with the Soles of the Feet Chakras and the Hara Line. This creates a three-way anchor that was able to effectively anchor the subtle body systems to the planet in a supportive way, and to provide sufficient grounding.

With the advent of the Upper or Higher Chakras, things have shifted and there is a need to utilise this system better, if indeed one simply stays with this system. And that is that there needs to be an extension of resonance. This means that there needs to be an 'Echo' of energy from the Earth Star that resonates upwards.

The upwards reception of grounding energies provides Chakra support in a 3D world.

This is essential with the influx of higher energies and frequencies.

Therefore the first step in the process is to balance the Earth Star (by clearing and activation) and then to align the triangle anchor with the Chakras of the Soles of the Feet.

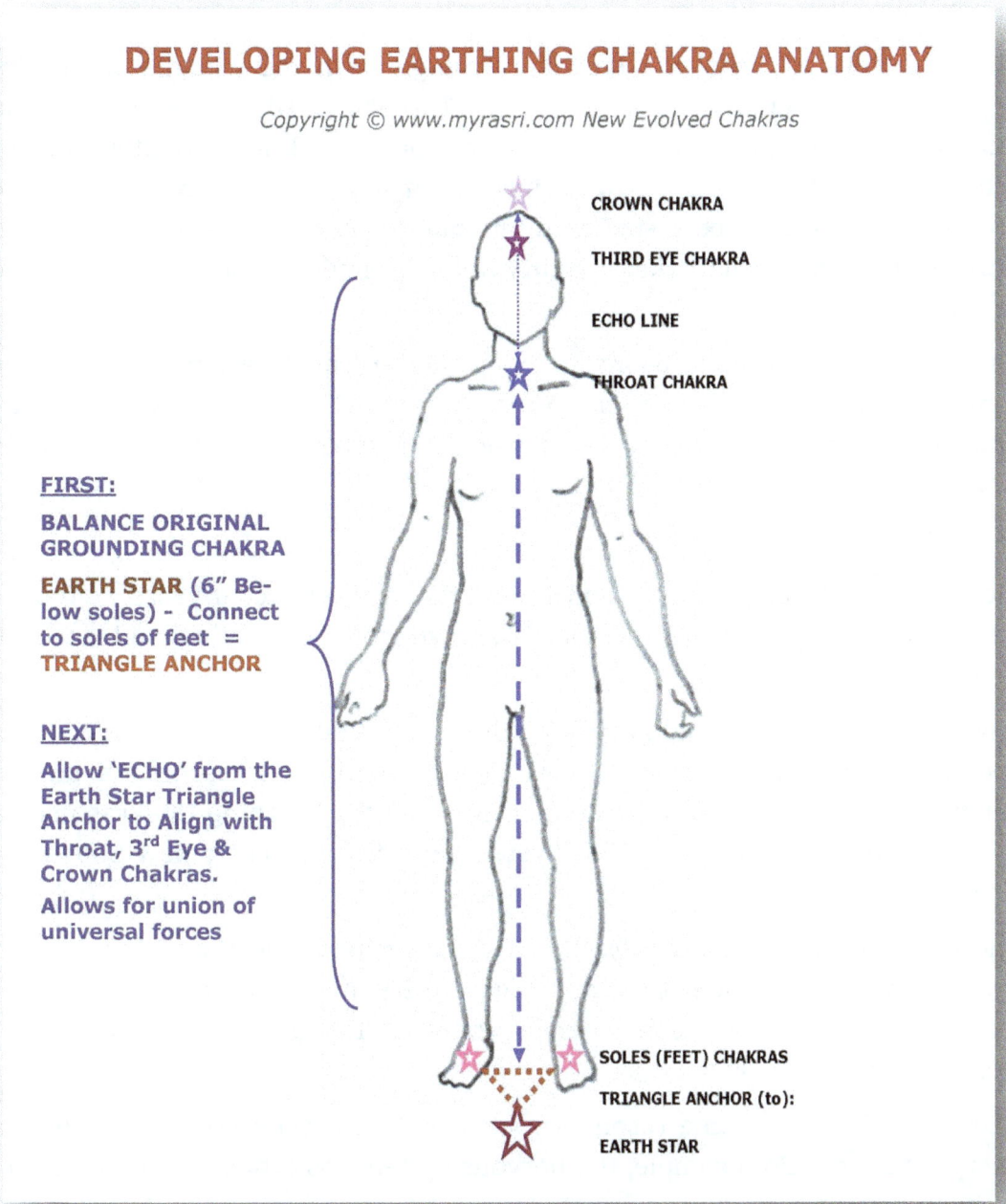

The next step is the 'Echo' process; energetically bring or 'echo' the Earth Star Resonance up through to the Chakras to allow grounding of the Main Chakra system via association through frequency with the Hara Line which also passes through the Central Core Channel.

The Central Core Channel houses several energy systems on several dimensions.

This step aims to 'echo' the Earthing Triangle with the triangle of the three upper Main Chakras comprised of the Throat, Third Eye and the Crown Chakras. This way, one can ensure that the corresponding Earth Star frequency echo is present in each Chakra, thus confirming the ability for the lower grounding energies to be assimilated into and through the main Chakra system. This helps ensure each Chakra's ability to be 'grounded' more readily when and as required.

The grounding echo now resonates along the central Hara Line and effectively connects the Earth Star with the Throat Chakra, Third Eye Chakra and Crown Chakra. Any misalignment or discordance is now better balanced to allow free flow of energies.

STAGE 2

Alongside the development of the Higher Chakras over recent years, so too have we been developing more advanced and effective grounding and anchoring systems.

Since the first five new Earthing Chakras became not only obvious but commonplace in 2009 I have been working with and teaching a different earthing system. This became known to me as the Earthing Chakras and was the basis for the Earthing Chakra System and this particular new Subtle Body Anatomy Matrix.

The frequencies of the Hara Matrix – which includes the Hara Line, the Hara System and its associated anatomy - and the Earthing Chakra Matrix are quite different and the anatomies are separate, though may appear to be superimposed at the Earth Star.

There is, of course, some resonance with both, but they are run on differing energy systems. For example, the nervous system has echoes with the Major or Main Chakra system, but is separate to it - one is physical and quite apparent in 3D, whist the other runs on ethereal fluidum (or fluidium) - which has been traced and recorded by TCM (though not yet formally recognised by the AMA or general medics, unlike the mirroring nervous system which *has* been recognised).

It is important that the Earthing Chakras maintain a connection to each other, and to the Earthing Chakra Matrix as a whole, and that each are operating correctly, and in harmony; thus allowing a clear flow from Earth energies up into the Main Chakra Matrix and Higher Chakras and through to the New Cosmic Gridding Systems.

The new Earthing Chakras are similar to other Chakras in that they work with Light frequencies, but these particular Light rays are fed through the Earth wavebands and harmonics. They utilise the bandwidths, resonances and waveforms of Light that are fed from and come through the Earth; these are infused with the Blood-Light of the Planet - which also contain the myriad of mineral and chemical nutrient frequencies, electromagnetic infusions and related energy vibrations. These are of course, when correctly connected and integrated, naturally grounding in their very nature and are a positive complement to the higher, finer and more elevated light, cosmic and star frequencies radiating downward and across on the surface of the Planet.

In this way, we can better utilise the upper frequencies emanating from the atmosphere, the sun, the various star systems and the Cosmic winds in general, the new incoming energies as well as the frequencies emanating from the Earth and that are processed via the Earth itself (or should I say, Herself?).

This system supports and completes the cycle of energies that immerse, saturate and bathe the planet and humanity.

First Things First

Preparation to Work with the New Evolved Earthing System

In order to make the most of the information in this book, when one is performing diagnosis or any type of energy work or any of the exercises, first ensure proper or correct connection to one's own Divine or Spiritual Source.

A clearer access to Divine Source can be gained through first clearing the Light Channel that exists via the Light Gateway above the top lip. This is described earlier in the book. Clear all blocks along the pathway and clean any filters that require it.

To further ensure correct alignment for healing and accuracy, next ascertain that the Central Core Chanel is clear and activated before proceeding to diagnose and balance. This is important for both the client and the practitioner when doing healing work. (And it is important for self balance regardless.) It will also ensure correct connection to one's true Spiritual Source. This reduces error, ensures neutrality, and the highest results.

Clearing the Central Channel and balancing the *Core Elements* allows the flow of energy to move unimpeded and also to be better anchored in the body.

For your convenience, I have made available for you the **Psychic Body Tone Meditation** (also called the *Psychic Body Toner*) in guided meditation form at http://www.myrasri.com/new-healing-store. It is also outlined as the **Psychic Body Toner Meditation** described in my '*Secrets Behind Energy Fields*' book which is currently available as an ebook and also in paperback.

It is hoped that the following diagram will assist with this.

Though initially designed to provide a stronger core for the Psychic Body, the exercise also provides an introduction to the Earthing Chakras and helps to prepare for the upcoming and current incoming energies that are currently engaging and processed through the planet.

It also provides a basis of stability for the body to house incoming frequencies from the Upper Chakras and Solar-Cosmic Light and to assist with the safe merging of these with the upcoming and upwelling energies and frequencies through and from the planet.

More precise alignments follow, as this is only part of the story.

The modules function maximally when aligned to specific normal Main (or Major) Chakras, and the Extra-Ordinary or New Evolved Chakras and the Higher Chakras. Those journeyers that have aligned them have felt and confirmed the difference that this sort of anchoring and definition brings.

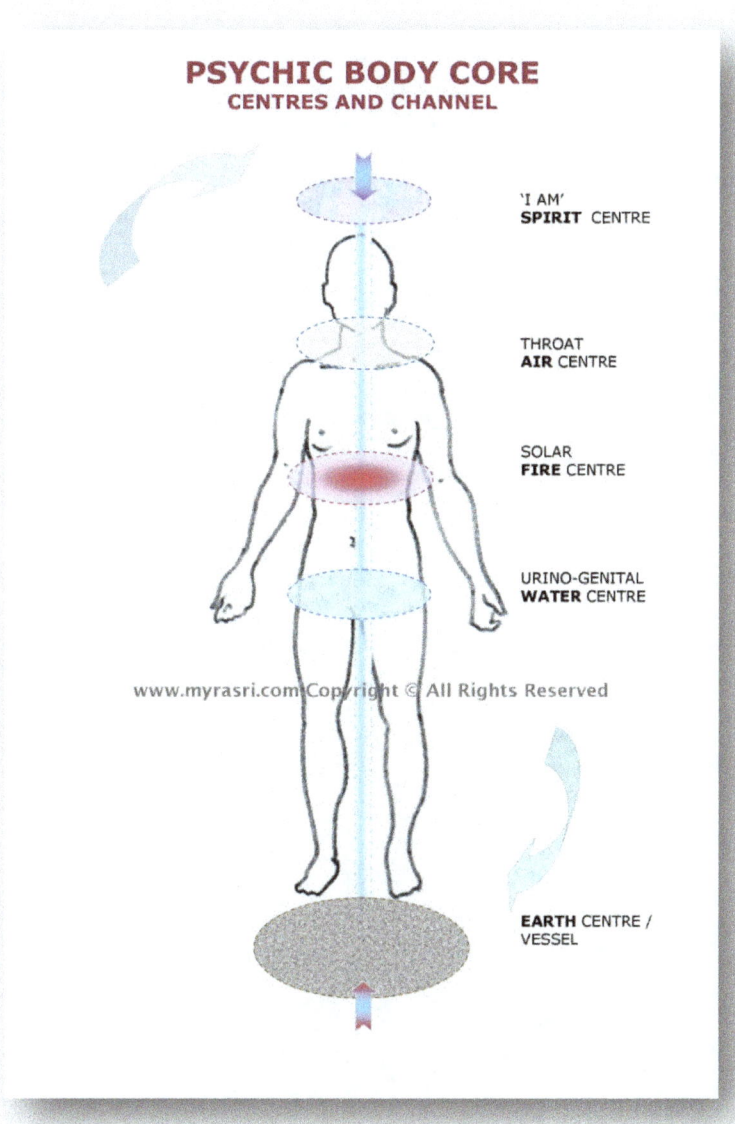

THE NEW EARTHING CHAKRAS AND EARTHING CHAKRA MATRIX

Working with the New Evolved Earthing Chakra Modules and Their Light Frequencies

This section aims to provide a guide to the functions of each Earthing Stage or Module and their associated Earthing Chakras as well as to provide a solid foundation for safe exploration and for balance of each individual Chakra and system. Each Chakra carries its own Light frequency that supports the Soul and its Journey when functioning correctly.

After the initial alignment of the Earth Star in the updated version, we commence with Stage 2; There are currently three modules or phases, each one reflecting either a person's evolutionary status, or hinting at their current destiny and path this life-time. Not all Souls require all modules to be activated in order for them to function.

At present.

Though it is my observation that *all* require the first module to do so.

First Module – The Recalibration

There are generally the first five Earthing Chakras for the ordinary person regardless of their interest in pursuing a spiritual direction. This first module called The Recalibration, seems to apply to everyone as it realigns current human functionality with the new incoming energies. Its purpose is to provide an updated and upgraded foundation that supports the physical body, and all of its energetic and possible potential energetic functions. This is necessary, and for Sensitives it is essential, for the correct utilization of the current energetic frequencies and for the foreseeable future frequencies.

Second Module – The Platform

Those that are questing or on a spiritual journey will find that they have evolved or developed the next stage – The Platform; which is the Sixth Earthing through to the Eighth Earthing Chakras. This can be an immense aid in current healing frequencies, as it works with the Higher Chakras very beneficially.

Third Module – Higher Function

Spiritually connected Souls will also be working with or developing the next phase or module; that of the Higher Function.

Fourth Module – Future

Whilst Advanced Spiritual beings will be working with these Chakras through to the Twelfth Earthing Chakra. The Twelfth concerns those who are working with creating a better future. Not just in their own lives, or indeed, circles.

Are there more beyond these? Yes, for a very few Souls, there are.

I have only yet met two other people working with the Thirteenth Earthing Chakra, and only one other person working with another beyond this. We are currently mapping this for future broadcast to those that also reach this stage. For as we develop, and as consciousness grows, more people can, by energetic and spiritual association, also activate to these further stages and energies.

HEALING THE EARTHING CHAKRAS

Observations of the many possible varieties of appearances for some of the Chakras have been noted for your information. This is to assist you as a kind of guide to sensing and consequently allowing the type of structure that constitutes your particular Chakra formation. You will find the observations and descriptions in the Chakra Clues descriptions. The Chakras themselves can be quite varied person to person, though they all share similarities. Some Chakras can appear as balanced energy shapes or vortexes, some can be like donuts, or spheres. Some can be complicated or complex, whilst others can be simply constructed and appear very smooth. None of this matters; only the accuracy through discovering, clearing, initiating and activating *Your* Chakra.

There is no right or wrong and there may seem to be some diversity in appearance or feel.

However, where there is a sense of ill-ease, incorrect spin or orbit, a cloudy or shaded look, or any tears, rips or holes, then be assured that the Chakra requires assistance and needs repair and clearing. This can be for a whole variety of reasons, too numerous to mention here, though we have included many discovered ones for expediency.

Chakras can become disresonant with each other when undergoing challenges or shifts, and they may need excavation, alignment or simply re-connection. If you have the tools to track back to the original cause of the imbalance without force, then you can make major and permanent beneficial changes.

Using the suggested **Balancing Techniques and Tools** outlined in this book, you can support the Chakra back to wholeness and activation again.

The **Keywords** listed can be very powerful triggers. For instance, in the Fourth Earthing Chakra, the word 'dolphin' covered a past life memory of someone who remembered being with dolphins on another planet. Strange as this may seem to some people, others may well experience a resonance or kinship with this experience, and indeed several students did so. Their Chakra meditation helped them to remember and to integrate certain aspects of that life and its experiences. As soon as they had made peace with this memory and retrieved the associated lesson, the Chakra shape shifted and took on another form which gave them a more rested sense.

The Key Chakra Codes Statements; Each Chakra has a series of specific statements that either triggers issues or assists to confirm when there is a shift in that Chakra. At the end of these specific proclamations, there are three further *confirming* statements that are general to *all* of the Earthing Chakras. These may be used as a final completion check at the end of the first activation. And also as a quick test for the Chakra during any follow-up-balance situation.

These **Confirmation Statements** are:

This Chakra is now 100% Clear and Whole

This Chakra is now 100% ready for initiation and activation

This Chakra is now 100% initiated and activated

INITIAL ACTIVATION

I have found that meditation on the Chakras in sequential order, usually a module at a time, may for some people bring about the easiest introduction between the new energies, the new Chakras and the existing systems.

In certain crisis situations in a healing session though, an **Earthing** Chakra may be indicated *prior* to the client experiencing a full Earthing Chakra balance. Usually the problem is in the first Five Earthing Chakras, for these are the essential Chakras to health and healing; all of the other modules being founded on these. The same tools and information listed here regarding the identified crisis or problem Chakra will apply. In this case, it is wise to focus on the problem Chakra, then to ensure that it is connected to the other four Chakras, and finally that the Fifth Earthing Chakra is also stable.

And then that it is connected to the appropriate Connection Points.

HEALING A PREVIOUSLY BALANCED CHAKRA

Once having balanced, cleared and / or activated an Earthing Chakra doesn't mean that it will never require attention again. In fact, it is an advanced indicator of when things have gone awry energetically. I very rarely refer now to the Main Chakras in my work, as the new energetic Chakras and anatomy seems to assist in balancing the Main Chakras back to equilibrium once the new Chakras have been addressed. Though possibly this is usually because the sort of client I now have seems to have advanced anatomy or is ready to activate it.

Issues that can emerge once the new Chakra has been balanced are not limited to life issues – that is, issues emanating from current living and current relationships. They can sometimes be triggered or revealed simply because of a new influx of Cosmic or Planetary energies, providing us opportunity to heal at far greater levels. There are many reasons for working with these Chakras, and their individual function and ability is a great guide as to the particular issue.

The Chakra Clues descriptions can assist you to determine what color, shape or component has been compromised, and thus guide you to assist in restoring this to how it should be again for full and optimal functioning. Each healing process itself, each healing session, has its own history, progression and story.

When a Chakra is indicated as being imbalanced, it may be the *cause* of the issue the client is presenting with. Or it may be a *symptom* and a consequence of it. As long as your overall intention is to clear the *cause*, and you understand the difference between both, then you will be able to rebalance or activate the Chakra correctly.

A word to **Earth Healers** here if I may. Having been involved in Planetary healing, I realize that now is the time for me to allow the Planet to heal and evolve herself. If one stays too connected or too available for the Planet, she will indeed use our energy and resources. But then what have we left to hold the Light we need to hold for the shift in Humanities consciousness? The Earthing Chakras purpose is **not** to link you to her problems, but rather to link you to the resources that are essential for evolved living and to assist in circulating the energies of Light **through** the Planet. This clears old history and hurts and allows healing to the Planet *indirectly*.

ORDER TO THE SYSTEM.

There is an order in these systems and they are best addressed consecutively. Currently the first five Earthing Chakras are undergoing calibrations and recalibrations with the new Incoming Energies. This may continue for quite some years to come as the energies shift, change and evolve.

The Modules or Stages are:

- 1 – 5:   **THE RECALIBRATION**
- 6 – 8:   **THE PLATFORM**
- 9 – 11:   **THE HIGHER FUNCTION**
- 12:   **THE FUTURE**

When working with The Earthing Chakras initially, they need to be balanced in numerical order, one at a time. This allows for correct consecutive alignment, permitting the flow of energies to build to support the more advanced Chakra energies. This then allows for initial methodical foundational placement and anchoring of each Chakra. Later, balances that are a result of further shifting Planetary or Cosmic energies can be addressed without having to attend to each and every Chakra.

For instance, the first three Chakras are holding strong, but the Fourth Chakra has been upset or activated by family issues or karma, or ancient memories have been triggered by a recent event or progression. This then may compromise or tax the Fifth Earthing Chakra too. But balancing the Fourth may also be sufficient for the Fifth to regain its full functionality again without it needing a further balance.

Then simply checking that its connections are still in place may be all that is required. And if the connections have been disconnected, it is a simple matter to re-connect these again, thus providing full stability to the module again.

1 – 5: THE RECALIBRATION

These Chakras figure largely for most people as these Ancient Chakras are reawakened and restored. They assist in the calibrations with the new incoming energies.

KEYWORDS

Physical systems, DNA, restoration of original anchoring, awakening of lost or shutdown systems, human healing.

Briefly, the first five Chakras are connected with or responsible for:

    1st Earthing Chakra; Plant World

    2nd Earthing Chakra; Mineral World and Kingdom

    3rd Earthing Chakra; Animal Kingdom

    4th Earthing Chakra; Earth Archives and Codes

    5th Earthing Chakra; 3D Third Dimensional Transducer

Together, these constitute the Recalibration Stage, whereby the basic human principles are rebalanced to the new Incoming Energies. These replace the currently recognised earthing systems and supersedes the Earth Star system.

WORKING WITH THE RECALIBRATION

This module and indeed all of the Earthing Chakra anatomy is an intelligent system, and is connected to clearing many issues associated with;

- Being human
- Being on the Planet as a human
- Being on the Planet in any form
- Planetary issues and / or memories
- Past Planetary trauma or husbandry

In the first module, each Earthing Chakra is approximately 2' (two feet or sixty centimetres) below the one above it, starting from under the feet.

As discussed in the Hara Section, the Earth Star Chakra is almost immediately under the feet and has also been known as the Grounding Chakra, and has been considered by some to be a part of the **Hara Matrix**, as it connects to the Hara Line.

This connects the direct energy line of the individual (via its thin laser blue-white-light) to the Core of the Earth and to the Original Divine Source or First Experiential Incarnation or Monad / Separate unit of Consciousness.

The frequencies of the Hara Matrix and the Earthing Chakra Matrix are different and the anatomies are separate, though they may appear to be superimposed.

There is, of course, some resonance with both, but they are run on differing energy systems. For example, the nervous system has echoes with the Major Chakra system, but it is separate. As mentioned previously, the Nervous System is physical and quite apparent in physical 3D, whilst the mirroring Meridian system runs on ethereal fluidum and consequently not visible to the naked eye.

It is important that these five Earthing Chakras are connected to each other, and that each are operating correctly and in harmony, thus allowing a clear flow from Earth energies up into the Main Chakra Matrix.

DEVELOPMENT OF THE FIRST FIVE EARTHING CHAKRAS

It may also be of assistance at this point to provide some understanding of the development of the first five Chakras, as these Chakras provide a simpler and fundamentally more accurate access point beyond the Base Chakra to reach recorded aberrations or frequencies that require attention in order to move forward to one's higher evolution. And greater Spiritual connectedness.

SEQUENCE OF THE FORMATION AND DEVELOPMENT OF THE FIRST FIVE EARTHING CHAKRAS:

1ST, 2ND, 3RD Earthing Chakras: These develop under the wings of the parents or guardians, in effect imprinting the embryonic Chakras with the 'tone' surrounding the birth process and event, the family and cultural codes of practice and with the geo-location-al vibrations of the place of birth – especially from birth to the first 2 years of life are the most influential.

The family (usually unknowingly) imprint or impact these Chakras with their own personal templates as the initiating resonances. These family resonances affect the developing templates of the unborn, and these are further and inevitably developed, or they may be inhibited, depending on the overriding purpose and make-up of the Soul, its own ability regarding particular genetic potentialities and suppressed programs and upon the chosen Soul journey.

Geographical locations (geo-locational) issues and frequencies that impact or are absorbed by the developing embryo are very different for someone born in the wilds of Africa as opposed to the slums of London, or the mountains of Tibet. The same applies to someone born into an area of poverty as opposed to being esconced amongst the rich and entitled.

4th Earthing Chakra: This is the first Earthing Chakra to be developed in the womb during the **third trimester** and is seeded within the Base Chakra until birth. After birth it begins a slow descent, in an attempt to allow for a gentler assimilation of incoming energies and information that further reiterates its coded contents. This also assists to avoid shock from ancestral possibilities and archives to the incoming intelligence and Soul/spirit of the being. Then it begins its connection, grounding and reinforcement into Earth realities.

Since the new energy shifts beginning twenty or more years ago around the mid 1990's, it would appear to me from my own research and findings that the generations born since then now develop the Fourth in the womb. So this was the first Earthing Chakra that has been evolved as a 'norm' for humanity and following generations.

Around this Chakra, another Chakra forms providing a measure of protection and shielding and this later becomes the Fifth. In this manner the Fourth is housed in the Fifth Earthing Chakra like a bud. At birth, this bud yields and releases the Fourth Earthing Chakra which begins to emerge at or shortly after birth.

As the Base Chakra develops and unfolds, so the Fourth becomes more defined at around nine months of age.

The Fourth tends to be impacted from its environmental frequencies until it can fully benefit from the nutritional and anchoring support provided by the Fifth at around age 10 years.

The Fourth Earthing Chakra:

- Is usually in place by age 3 – 4 years
- One may experience challenges connected with this Chakra and its associated issues at one or more of the following ages; 13, 18, 27, 39, 50, 63, 70

5th Earthing Chakra: In the womb, this Chakra begins its formation during the **second trimester** whilst still held in the embryonic Base Chakra. This Fifth Chakra is present at birth and acts as a malleable Template; then it begins its slow descent and further development, interacting, absorbing and utilising the environment and resonances surrounding it. As it emerges and forms to very slowly develop as a Template, it also provides support and nurtures the preceding Earthing Chakras. It is usually fully developed and programmed by age 10, when it is also often necessary to assist and support growing awareness held in the 4th.

Base Chakra: It is important to note that the Base Chakra itself impacts on the formation of the first five Earthing Chakras. During the **first trimester**, many life systems are already set down and these can naturally influence, impact, or enhance formation and development. I suspect that these new Chakras are to provide a connection to a higher source of energies that can override the basic and persistent generational patterns for humanities better evolution.

Sequence:

So the sequence of formation can be seen as this:

First Trimester; Base Chakra begins to form. This is influenced by tribal and family stories found in the DNA and interacts with the Soul's personal blueprint. This is one's own genetic map which forms one's physical components; this is connecting to and stimulated by the energies of both parents. The job of a Spiritual Geneticist is around identifying and working positively with these components and related aspects.

Second Trimester: Fifth Earthing Chakra begins to form around the 4th in utero month and is held in the embryonic Base Chakra.

Third Trimester: Fourth Earthing Chakra forms and is housed and influenced by the Base Chakra, allowing for a personal expression of its inherent qualities.

Birth: The Base Chakra is the first to emerge and takes up to five months to begin to develop and define itself. The Fifth Earthing Chakra slowly descends from the Base until it becomes defined at around nine months of age.

Nine Months Old: The Fourth emerges from the Base Chakra and is usually in place at around age three to four years.

The First, Second and Third seem to emerge during the second year, separating or unfolding as they develop. They are imprinted, impacted or impressed whilst still not fully formed or defined in the womb, and out of it after birth.

The Fifth undergoes further development, continuing to receive information, impact and impressions until fully developed (and houses a lot of programs) at around ten years of age.

This is my observation, testing and assessment of this process, and of these Chakras early formation and development.

Comment

This process may provide further explanation as to issues arising later in life, and connected with these Chakras, which were already forming in early pregnancy. These findings are based on healthy child development in the womb. If there are or were any abnormalities, these Chakras may not develop enough to become fully active. It is my understanding that this can also explain that developing Spiritual Consciousness may not be their journey in this life.

This is perfectly acceptable.

For other Souls, their journey may be to work through and move beyond past family limitations and processes, whether directly part of the DNA or of the family mindset. This usually occurs after childhood socialising and family orientating has been completed, and as they move toward their own self-awareness. Around age 28 to the early 30's, which is often related to their Saturn Return cycle, they have an opportunity to develop beyond family lores, laws and mores according to their Soul's own inner mission.

MODULE 1 — EARTHING CHAKRAS

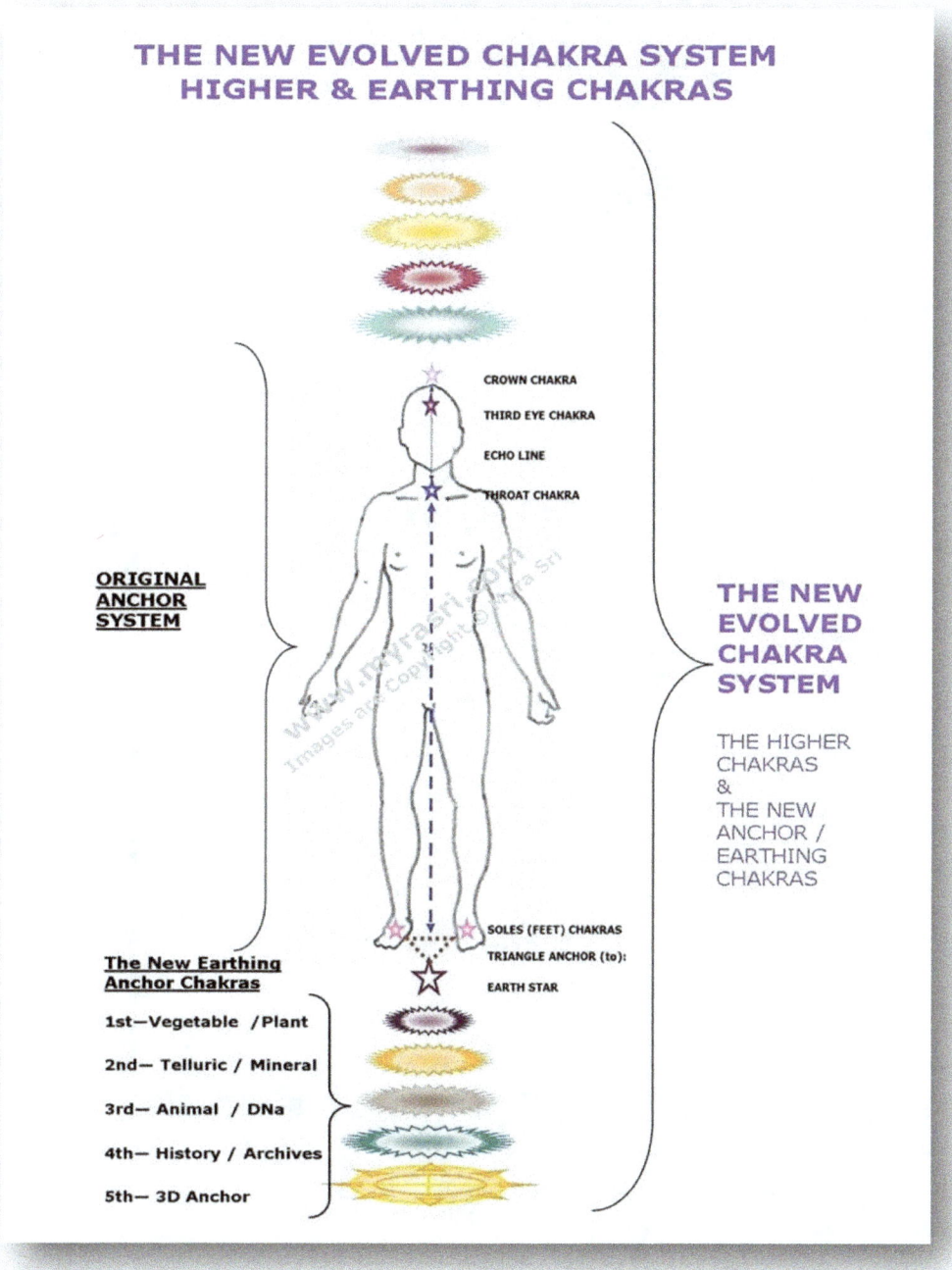

Anatomy of 'The Recalibration' Earthing Chakras 1-5

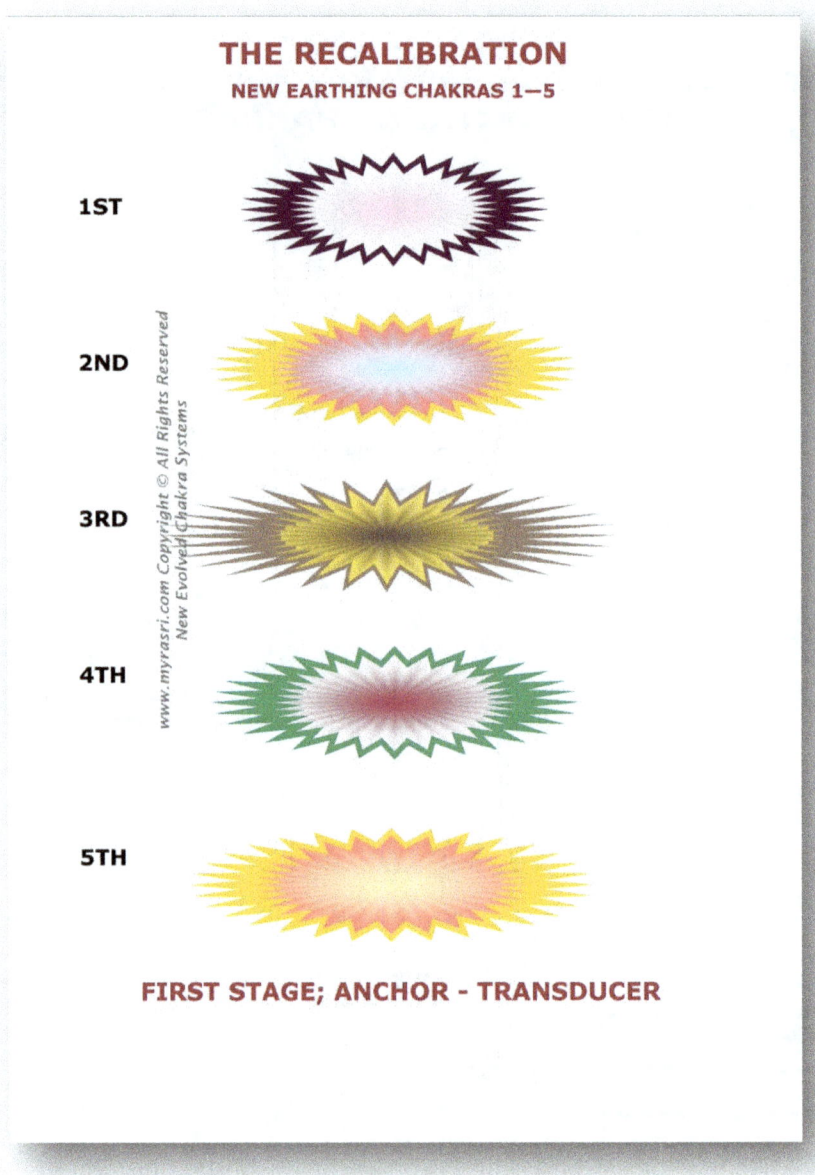

Recalibrations Chart – Connections

		CHAKRA	MAIN PURPOSE	CONNECTIONS
1	2'	**Plant** World	Interaction, compatibility, utilization	Navel, Spleen, Adrenals, Feet chakras
2	4'	**Mineral** World	Chemical compatibility, crystals, air, oxygen, hydrogen	Sacral, Base, Crown Chakra. Knees
3	6'	**Animal** Kingdom	DNA, Ancestors, Animal husbandry, nutritional compatibility	Base, Solar Plexus, 3rd Eye, Hand Chakras
4	8'	**Earth** Archives and **Codes**	Space Dust Codings storage, Star Seedings, Purpose and Destiny	Base and 7 Main Chakras, Feet, hands, Transpersonal Chakra
5	10'	3D Reality and **Grounding**	Gold and Orme Charge access and storage, Anchoring	Sacral, Navel, Throat, Crown, Transpersonal, Amygdala, Pineal, Eyes, Link +Heart, Navel, 'I Am'

Each Chakra is positioned approximately two feet or sixty cms below the previous one.

Earthing Chakra Nadis or Cord

It is worth noting here that when exploring the Earthing Chakras, there are a couple of points of interest that are worthy of explanation.

In the Main Chakras, there is documentation and observation of the two main Nadis in the central channel of these Chakras.

The most commonly known are the Ida (left channel), the Pingali (right channel) and the central Nadi channel called the Sushumna. They appear to twine around each other, crossing over and creating an interesting picture which looks very similar to the medical symbol of the Caduceus; two snakes entwined round each other.

In advanced Souls I have worked with, I have often found that the Ida and Pingali are not easy to trace, and instead there seems to be an integration into a stronger Sushumna. When we extend this channel down to the Earth Star - should we chose to work this way to connect the base to the first and subsequent Earthing Chakras – we may find varying channels to work with.

In some people, the centre channel is easily traceable; descending downwards it first encounters the diminishing Earth Star to reach the First Earthing Chakra, and continues in a centre channel manner through to all of the Earthing Chakras.

I have seen in a few people that there was no centre channel until the Fourth Earthing Chakra. Instead, the method of energetic connection from these Chakras to the Base Chakra and beyond lies in two separate energy channels. These appear to emanate directly from the Soles of the Feet. One person said that they felt two separate channels directly from their feet, which felt like rubbery attachments to their First Earthing Chakra, and then they joined and there was only one channel below that. My conclusion, based on what I knew and learned about the persons involved was that they were not fully integrated spiritually, and were struggling with karmic issues that they were not yet aware of. On some level, they were un-integrated; developing but not quite integrated.

In other words, they were still torn or conflicted in some way as to how they saw themselves, in who they really were and in how they actually operated. To be kind about this, this illustration and observation could also be viewed as an Initiation; for them to integrate all aspects of what they presented and of what they constituted, and to do it in a spiritual and ethical manner.

One of these two was actually taking energy from anyone who worked on her energetically, as well as taking energetically from others around her. She wasn't yet ready to step into the Light fully, often relying on an inner picture of herself that was based on past life energy manipulation. It is hard to tell someone like this what they are actually doing energetically, for they do not want to hear anything other than what they choose to project and are just as likely to send negative energy toward one intentionally instead of simply ripping off one's energy.

My recommendation is that when working with someone who cannot see their central channel but instead they find it easier to work with the two-channel system for means of envisioning, establishing and clearing their Chakras, then approach their system in a supportive (and possibly cautious) manner as they are still somewhat split and possibly still 'in-process' in certain areas. Wishing to balance these Earthing Chakras is a positive sign from them and hopefully an indication of intent to progress, and this in itself can provide a means and opportunity for better integration.

Given time working on these levels, they will 'normalise' or progress to the single central channel.

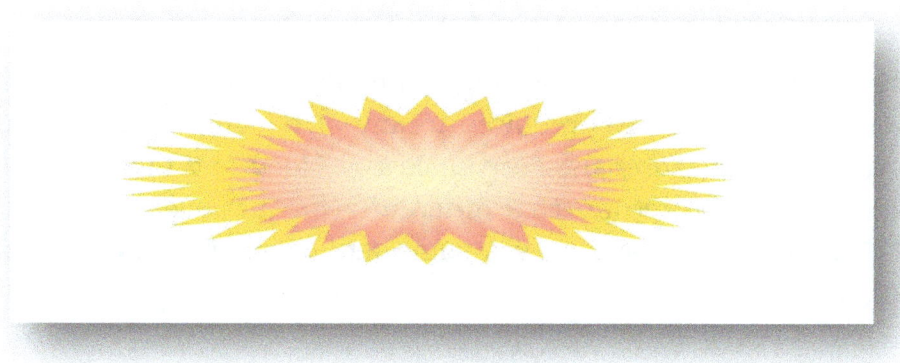

First Earthing Chakra

*The First Earthing Chakra connects us to the **Plant World**, and benefits the ability to interact with the plant life that surrounds us on Planet Earth.*

This includes flowers, trees, flora and herbs, and indeed, the foods that we eat that are sustained by these elements. As the existing energies shift, it affects not just the Planet, and not just our energy and consciousness, but also all that grows upon the Earth and in the Earth. Contaminants and chemical herbicides in our food can sometimes imbalance this Chakra.

The function of this Chakra is to Allow for Nurture by Nature. It is located approximately two feet or sixty centimetres (2' or 60cms) below the feet.

Keywords

Nature / Nurture; Nature Spirits / Devic Energies; Effective and Beneficial plant, herb and flora Interaction; Compatibility with and Utilization of Plant Life and all harvested foods; Human Physical blueprint; Veils, digestion, alimentary tract; ability to utilize what we take in physically; interaction / absorption / utilization; correct detoxification.

Ability to *convert foods*

Chakra Clues

When examining and exploring this Chakra, the colour range is generally of rich maroons, reds or browns. Though one client who had a lot of Venus memories and energies found that her's was a very soft green. The colours 'feel' very earthy and rich when balanced. It can also contain traces or threads of platinum. It seems to respond to a gentle approach better than a direct or commanding approach.

Connections

Then it has been balanced, and the statements listed ring true, further check if connection or reconnection is required to any of the following: Base Chakra, Navel Chakra, Spleen, Adrenals, Feet Chakras. Blood and Circulation. These may simply need to be reconnected differently (or just even consciously). If you find that any of these are not yet connected, it may indicate further issues that need addressing.

Key Chakra Codes Statements

Statements that can reveal, diagnose, initiate and activate include:

I now align and balance my 1st Earthing Chakra – I am aligned with the plant world and nature, and with the spirit and intelligence of nature easily and safely

My physical DNA remains human yet now resonates with ease to nature

My ability to safely assimilate the energies of the planet are enhanced

I align with the telluric realm safely and appropriately and I embrace the magnificence and variety of seedings from the solar winds, cosmic sources and earth incubations

My DNA is rebalanced to the New Light Code energies on this level

This Chakra is now 100% Clear and Whole

This Chakra is now 100% ready for initiation and activation

This Chakra is now 100% initiated and activated

SECOND EARTHING CHAKRA

*The Second Earthing Chakra connects us to the **Mineral World** and Kingdom and the Telluric Realms.*

This Chakra enables correct chemical uptake and interactions through and from; nutrition, the environment, water, and the gem, mineral and crystal kingdom and their energetic support. The creation of a Planet involves gases, fluids, matter, electrical currents and space seedings.

When this Chakra is out of balance our kidneys can suffer as they can become compromised or overloaded more easily. Contaminants and chemical herbicides in our water supply can sometimes cause imbalance in this Chakra.

This Chakra also rules our ability to utilise the composition of oxygen, hydrogen and carbon dioxide which are the main components of the air we breathe. So when not activated or balanced properly, the lungs can also be compromised; or the air we intake is not welcomed, assimilated or utilised correctly.

The difference in the particular vibrations or frequencies of land and its minerals and composition can also be a factor in this Chakra. Consider the difference in feel and effect of say salt or even cheese from differing parts of the globe. Minerals and natural products carry a different vibration depending on where they originated from. Each region has its own energetic imprint that can imbue and be carried by an item from that region. This is also true regarding what minerals via food, water and air were available and significant during gestation, and the early years. Energies impacting at birth may be positive or otherwise. These can all imprint on this Chakra. And the difference in the frequencies where we may find ourself in later life may be at variance, or disresonance, affecting quality of assimilation and of health..

The Second Earthing Chakra is located approximately a further two feet below the First Earthing Chakra, which is roughly four feet or one hundred and twenty centimetres below the feet.

KEYWORDS

Chemical compatibility; mineral utilisation and compatibility; crystals, air, oxygen, hydrogen. Geo-location issues and frequencies (issues due to being located in a particular geographical situation), Leylines or their connection points. Aura hydration and support; cells and cellular level; chemicals mini-factory / Sun

Ability to *convert gases*

CHAKRA CLUES

When examining and exploring this Chakra, you may well find that it holds a collection of colours, usually a full spectrum of a particular colour such as earthy multi-browns, creams and silvers. It also tends to golds and metallics, and can have a crystalline, almost lattice-like feel to it. Occasionally it can be a pale blue. Copper and zinc can also be traced in its configuration. There may be inclusions of patterns and formations similar to cellular receptor channels found in the human cell structures. These all facilitate better absorption. Its 'echo' supports bodily function.

It has been observed to appear as a Spiral Galaxy in some cases, whilst in others it appears to function as a kind of mini SubAtomic Chemical factory. It is often seen as a rotating Chakra or system.

Special Note for Sensitives

In those Souls who have had trauma through Reptile species (past or present), this Chakra can appear to be reduced or worn down; the Reptile energy has the action of attrition and grinding down on some Sensitives. This can result in a continual and constant weakening and exhaustion. After clearing all energies connected with this species, and clearing any associated impacts and taints, it would be wise to reclaim one's self as a *human* again...*and* as one living in this *current* Time and Space:

CONNECTIONS

Check if connection or reconnection is required to: Chakras; Sacral, Base, Crown Chakra. Knees. Liver.

KEY CHAKRA CODES STATEMENTS

Statements that can reveal, diagnose, initiate and activate include:

I now align and balance my 2nd Earthing Chakra – I am aligned with the mineral world and kingdom

I easily assimilate appropriately the minerals, chemicals and gases that enhance human life. My lungs breathe in more life and light

My crystalline body is enhanced daily. I am supported

My DNA is rebalanced and in harmony with the New Light Code energies on this level

I am now myself again, living and functioning as a human ...(wo/man) at ... (current living place), Planet Earth on the... (day, date and year).

This Chakra is now 100% Clear and Whole

This Chakra is now 100% ready for initiation and activation

This Chakra is now 100% initiated and activated

THIRD EARTHING CHAKRA

*This next Chakra connects us to the **Animal Kingdom**. It also holds many aspects to do with ancestry and humanity.*

This includes the inherent aspects of the hu*man* being on the DNA level, from our earthly (Gaia) ancestors (whether by 'nature' or by extra-terrestrial - or other - genetic modification) and our relationships with all things living and moving, particularly animals as opposed to insects.

It is also connected with our ability to relate to animals in a husbandry or caretaker sense. For those blood groups that require animal protein for health, it enhances the ability to better utilise all nutrition from animal products. In so doing, it can also assist with breaking down any negative or fearful vibrations that accompany some meats, keeping one's vibration clearer.

Our ancestry also affects functioning of this Chakra as these ancient resonances may imprint us before and after birth. Some Ancestral issues can be stored in this Chakra that are not helpful or compatible for our Soul journey. There may be Karmic records, Ancestral Codings, blames and / or taints held in this Chakra. Or any number of Ancestral skeletons in the cupboard, the energies of which remain unresolved yet are handed down through the following generations.

The location of the Third Earthing Chakra is approximately six feet or between one and a half and two metres below the feet.

KEYWORDS:

Animal in hu*man*; Genetic Modifications – historic; Ancestry and bloodline origins; Animal Food Products; an important Physical DNA anchor; it processes and detoxes a variety of allied issues and substances to provide greater nutritional compatibility and stability; **Etheric** Alignments with the elements and making friends with them (earth, fire, wind, water); Shamanic, Ancestral Commands, Dead Bones, Cannibal issues; Indigenous Incarnations; Centaurs, Totems, Shape-shifters; Sacred Geometric symbols; the opportunity to delete old ancestry stuff and activate good ancestry stuff

Ability to *convert living vibrations*

CHAKRA CLUES

When examining and exploring this Chakra, you will generally find that when balanced it is of a High Spin rate and is more in the shape of an Orb than a thick flat ring, donut or star. It tends toward a weave-like and fine filamental structure, oozing with golds, platinums, precious metals, and in some cases, symbols from the periodic table. There was also a sense of animal patterns and colourings in one student's experience.

CONNECTIONS:

Check if connection or reconnection is required to: Base Chakra, Solar Plexus Chakra, 3rd Eye Chakra, Hand Chakras. Kidneys and Kidney Chi.

KEY CHAKRA CODES STATEMENTS

Statements that can reveal, diagnose, initiate and activate include:

I now align and balance my 3rd Earthing Chakra – I am safely aligned with the animal world and kingdom

I no longer absorb ancient or current stress vibrations from what I eat, and I choose to let the resonance of the life-force which sustained all living things also support and sustain me no matter what my choices are in the foods I eat

I respect all living things, including my own physical flesh and its material aspects, and including my genetic ancestry and heritage, no matter the source or origin of my Soul and spirit

I can safely and easily now release past ancestral blames, shames and codings and reclaim myself

My DNA is rebalanced and harmonious with the New Light Code energies on this level

This Chakra is now 100% Clear and Whole

This Chakra is now 100% ready for initiation and activation

This Chakra is now 100% initiated and activated

Fourth Earthing Chakra

*The 4th connects us to **the Earth Archives and Codes**.*

This Chakra bridges as well as connects us to 3D and 4D Earth Destiny and Karma, Earth History and Future Plans. We are already in a 4D world, and many are embracing and moving into other dimensions.

Codes hidden in the 4th Earthing Chakra are from the beginning of time on Planet Earth. (And possibly from previous incarnations of the Soul and Entity that resides in this Planet.) These codes naturally include some degree of access or records of connection to the Planet or even to the Master-Mind that created this Planet.

There may also be some of us who have access to other-Planets or Stars that have contributed matter (through Space Dust distributed on the Planet via Solar and Cosmic Winds), and there may be those of us who have some prior knowledge through direct incarnation of these seeding Planets or Stars. This access can lie dormant in this Chakra until triggered later in life by a déjà vu experience or by incoming light or by vibratory transmissions of specific frequencies that resonate with them.

This Chakra also provides fuller access to earth electromagnetics – EMF. As the Earth moves through the energies of the Cosmos, and also experiences the shifts of energy and the regular changes in polarity of our Sun, its electromagnetic field is affected. This creates changes in its vibration. Because our own EMF is not resonating in the same way as the Planet's, we then need to re-align our EMF to be harmonious with the Planet's again.

The Earth EMF polarities change approximately every ten or eleven years, and our own EMF needs to adjust to match these in a harmonious way.

This Chakra, together with the Fifth and the Seventh, may also retain past or ancient Radiation damage or resonances. If this shows up in any one, it is a good practice to check that all three of these Chakras have been cleared of this toxic issue.

The Fourth Earthing Chakra is approximately eight feet or two and a half metres below the feet.

KEYWORDS

Space Dust Codings storage; Star Seedings memories and resonances; Purpose and Destiny; Leyline Akasha; Hidden codes since the beginning of earth time; 3D and $4D^h$ Earth destiny, karma, history and future; Responses to light and vibratory transmissions; fuller access to Earth Electromagnetics.

Earth memories, Input, reactions, beliefs, patterns, Old contracts, StarSeed records, Sea Turtle, Ocean, Waves, Dolphins, Fish, Fairy, Water eddies, Mathematics, Rainbows, ability to be released from certain types of incarnational Karmic Destinies, clearing of collective unconscious, No Time-No Space, Atomic Strength, Bleed through of Planetary Etheric Information, Major Species etheric interchange. This Earthing Chakra is the first to develop in the womb, is held in the Base Chakra till birth, and then has a slow descent into reality in childhood.

Ability to *convert electro-magnetics and etheric information*

CHAKRA CLUES

When examining and exploring this Chakra, you may find that it can be a variety of shapes – colours generally tend to teals, aquas, turquoises or a greenish spectrum. Brass, emerald, iron, shell (ocean) threads or resonances are associated with it.

Shape and structure is dependent on one's hereditary DNA and one's Star-Soul structure. Shapes and form may shift over time. And it is likely to change again after working and activating the Eighth Earthing Chakra.

CONNECTIONS

Check if connection or reconnection is required to any of: Base and All the Main Chakras, Transpersonal Chakra, the Feet and Hands. Spleen.

KEY CHAKRA CODES STATEMENTS

Statements that can reveal, diagnose, initiate and activate include:

I now align and balance my 4th Earthing Chakra – I am safely aligned with the telluric realm on a Planetary level

I now align safely and appropriately to my **Earth Archives and Codes.** *I am no longer held by the Planets historic memories and traumas. I have easy access to the vision I saw before this incarnation. The ocean intelligences now help me at* *the atomic level*

I easily release ancient traumas of the Earth that I may have picked up, or I may carry

I easily resolve and release planetary and earth karmic resonances as I surrender them to the light for transformation and higher learning

My Electromagnetics reset easily, appropriately and safely to the New Alignment Frequencies, and I easily adapt and align with Earth changes

I am renewed and energetically supported by this Earth as I sleep

My DNA is rebalanced to the New Light Code energies on this Earthing level

This Chakra is now 100% Clear and Whole

This Chakra is now 100% ready for initiation and activation

This Chakra is now 100% initiated and activated

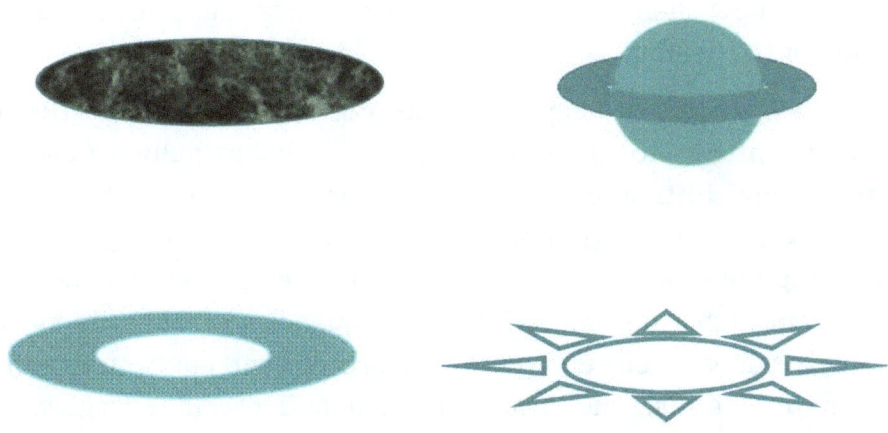

Fifth Earthing Chakra

Connection to Planetary frequencies of Gold and ORME. ORME: Orbitally Rearranged MonoAtomic Elements; Light enCoded Molecules and Atoms, a newly discovered form of matter sometimes referred to as 'exotic matter'. Some have linked this to the 'Philosopher's Stone' and 'StarFire'. The Ancient Egyptian esoterics knew of this substance, and it appears to be more readily available energetically to us all in these times.

The Fifth Earthing Chakra is an important Connection Point, and it further functions as the Anchor that stabilises and seals the previous four Earthing Chakras. In its own rights, it is a major Transducer of energy and helps maintain our ability to ground correctly. It replaces, or rather supersedes, the Earth Star in functionality, as its effects are more comprehensive and it is equipped to connect to other connection points for consistency and steadiness. The grounding ability is directly in relation to and as a demand for greater anchoring and security for the spiritual Upper or Higher Chakras.

This Chakra helps to seal or complete the previous four Earthing Chakras, and provide a good basis for most people in these changing times. Some energy work may require attention to this Chakra to enable the anchoring-in and integration of the new changes brought about by a healing. This supports long term retention of the healing.

Though this Chakra helps to keep us connected to **3 Dimensional Reality**, it works in a different way to the 4th Chakra. This Chakra helps to compensate for the destabilising shifts in energy so as to anchor and ground us better. It helps keep us solid and functioning in harmony with human 3D limitations whilst supporting the more refined energy fields; we can better cope with and utilise the current higher and more intense frequencies through its 'downstep' abilities. It also supports our energy to stay present and connected, enhancing our ability to fully utilise the incoming Gold and ORME energies. These frequencies are also strengthening and repairing to etheric and other subtle body energies. The Gold frequencies are especially necessary for a healthy charge to the Aura and all energy bodies. One can further assist in keeping this Chakra balanced, once it has been aligned, with homeopathic Aurum (Gold) and / or gold suspension fluid (Colloidal Gold).

The ORME assists in higher functioning connectedness and in maintaining a correct orbit or rotation speed. One which more readily adapts to the current shifts and changes in frequency. This is extremely important for the Major Chakra System functionality as these in-body Chakras require this level of alignment and connection to interface and maintain the new 3D -4D physical energetic aspects. [A candle cannot stay lit if there is no inner wick, not enough oxygen or no more wax. The flame requires the right environment to prosper.]

The Fifth sits at around ten feet or 3metres below the feet. It is a primary structure for initiating connection to the new Galactic Gridding System, which is part of humanity's ultimate evolution.

KEYWORDS

Gold and ORME charge, access and storage; Gold and ORME utilisation for healthy Aura; Major Anchoring point for Higher and other Chakras; Helps to sustain main Chakras; Help us to function in 3D solidity; bridges 3D and 4D in current energy shifts, Gold and ORME *utilisation* is essential for a healthy Aura; First module Recalibration sealer and Transducer.

Ability to *convert higher energies*

CHAKRA CLUES

When examining and exploring this Chakra, you may find: It tends to be osmotic and etheric in nature and structure and can give a sense of functioning like a mini laboratory. Often of Metallic composition (sometimes of mixed metals), it can appear to have 'pores' or receptor sites similar to those in human cells). The Fifth can also often hold family and ancestral codes that are connected with cellular functionality and may also affect one's chi on an energetic level. This is a different level of ancestral codings than the Third Earthing Chakra and is generally more connected with human higher involvement in Planetary history.

For some Soul's this Chakra may appear as a symbol. This symbol may remain throughout their lifetime if they have reached and integrated the source of their origin, or it can change depending on how much further evolving they need or choose to do.

Colours can be: Bronze, pale ruby, electric blue, helium. One client's Chakra had snow like energy surrounding it. Another client's was that of soft molten gold that she felt was a 'healing juice'. One of my students shared that the gold and ORME bathing felt like 'little cleaners; joy on steroids, happily polishing'.

Correct Orbit and a vertical plane are important with this Chakra.

CONNECTIONS

Check if connection or reconnection is required to: Chakras; Sacral, Navel, Throat, Crown, Transpersonal, 'I Am', Link-and-Heart. Amygdala, Pineal, Eyes, Adrenals Axis and Adrenals Matrix.

This now becomes a Gateway for Higher Consciousness to connect to.

KEY CHAKRA CODES STATEMENTS

Statements that can reveal, diagnose, initiate and activate include:

I now deserve to benefit from Gold and ORME

I now align to the liquid Gold and ORME codes and frequencies, and I stabilise my Earthing Chakras

I now utilise Gold and ORME energies easily and safely

My Aura now permanently retains Gold and ORME as is needed

My connection to the **New Golden Galactic Gridding System** *now proceeds*

I now allow healing at the Soul level and at the subatomic level

I align to the Symbol that is me

My DNA is rebalanced to the New Light Code energies as a ...(man/woman) on Planet Earth in the year...(date) on this level

This Chakra is now 100% Clear and Whole

This Chakra is now 100% ready for initiation and activation

This Chakra is now 100% initiated and activated

First Module: Anchoring

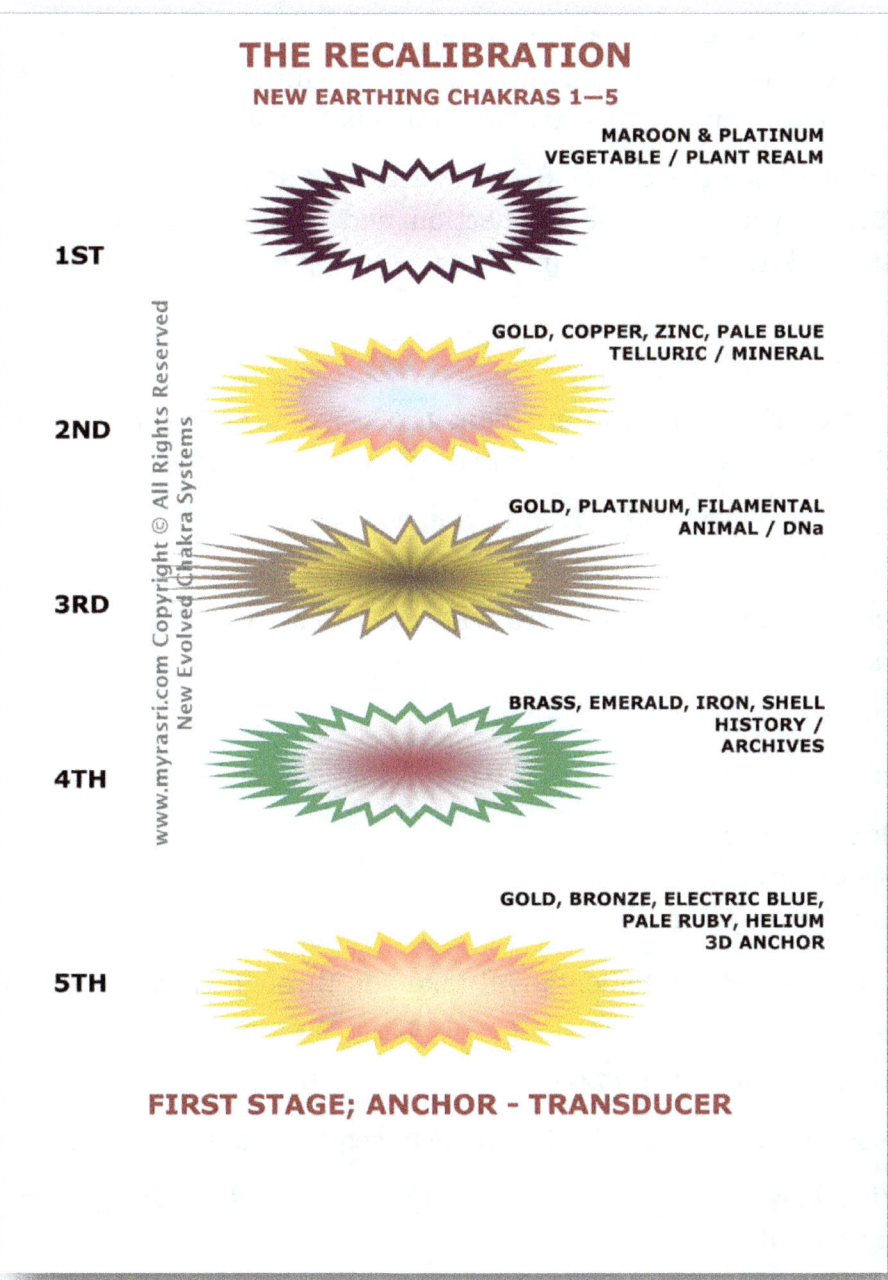

Perform the Calibration Anchoring

Now that we have balanced, cleared and initiated the first five Earthing Chakras, we can progress to 'seal' them and to anchor in this section of the new evolved system.

This next exercise is very important to *complete* the Recalibration and Upgrade Process. This then allows for proper 3D Anchoring and completes the Transducer requirements at this level and for this Module.

It is important to see these first five Chakras now as a whole, as a complete section. Before you begin the Connection and complete the Re-Calibration below, first check to ensure that in its entirety it is clear of all residual hooks etc.

Calibration Statements

My first five Earthing Chakras are now 100% free from residual hooks and drains, and the residue and muddiness of others or of the Planet

All of my first five Earthing Chakras are now fully recalibrated to the new Incoming Energies

I am now 100% correctly recalibrated and ready to activate this section, and to Anchor in at this point safely

Connections

Now that the Fifth Earthing Chakra is balanced, it is ready to connect to:

- Link Star Chakra
- Heart Chakra
- 'I Am' Gateway Chakra

To do so, the following statements will take you through each 'lock-in' step in order.

Key Chakra Codes Statements

Statements required to initiate and activate in sequence are:

My first five Earthing Chakras now easily, safely and willingly harmonise, anchor and 'lock-in'

My Gateway to my Higher Consciousness now engages

[Instruct 'lock-in' with each of the following Chakras as you engage and 'lock-in'; Allow time for each connection and allow yourself to feel your own inner command directed to the areas involved:]

I now lock-in at this Fifth Earthing Chakra level:

~ To the Heart Chakra

~ To the Navel Chakra …

~ To the Link Star Chakra

~ To the 'I Am' Chakra …

I am now stabilised at this level and where appropriate, I am ready to evolve further

My Fifth Earthing Chakra is now fully locked in and activated as The Anchor for my Earthing Chakras

1 - 8: THE PLATFORM

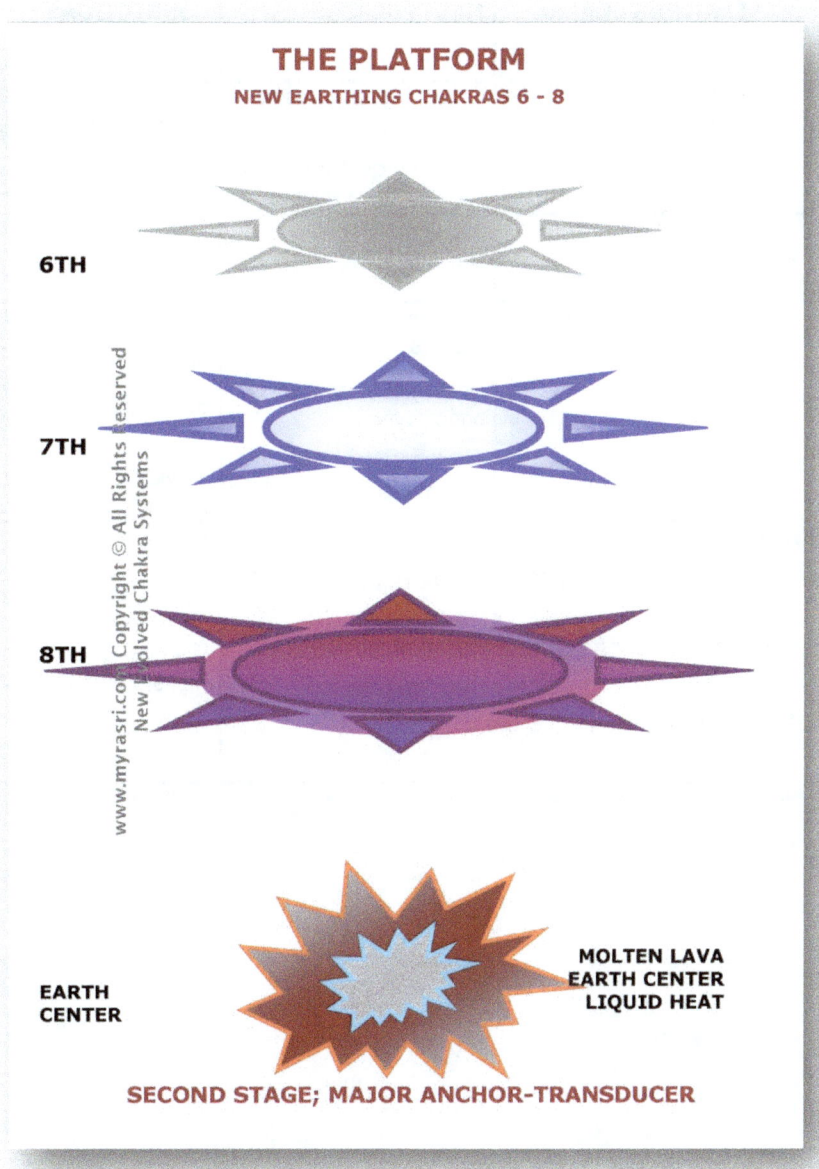

The Platform Chart - Connections

THE PLATFORM: 6th – 8th EARTHING CHAKRAS MATRIX

	Approx	EARTHING CHAKRA	MAIN PURPOSE	CONNECTIONS
6th	13'	Self Recognition & Re-union	Grounding for Access to Spiritual DNA Access ancient trauma & toxic shock to release	Activation of the 6th & 7th Earthing automatically triggers 8th Earthing.
7th	16'	Purpose & Destiny	Aligning DNA of physical, soul and spirit	
8th	19'-20'	Freedom Preparation	Release of old allegiances Healing of ancient shock and trauma Establish Earth Energy Transducer	Earth ElectroMagnetics StarSeed Anchor Seals Earthing Chakras 1st -7th Provides Platform for Soul Healing
ESTABLISHING THE PLATFORM: CREATION OF NEW GROUNDING PLATFORM AND STAR / PLANETARY ANCHOR CLEARING OR DEMOLISHING OF ANCIENT STRUCTURES, AND ASSOCIATED SHOCKS AND TRAUMAS ON CELLULAR LEVEL. CONNECTION TO GAIA, ALIGNMENT TO GAIA				When correctly balanced, cleared, activated and aligned, connects back to 5th Earthing, Heart Chakra, Link Star Chakra and Higher Spiritual Chakras

6 – 8: THE PLATFORM - OVERVIEW

This next series of Chakras builds on the Recalibration module.

KEYWORDS:

New Platform; New Foundations after the breakdown and Demolition of existing limiting structures and restrictions. Corrected DNA alignments. Old wounds addressed. Self Healing, Soul Healing and Unity.

WORKING WITH THE PLATFORM

Most humans are developing or reclaiming and clearing to the first Earthing Chakra module, requiring trigger words to assist in clearing, diagnosing and activating these first Chakras correctly. The activation words and tools listed were, generally, more than sufficient to enable the shifts and modifications required to prepare them for this next section. These same statements would, in some cases, have triggered issues that would require energy healing and clearing to speed up or to clarify the process.

The purpose of this second stage is to allow going beyond the limitations of the human experience. To do so, we must address those buried, forgotten, hidden or already arising issues that keep us shackled in any way on levels that are not immediately obvious or normally accessible. The key trigger words now need to be combined with essences for support.

In more advanced Souls, those who have evolved this next set of Chakras but haven't yet fully cleared, activated or aligned them and the associated issues, will find that the balancing and healing approach is more subtle and requires a different management.

For the Sixth, Seventh and Eighth Earthing Chakras, again work with each Chakra in consecutive order. When each one is properly aligned, you can safely proceed to the next.

However when it comes to the Eighth Earthing Chakra, please allow more time, as this is a major point and it can seem like once it has been activated that it begins to affect all of the previous seven Earthing Chakras. This can result in a fresh energy flow throughout all of these previously balanced alignments, and as the new energy flows through, it performs a kind of re-setting. Because the Eighth is a major pivotal point for the Soul journey and the spiritually journeying, connecting this point provides a different energetic translation of the incoming (and operating) energies and frequencies. This is fed through the Eighth and this new translation helps to 'lift' the tone of the whole Earthing System, and to enhance the spiritual connectedness, and thus the total experience, and the journey.

This can result in a re-setting of some or all of the Chakras whereby they may change shape, colour, tone or spin. Some can even change appearance totally. This simply indicates that the connection to the Higher Ascension energies has now allowed them to become more of what they are or were originally intended to be.

And may also demonstrate just how compromised their systems had been initially. It can also indicate a real and clear connection to their true StarSeed nature, or show a new visual realignment of their Crystalline nature and their Soul Body.

This second series of Chakras are positioned slightly further apart than the previous five. They are generally spaced at around three feet or 90 centimetres to one metre apart. This means that the Sixth through to the Eighth generally range from approximately thirteen to twenty-two feet (four to seven metres) under the soles of the feet.

Healing the Platform Chakras

6th Earthing Chakra

I have generally found that healing this Chakra often requires some other energetic form of support to complete the balance. Generally by means of an essential oil, essence or energetic balance.

Support Essences

A support essence can be an essential oil, a flower essence, gem essence, Shell essence, a homeopathic frequency, herbal essence, AuraSoma or some other form of vibrational essence or medicine. Some people may have access to colour frequencies. Whatever is indicated as a healing support frequency that you work with or are familiar with, and that indicates as appropriate will serve.

It may be that using essential oils engages the olfactory sensory organ as well as the nervous system, thus providing an extra etheric boost that supports the shifts and energy systems.

Using or requiring essences such as flower essences, Shell essences or gem essences will also engage the gustatory senses, digestive system and of course, the nervous system. And requiring a spray of essences of some form can indicate that the Aura itself and the etheric fields are being further supported to make the shift more easily and elegantly.

Of course, sprays can also assist in cleansing and purifying the Aura, depending on the sprays constituents and actions.

Energy Work

When energetic work or balance is indicated, this may be in order to more easily access a vibration in the healers field, or some resonance that they carry that comes through during the healing, especially if they have already balanced and initiated their own Sixth Earthing Chakra.

I initially found that there was some simple balancing of certain Chakras (main or Upper) that quickly assisted my client to move to this next level of energy. However, my own Earthing Chakras had already been fully balanced down to the Twelfth, so there was little to do to introduce the new resonance and activation for the client. For those still working on their own Sixth to Eighth

Chakras, there may be a combination of oil, essence and energy that is required.

7TH EARTHING CHAKRA

Working with this Chakra may well bring up some ancient or deeply buried and difficult issues to attend to.

This may well include DNA clearings and releases. Often, the energies involved emerge from the cells themselves, and over time the body also has to deal with the ensuing toxic fall-out as the old is sloughed off and moved out of the energy systems and the body itself.

Time may be required between working with this Chakra and moving on to the next. That is my strong suggestion. And to prescribe that the client or journeyer sets aside time to allow for some fun and to partake in appropriate social needs as part of their healing homework.

8TH EARTHING CHAKRA

As opposed to the previous two Earthing Chakras, you will find the Eighth very different to work with. When the Sixth and Seventh Earthing Chakras have been balanced and they are ready for the next step, there is generally very little active involvement required by the practitioner or facilitator. It seems that somehow this Chakra begins to balance itself, gathering energy as the previous two are cleared and aligned. This Chakra may well then begin to 'kick' into function without a lot of balancing as the Sixth and Seventh are aligned.

However, it will still require some work, though less intensive as the previous two in clearing any arising issues.

Due to planetary shifts, this Chakra can sometimes be affected and misalign itself even after activation. This is not necessarily due to anything other than the powerful impact of unseen esoteric, etheric and cosmic forces on the Planet, and subsequently upon us that dwell here. Not everyone will notice this, especially if they have not yet activated these Chakras, but the impact may affect the Sensitive, the Healer or those who are Earth Workers – working with healing the Planet.

Sometimes an ancient issue may arise, and only arise now because of the energies that the Planet is traversing that trigger the issue. This can well affect the Eighth too, or indeed any of the other Chakras.

When the Eighth indicates it is again out of balance, wherever possible, attend to the ancient memory, tracking it to its cause in order to completely winkle it out of the Chakra and any associated energy systems or connections.

When it appears to be damaged in some way and its spin is badly affected, I have found that working with the molten lava of the heart of earth can repair and rebalance any effects of interference or damage.

Use the energies as a homeopathic frequency: Imagine the molten lava in the heart of the Earth, and allow a gentle distillation of the energies to be applied like a paint onto the Eighth Chakra, gently bathing all of the surfaces of the Chakra and finally, bathing it gently so that it washes through and out again quickly. It appears to soothe it and replenish it, allowing it to gather itself again and to stabilise and realign again. Also, taking an Iron Supplement will assist in quick recovery and correct 'tone'.

After the Eighth is balanced, then the next step for this section or module is to focus on its function as the main Transducer, and on the effect that initiating and activating this as The Transducer has on *all* of the preceding Chakras.

SIXTH EARTHING CHAKRA

Self Recognition and Reunion. Soul fragmentation and shock healing. Symbols. Light beings and light bringers connections. Unhealed blockages and protections addressed.

Once this Chakra is aligned correctly its purpose is to enable proper grounding for the further advanced processing of one's *Spiritual DNA*. This means that not only can we now easily and readily access much more of our spiritual DNA with its wealth of qualities, attributes, recognitions, information and covert understandings, it also means that on a practical level we are more able to access the blockages that have built up over various impactful experiences. This needs to be addressed for us to move forward. Over time, buried and unresolved experiences on the spiritual level, experiences that we may not have had the tools to deal with, or that it was not safe to explore, these experiences need to be excavated, exorcised, cleared and resolved. The covering up or burying of these events can cause a covering-over or quarantine. These can create blockages. Blockages that have enabled us to function regardless of the hidden pain or wound. But blockages that are no longer supportive for us and that we are now ready to outgrow; now we can evolve and develop beyond them.

These blockages have allowed some mending of the spiritual woof and warp of our etheric and subtle body structuring to be protected and insulated to some degree which has facilitated and allowed a measure of functioning. Now we are at a time in the Planet's history where we are being called to further responsibility and awareness of a new consciousness, and it is important that these Chakras are now recognised, accessed and aligned.

Registrations of Toxic Shocks that have been held in our energy bodies from past Planetary and past Civilisation Destructions and Annihilations are now accessible through this Chakra. These issues have caused huge problems for many, creating impediments to our embracing freely and fully our spiritual sides on this physical plane.

There may be impact from or absorption from Ancient Radiation damage or retention. If this shows, then accessing this Chakra can allow old resonances to emerge, providing the opportunity for a deeper healing; this includes similar resonances that have been previously trapped in any of the previous Chakras.

In this case, recheck the Fourth and Fifth Earthing Chakras again, and bear the same in mind when working with the Seventh Earthing Chakra.

As mentioned earlier, Oils for trauma, essences for etheric shock and for energy system protection can assist in soothing this Chakra during the healing process. If you have access to them, use gem essences, Stellar or Star essences if and where indicated.

This Chakra is a further 3' below Earthing Chakra 5, and is located approximately thirteen feet or four metres below the soles of the feet.

KEYWORDS

Grounding at this point to enable enhanced Access to and balancing of one's Spiritual DNA. Ancient trauma and toxic shock in this Chakra or module can now be released. Access to historic issues on the Spiritual level that have not been dealt with or that require healing.

Soul Healing / Etheric Shock effects, Re-Alignment with elements after healing (See Third Earthing Chakra), Radiation damage / retention (check Earthing Chakras 4, 5 and 7).

Ability to *assimilate and convert on a Soul Level*

CHAKRA CLUES

When examining and exploring this Chakra, some of the things that may emerge are connected with issues arising that have been buried or unresolved through the ages. Due to the nature of the energies involved, we are given a chance for reconnecting with our own personal Spiritual DNA. This is quite separate from our physical Human DNA. It allows for the following:

- Star / Divine Source Alignment

- Spiritual DNA Access in order to clear blockages, and remove Protective Bandages

- Access to one's Spiritual Source in order to bring down inherent higher qualities, understandings, support and attributes

- Past planetary toxic shocks can now safely emerge, to be balanced, resolved or released for trauma [past planetary and civilisation destructions and annihilations may emerge for release and mending.

Part of the healing is often to recognise, love and accept our part (if any) in these events.]

The appearance of the Chakra can be a little different from earlier ones. For instance, it may appear to have 'fins' on its surface, or even a form of 'baffles'. It has more often than not a sense of Metals about it: iron, steel, brass, titanium; if damaged, it may need some form of energetic visualisation to kind of 'panel-beat' it or 'iron-it-out' and back into its proper shape, whatever shape that feels appropriate at the time.

Here is how one Chakra looked before it was 'iron-ed' out, and yes, later on at 8th Earthing Chakra you will see the significance of *Iron*.

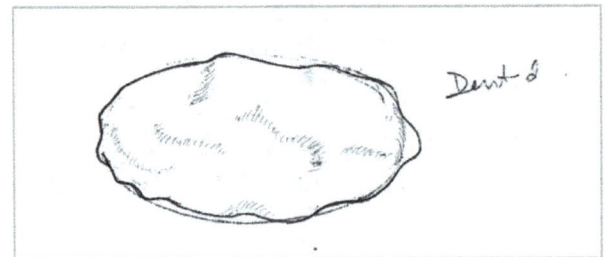

And here is one with a damaged 'baffle' or flange.

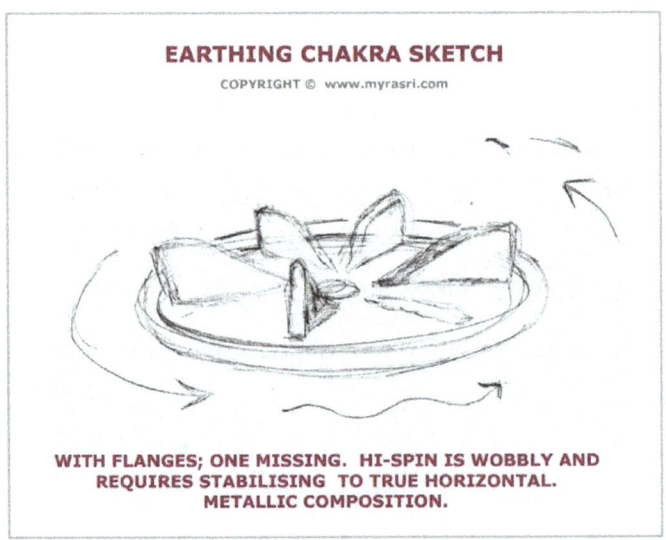

Besides the trigger statements, it may also require an essence or a sound to fully synchronise or activate it. Cymbals, a 'singing' brass bowl or whatever is close to hand that is appropriately acceptable energetically can be 'tested'.

(One person required a Hum sound, another wanted the sound 'OM' and someone required their name to be sung in order to initiate fully. And these were the perfect sound for the client at the time.)

The aim is to clear, to heal and to seal.

CONNECTIONS

Check if connection or reconnection is required to:

Fifth Earthing Chakra, The Nervous System, the Heart (as a Gland), the Gonads or the Ovaries.

KEY CHAKRA CODES STATEMENTS

Statements that can reveal, diagnose, initiate and activate include:

I now recognise myself

I am now reunited with myself

I now align and balance my 6th Earthing Chakra – I am aligned with my true Spiritual DNA.

*I **safely** release the need for spiritual bandages or splints, or for spiritual protection born of fear, wounding, lack or trauma. I am safe*

Past blockages and shocks now gently and surely clear and make way for my spiritual gifts, qualities, capabilities, attributes and recognitions and merit

I allow full healing. I am connected to and supported by my Spiritual DNA.

This Chakra is now 100% Clear and Whole

This Chakra is now 100% ready for initiation and activation

This Chakra is now 100% initiated and activated

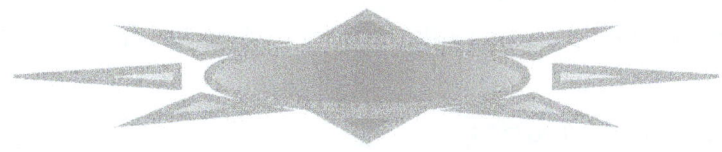

SEVENTH EARTHING CHAKRA

Purpose and Destiny. Integrating and Aligning all of the separate DNA's – Spiritual DNA, Physical DNA and Soul DNA - in harmony and to enable Purpose. All parts of the Being engaging and moving forward together in harmony.

Harmonising and freeing up the main Earthing Chakra Matrix comprising the first five Earthing Chakras assisted with our connection to Earth, to 3D, to 4D, and an increased functioning on the practical physical and mundane levels. This Chakra's importance is because it allows the DNA of our earth body and its energy systems, together with our Soul and our Spirit to now move into alignment. When balanced, a deeper inner harmony now resonates throughout the systems, *but* this also creates fall-out as some instances and inconsistencies have registered at different levels within these separate aspects of ourselves, and so the balancing process now initiated inevitably throws up any remaining cohesion differences to be dealt with.

As part of the healing at this point, be prepared to nurture the physical body again as one moves through to the completion of this particular process, whilst also practising or maintaining an emphasis on having some fun; in order to allow greater ease of movement through this alignment.

This Chakra is positioned approximately sixteen feet or almost five metres below the feet.

KEYWORDS

Aligning the DNA on the Physical level (balanced in the Recalibration module) with the DNA on the Spiritual level (balanced in Sixth Earthing Chakra) and one's Soul DNA. Initiates the connection of the now newly (and automatically) recalibrated Link Chakra to the Galactic Gridding System.

Check for DNA Shock or Interference of any sort from any source; including such issues as splicing, incompatibilities, implants or imprints.

Check for Holographic integrity; Clear any rogue programs, sabotage or Trojans if present.

Main Keyword – DNA Integrity

Chakra Clues

When examining and exploring this Chakra, I was amazed to see it moving with an extremely FAST HIGH SPIN. It had flashes of blues and pure white Light as it moved, and threaded through and from it were pearlised blue threads. My experience was that of a sense of it not moving smoothly, but seeming to 'catch' on something which created a kind of shudder, together with shutters or flashes. There was a sense of different gears attempting to synchronise together, and the release of a kind of energetic 'fall-out' as it moved through the different blocks or frequencies that had kept it misaligned in some way.

Any disresonances between the different DNAs will now be highlighted, and will require clearing and support. As it harmonises all previous Earthing Chakras, assists the Soul, Physical and Spiritual DNAs to align and increases function abilities, its construction may reveal gold, brass, bronze and / or spirals of pale rainbows. Focus on support now as working with this Chakra is also preparation for the Eighth Earthing Chakra to reveal itself; this will begin a process of self-activation and instigate a process whereby it will initiate its own programs as part of ascension preparation.

Connections

Check if connection or reconnection is required to previous Earthing Chakra or Chakras.

Activation of the Eighth Chakra commences when the Sixth and the Seventh Earthing Chakras are balanced.

Key Chakra Codes Statements

Statements that can reveal, diagnose, initiate and activate include:

My Soul DNa, my Spirit/ual DNa and my Physical DNa now safely align and harmonise together

I now choose that my Physical DNA is 100% Human in order to fulfil my Human purpose and destiny according to my own Soul's true purpose

I am now One with my Purpose

Action Support Statements

I now align and balance my 7th Earthing Chakra

I align and safely release disresonances between my different DNA systems, allowing them to emerge, to heal, to clear, and to harmonise

I nurture my physical vehicle as I welcome and accept this Chakra

This Chakra is now 100% Clear and Whole

This Chakra is now 100% ready for initiation and activation

This Chakra is now 100% initiated and activated

EIGHTH EARTHING CHAKRA

Freedom and Ascension Preparation. Connect to 'Home'. Transducer, Platform. Dissolution of old allegiances and structures enslaving the Soul or Being.

This Chakra now requires clearing and correct alignment in its own right, and then to be appropriately connected to the previous Chakras and relevant Connection Points – as listed. The process was already initiated as the Sixth and Seventh were cleared and activated. Now we focus on checking if any further clearing or support is required.

The Eighth Earthing Chakra governs this initiated new system of Earthing Chakras (First Earthing to Seventh Earthing) as they are being realised and aligned, by establishing a higher functioning through the control and transducing of Earth Electro-Magnetics, frequencies and vibrations. This in turn creates our individual energetic platform and stabilizer or 'landing pad' which allows for anchoring of the Starseeding heritage (incoming through the Higher Chakra systems and the associated Light Bodies) of vibrations, codings, values, geometric alignments, pattern-ings, freedoms, powers and alternate dimensional slipstreams, so that the memories of free travel between dimensions hidden in our Starseed memories can be incorporated into our present perceptional reality again for our fun, play, potential productivity and creativity in the cosmos and inter-dimensionally.

Disresonances between the different systems – often governed by DNA and past experiences – are now smoothed and harmonised as integration takes place through all these systems. They now co-exist with ease, aligning themselves to the one purpose, that of the Supreme intention of the Soul.

With this Chakra fully cleaned and cleared, balanced and aligned we can truly recognise the winds of heaven dancing around and within us, and our dance between the winds and in the heavens. Wonder returns to refresh our energies in ways we have never experienced before, joyful awe at the journey and the arrivals, and the destination platforms being prepared to catapult us to a higher college of experiences and creations yet again. Jadedness will lapse, boredom at the recycling of drama and conflict will be forgotten, hope will be our shadow and our moon, and peace will be the sun we turn to face. When the other previous Chakras are aligned, then this Chakra will gently move into place over a short period of time. This then acts as a kind of 'sealing' of these lower Chakras, only dislodged by self abuse or huge atomic shock.

This major Chakra is located approximately nineteen or twenty feet (five to six metres) below the body.

KEYWORDS

Release of and Dissolution of Old Allegiances. Clearing of old Structures, Healing of ancient shock and trauma. The establishing of the New Earth Platform, Foundation and Energy Transducer. Stabilization of the Earthing Chakra System. Birthing of the New Consciousness.

Anchoring of vibrations, codings, values, geometric alignments, pattern-ings, freedoms, powers and alternate dimensional slipstreams; provides access to appropriate memories of free travel.

Main Keyword: The Platform – is Established.

CHAKRA CLUES

When examining and exploring this Chakra, accepting its importance will assist in its automatic balancing, already triggered as the Sixth and Seventh Chakras are cleared.

This Chakra will appear as larger and more solid than previous Chakras, as its function is a comprehensive one. It can often appear a bit more elaborate than others, but this is not necessarily an indication of anything other than the technology of the Soul's own StarSeed capabilities.

It is a major Gateway and a Waveform Platform, handling and transforming incoming energies to safe voltage, frequency, range and loading. It also deals with vortex energies, and may sometimes have this feel about it, demonstrating opposing energies in vortex, or varying spirals of frequencies. It is a rather amazing piece of advanced etheric anatomy technology.

The actions and processes initiated in this Chakra now incorporate the following:

- Transduces and Stabilises to the Earth EMF Frequencies and Vibrations
- Energetic Platform and Anchoring for supportive Starseed vibrations and broadcasts

- Memories may be triggered, that can create an increase of fun and play potential if one has experienced a serious incarnation
- Activates the Sealing of the previous Chakras

IRON SUPLEMENTATION

An interesting factor to this was the discovery that when one's own Iron supplies are depleted, and this Chakra is activated, it can increase a temporary need for more Iron in the diet. It is not always readily available in a vibrational support essence that I am aware of. I was alerted to this when I personally found that I had a sudden overwhelming desire for a Guiness – an Iron-laden beer – to fortify and help rebuild this Chakra. Interesting when one considers that I don't like beer, and hardly ever drink. The Iron in this type of drink is made extremely effective because it is carried into the body via the alcohol, which has the ability to penetrate the blood-brain barrier very quickly, transporting whatever is in the alcohol immediately into the brain. This then begins a work and change within the physical being which obviously supports the etheric and energetic changes. I also found that bathing the Chakra with the energy of the Molten Earth Lava in order to support, repair, stabilize and assist with its correct spin was very effective. So do not be surprised if balancing this Chakra reveals a need for further Iron Supplementation as the Chakra system sets itself to its higher capacity and functionality.

CONNECTIONS

Ensure that there is correct and safe connection or reconnection to Earth ElectroMagnetics (EMF). Ensure that this Chakra fulfils one of its functions as a StarSeed Anchor and that it Seals the Earthing Chakras First to Seventh. Establishing these connections ensures its function to provide a Platform for Soul Healing;

- Soul Connection Point near Navel (Tan Tien)
- Liver
- Eyes
- Pineal Gland
- Inner Earth and Outer Cosmos Energies
- Earth Light (Earth Blood Pure Liquid Light)

KEY CHAKRA CODES STATEMENTS

Statements that can reveal, diagnose, initiate and activate include:

I now accept and reclaim my True Higher Divine Purpose, free from restrictions or agendas of others

I break and dissolve <u>All Old Chains</u> and Allegiances <u>Now</u>

Action Support Statements

I welcome in the Inner Earth Energies, and bathe this Chakra with the molten heart of the Earth, allowing for this Chakra's birthing, strengthening, and activation

I now align and balance my new 8th Earthing Chakra – this energetic platform and anchoring Transducer now aligns, and stabilises

Memories of my Soul and co-creativity now liberate me

My eyes are 100% mine, and only I see from and through them

This Chakra is now 100% Clear and Whole

This Chakra is now 100% ready for initiation and activation

This Chakra is now 100% initiated and activated

HEALING THE EIGHTH CHAKRA

When viewing the Eighth Earthing Chakra, it may look like a disc on its side, horizontally, or like a spinning horizontal wheel. There may be warps on the disc so it may look corrugated or dented – depending on the impact of our journeyings. There may be a noise or grinding sense with it, as it tries to activate itself, or possibly an uneven whirring sound. It may look murky, muddy, rusty or chipped until 'balanced'.

Methods I have used:

- Basting it with molten lava from the centre of the Earth
- Basting it with molten metal, be it lead, iron (most common) or some other indicated metal
- Addressing the spin, axis and composition to stabilise
- Support with 'Fun' and 'Pleasure' homework
- May need Iron 'Hit' – Guinness or Steak or Iron Supplement

ALLOW TIME FOR THIS TO NATURALLY COMPLETE ITS PROCESS AND STABILISATION

Once this Chakra has been correctly cleared, aligned and activated, it is then time to address these three Chakras – Sixth, Seventh and Eighth – together as one stage; **The Platform**. This Platform is essential as a safe foundation of grounding, wholeness and connectedness for Spiritual Freedom and Ascension.

Establishing the Platform:

We are now at the point of Creation of the New Grounding Platform and Star-Planetary Anchor. This is to allow full Clearing and demolishing of Ancient Structures, together with Associated Shocks and Traumas on Cellular level. We also gain at this point correct and appropriate connection and alignment to Gaia.

The assembled and activated Chakras are now ready for Anchoring.

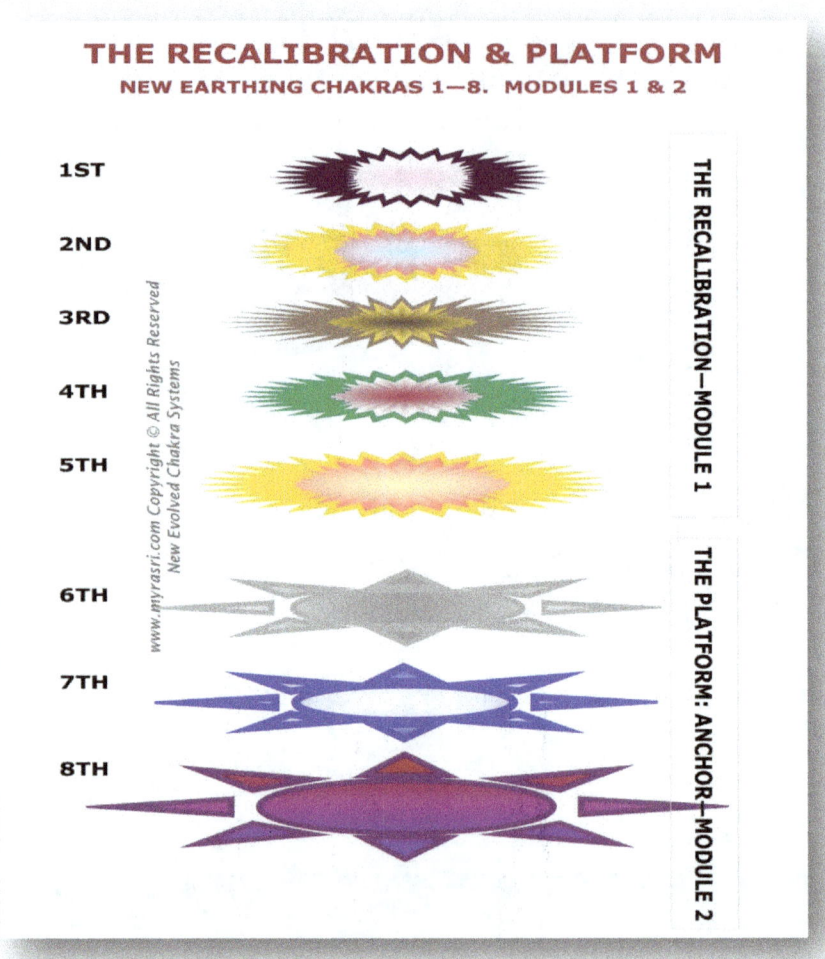

ANCHORING 'THE PLATFORM' EARTHING CHAKRAS 1-8

KEY CODE STATEMENTS

This stage of my evolution is now clear and I am poised to fully embrace all that I am and all that I can be

All of my Eight Earthing Chakras now balance, align and harmonise together, as I welcome my freedom and enhance my essence and presence here on Planet Earth

My beliefs and attitudes now reflect who I am on a Soul and Spiritual level, and these work together for me in this 3D reality

I now replace the cycle of drama, conflict, boredom, despair or enslavement with inner harmony and strength

I am ready to welcome true joy into all aspects of my being and life

My energies are now refreshed, my purpose and Soul Plan is now refreshed and I am ready to take my place on this Planet, free from shock and delusion

My Transducer at the Eighth Earthing Chakra is now fully and safely initiated and activated and I welcome in the new Light frequencies with ease and stability

The Eighth Chakra (as the Anchor for all of the preceding Chakras) now requires linking in and connection to the following Connection Points. Take care to do each connection one at a time, ensuring that each connection is completed before proceeding the next.

This Stage (Module) at this point is now safely connected to:

- The Fifth Earthing Chakra Anchor (Platform)
- The Heart Chakra
- Link Star Chakra
- and the Upper Chakras.

As each Connection Point position records the echo and vibrational frequency from the Eighth Chakra, the ripples from this action initiates a re-setting of their own inherent frequencies, assisting in lifting them to a higher and more effective level of functionality and grounding.

NOTES ON THE PLATFORM

TRANSDUCER BENEFITS

So as the 8th aligns, through the balancing, clearing, activation and initiation of the 6th and 7th, things shift and change – the play out of personal stuff is no longer the real game field or overriding reality – but the Soul is now given the opportunity (and now faces more clearly) the <u>results</u> or repercussions of current life circumstances and choices made, and begins to access and understand the deeper reasons why.

The scope goes beyond simply 'past lives' and their karmic consequences. And even beyond Genetic DNA and Ancestral Commands. We are accessing the Soul plan, destiny, purpose and blue-prints on a different level. We are now able to access OverSoul issues, Creator issues, Grand Planetary Schemes issues, Genetic Creation and Modification issues.

The Soul is now poised to gather momentum toward a new future – the foundational Earthing 'Base' has shifted from 'feet-on-the-ground' through the Earth Star or early anchoring system, to the new 8th Transducer Earthing Chakra.

There is now a real anchor from which to explore more safely through an improved connection with the planet, the stars, the cosmos; to arrive at the answers to those deeper Soul quests and questions.

COMPROMISED EARTH HEALERS

There are some whose energy systems have become entwined with the Planet, and these same helpers can unfortunately become involved with past Planetary issues, karma and associated problems. This then prevents them from being fully effective in their role as healers to the Planet and also in their own individual lives, as over-involvement prevents true clarity – and therefore effectiveness. When the Planet herself has issues and is struggling with the injustices lain upon her, one can be compromised when wearing the same vibration or resonance, and can also find their energy and efforts thwarted.

To truly help the Planet and be of real assistance, one cannot be as injured as her, and one needs to be able to separate energy connection in order to bring a more positive energy and outlook to the situation. It is my opinion that we best serve the Planet by holding our own Light as best we can.

CONNECTIONS

When correctly balanced, cleared, aligned and activated, this module is then connected back to the;

- Fifth Earthing Anchor
- The Heart Chakra
- Link Star Chakra
- and the Upper Chakras.

SOUL CHOICES

When the first eight Chakras are cleared, balanced and aligned this allows for speedier resolution of existing issues through the mirrors of past events and unresolved issues in this current incarnation.

Attention is then focused on the Soul's thrust or Core definitions that were essential to be set up in this life time through the huge restrictions in utero, in childhood and in circumstances.

The personal choices of the selected family that one was incarnated into; the individual family members, family genes or patterns of any particular parent or sibling, the culture, geography, nation or era-time; these are not all 100% under the control or responsibility of the incoming Soul's own volition. They may be able to inhibit some things, and they might not have been able to inhibit others, often those things which they wish to overcome and to go beyond.

There may have been a pre-incarnation selection process going on regarding possible combinations of genes, parents or families, national or geographic karma or possible technical or spiritual developments and timing.

There may have been counselling and advice given from major entities of importance to the Soul or responsible for guidance or mentoring of the Soul.

There may have been interference at some Higher Level, and consideration for a Higher agenda than one's personal Soul evolution.

There are many possibilities, choices and pathways that could be part of the equation to incarnate at this time, in this place, with these people.

It may also appear that one's pre-ordained 'mission' may feel like a 'sentence' to some, even many, when experiencing huge restrictions in early life.

Particularly if one is not fully aware of all of the concerned parties or 'investors', agendas, co-ordination or planning involved.

It is wise, therefore, to consider that some choices we had no control over; and that this possibly created a fear on some level that could have been registered in some part of our anatomy or memory back in the womb, as recognition dawned on the Soul as to what it had arrived at.

[The Spirit may know All, as it operates in other spheres, but when it comes down to things at a Soul level, and because it operates and functions differently, recognised or acknowledged fear or trauma is more likely to affect the human aspect detrimentally. This being said, the Spirit itself can even be damaged, though usually the Soul is somewhat badly damaged first before the Spirit is so affected, but not always.]

The effect of this can 'play' with one's inner guidance system, as the reality and potentiality of this earthly existence comes into full focus – creating a kind of Soul 'panic' which does not make for easy access to previous Soul knowledge and security. Nor readily to one's higher purpose.

This panic, fear, anger or hurt must be addressed for the Soul to feel supported and to remain 'safe' whilst continuing its mission.

9 – 11: THE HIGHER FUNCTION

9th To 10th Chakras approx 3' each apart = 25' – 32' or 7 – 10 metres below the feet.

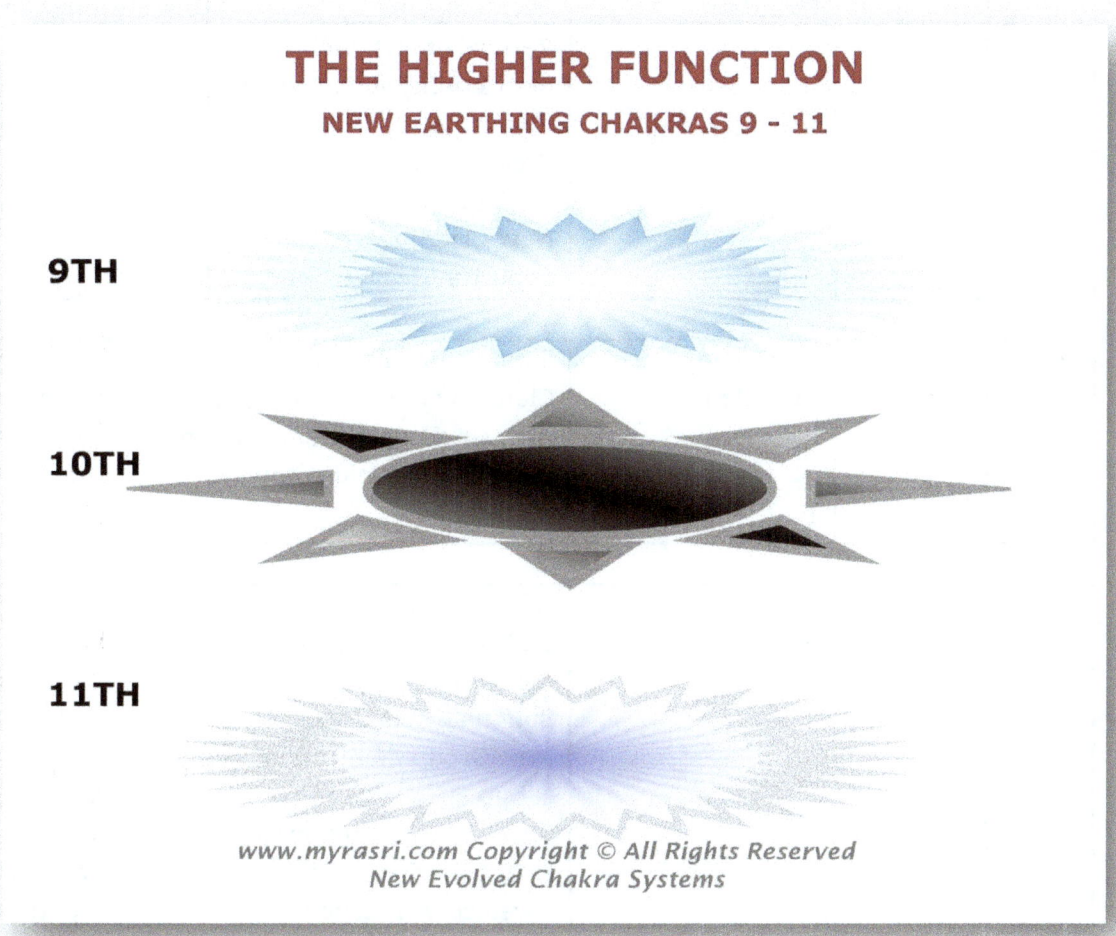

THE HIGHER FUNCTIONS: CHART

	Approx	EARTHING CHAKRA	MAIN PURPOSE	CONNECTIONS
9th	25'–26'	Freedom Foundation	Renovation begins with new template Release of Ancient restrictions, voluntary or involuntary Break down and release of Ancient structures New Gridding System opportunities	New Choices Ascension Wave
10th	30'–32'	Ascension Initiation	Establishing new foundations Claim own identity and purpose New Gridding Systems initiated as close down old pathways	New purpose in the New Ascension Energy Wave
11th	32'–37'	Utopia / Dystopia Polarity Exploded	New Highways and Gridding Pathways setting up Following own Spirit Spiritually comforted New Group Connections being set up Move into Co-Creatorship Duality and Polarity issues revealed or reconciled	Reconnection back to and liberation of the Female energy Balancing of Female with Male, demise of patriarchy
HIGHER FUNCTIONS: REVEALED, INITIATED and ACTIVATED. SOUL PURPOSE IS REDEFINED, SOUL CONNECTIONS REVIEWED, SOUL HEALING FROM OTHER INCARNATIONS, EXPERIENCES, DIMENSIONS and REALITIES IS ACTIVATED.			When correctly balanced, cleared, activated and aligned, new gridding connections of and Nadis commences. Brings one into new choices of purpose Can connect back to 8th and 5th Earthing, Heart Chakra, Link Star Chakra and Higher Spiritual Chakras	

THE HIGHER FUNCTION — 9TH — 11TH OVERVIEW

*The **Higher Functions**; Revealed, initiated and activated. In alignment with the possibilities and frequencies provided by the new Incoming Energies, the Soul Purpose is redefined, Soul connections are reviewed. New Gridding connections are now redefined and aligned.*

Now we proceed to a Renovation of existing structures on a Higher Level. We have realigned the energies of our Humanity and recalibrated it to the new Incoming Energies. We have reset our DNA's to allow for full integration. We have established a foundation and a transducer to cope with the new energies. Now we proceed to build on these and begin the creation or correct establishing of our new position and refinement to the next level. We are now moving to the preparation and establishment of new structures, connections, blueprints and potentialities for our own Spiritual healing and Cosmic healing. We are moving from service or enslavement to others toward self kingship / queenship.

Balancing this module is best undertaken when some time has elapsed since the reclamation or activation of The Platform. There needs to be some time for integration and energetic rest and equilibrium before commencing work on the Higher Function Chakras. Allow at least one month to three months between these two modules.

Ninth Earthing Chakra

Freedom and Ascension Renovation and Foundation. Demolition of the old, and preparation of the new at a Higher Level. Release of Ancient restrictions. New Gridding System opportunities.

We are now stabilized through the 8th Earthing Chakra, and this allows further release and realignments. This level cannot be accessed unless the previous Chakras have been aligned and connected.

Old ideas and ways of freedom are superseded as new information and energy is accessed via the Transducer Platform. The ancient programmed or dictated rules and traditions regarding 'Ascension' now give way to the Divine reality in 3D, 4D and beyond. Ancient rulers and their claims are now cleared and refuted as they no longer apply to this time-space-place reality. Occasions of induced, seduced, hypnotic, subconscious or enforced agreements and allegiances are now revealed for challenge and invalidation.

Twenty-five to twenty-six feet or seven to eight metres).

Keywords / Main Purpose

Claiming Freedom. Freedom foundation. Ascension Preparation. Renovation begins with the break down and release of any existing restrictive Ancient Structures, voluntary or involuntary. Restoration begins with creating, designing or accessing a New Template.

The Void is addressed, and alignment to a new framework takes place. We anchor here with the 5th Chakra above the head; the 12th Higher / Upper Chakra or Divine Threshold.

Main Keyword – Accessing Higher Function, Connections and Possibilities in a New Way.

Chakra Clues

When working this Chakra, one may well experience a lot of energetic activity. This is because releasing really deep and hidden issues requires a safe, stable and sure environment and foundation. The body, being and energy systems require this in order to open, explore and release things at this level. Consequently, one may well find some interesting reactions as old buried stuff is dealt with.

There can be a 'shattering' sensation as things are exploded apart, like a skin bursting, and the revealing and releasing of inner and outer restraints.

Reactions and actions can include:

- Shaking and disorientation for light-workers which can create a kind of smog. This smog can impact on others around them.
- Releases occur – old chains, archetypes, further blue-print interferences. One may also 'feel' these energies as they rattle whilst making their exits
- Persistence to prevent the desire to 'escape home' prematurely is supported
- Accesses and pulls more light in for the next stage of journey

Its colours tend to the Turquoises, Sea-greens or Pewter in feel and appearance. It seems to hold an inner Light which infuses one with a sense of inner-connectedness in *safety*.

CONNECTIONS

Connect, reconnect or resonate to:

- Divine Threshold – 12th Higher Chakra
- New Gridding System opportunities
- New choices
- Lungs
- Nervous system
- Signal / Survival Chakra System

KEY CHAKRA CODES STATEMENTS

Statements that can reveal, diagnose, initiate and activate include:

I Am One With My Freedom

I Am Free

Further Action Support Statements:

I null and negate all:

- *Old Codings*
- *Imprint-ings*

- *Pattern-ings*
- *Programs*
- *Allegiances, Enforcements*
- *Enslavements*
- *Punishments*
- *Mistake and Failure Debris and Residue*
- *Tectonic and Mummified Armouring and Bandaging/s*
- *AND ALL Frozen and Grafted / Implanted / Embedded Chains, Shackles, Fetters and Restraints THAT are being shaken up for Release, Discharge, Liberation, Dissolution, Conversion, Healing and Transmutation.*

I now sail easily through the 'smog' of releasing debris of humanity. I now house a higher and larger light frequency with ease and elegance

Renovation, review and refreshment now restores me

I am now fully willing to step into co-creation on a Soul level

The reasons to 'leave' this incarnation and 'escape' home no longer exist, as I now know at this level that I will inevitably return home

I am now fully open to recognising New Gridding System opportunities available in the Ascension Wave

This Chakra is now 100% Clear and Whole

This Chakra is now 100% ready for initiation and activation

This Chakra is now safely 100% initiated and activated

NOTE:

As this Ninth Earthing Chakra has connections that work with the Earth Gridding System, those who are really Sensitive and have had a history of standing up to the Dark may occasionally find that certain Dark Species attempt to connect in at this point to the energy systems of those who have opposed them in order to regain control or keep an ill-health frequency running.

This situation is not new – those who have been evolving and find themselves here again at this time may well have set themselves the challenge to use the energies of this current time era to dig deep to clear those things that have hunted and hounded them throughout time. This then, is one of your tools.

So rather than viewing this negatively, see the amazing opportunity that presents itself to you now, through the revelation of this particular Chakra and its domain and function; and its past connection vulnerabilities that you may well have had no previous idea about.

From the Ninth with its holding foundation of the Eighth, you now have a position of power to monitor from – for instead of viewing it as a weak spot, see it as your conscious access to self reclamation and victory! Now you are aware that you *can* clear this; and you can no longer be accessed secretly through any covert Earth connections.

Tenth Earthing Chakra

Ascension Purpose Initiation Process. Soul Healing at the Galactic level. Claim of one's own true Identity and Purpose at a higher level.

The preparation of new foundations, new anchoring, new energetic plumbing, new options choices and decisions as old decisions and pathways have now been closed down. Healing of deep grief of the Female and the Female Lineage of Light (Codes carried down through the Female energy).

This Chakra allows us to align to a New Pathway without bleed-through or interference of energies from old or unfinished commitments, intentions or choices.

We now start our own personal Ascension Process... Unique to each of us, we are getting ready to move up.

Twenty-eight to thirty-two feet or eight to ten metres below the feet.

Keywords / Main Purpose

Freedom Foundation. Ascension Initiation. Establishing new Purpose Foundations. Claiming of one's own identity and purpose. Closing down of old energy leakages in the direction of unfulfilled hopes, decisions and dreams. New Gridding Systems initiated for engagement as old pathways close down. Focus on Divine Soul Mission. Holds and anchors new grid and Nadi system.

- Completes upgrade from kinship to Kingship / Queenship
- Align to new chosen pathway, must close down other options
- Re-wiring for the move forward and a reality check for formulating goals and plan
- Ascension possibilities becoming clearer – as clarity progresses, choices of future destiny begin to emerge
- May appear as a symbol, geometric pattern or as a Thoughtform structure (of the Self)

Main Keyword – New Purpose in the Ascension Energy Wave.

Chakra Clues

This chakra may appear as a symbol, geometric pattern, or series of symbols or even as a crop circle design.

Or it may appear Iron-Like, with Steel Rods or Inner Spokes of Reinforcement. Qualities include; Metallic, silvery grey, Iron, steel. It may demand further Iron supplementation or support as for the Eighth Chakra.

CONNECTIONS

Connect or reconnect to:

- New Choices
- Appropriate alignment to The Ascension Wave (and New Era Energies)
- The Womb in the female
- The Fifth Earthing Chakra Nadis and the Galactic Gridding System

KEY CHAKRA CODES STATEMENTS

Statements that can reveal, diagnose, initiate and activate include:

I now stand in my own identity, my own karma, my own merit, my own rewards, my own Purpose

I deserve my freedom, and I deserve and claim it now

I now claim my own unique identity and my own true Purpose and Destiny in full alignment with my Higher Self and my Soul journey

My new creations are truly supported, crafted and imbued with free will, love and Divine inspiration, aspiration and integrity

Further Action Support Statements:

I now close down the many past un-actioned, unfulfilled and un-followed options and decisions in order to pursue the One, and I can still allow for other choices

I acknowledge and release all past promises and intentions that I have left unfulfilled, and I ask for these energies be withdrawn and recycled to positive use without harm to myself or others

I am at peace and resolved with my past endeavours, intended purposes and incomplete plans as I move away from them and onto my true Soul path and creation, and live in the moment

I now herald my energies, focus and intentions, allowing for clearer integrity and authenticity

From this point on, I am 100% free from anybody else's choices, decisions and intentions for my life and my purpose

It is now clear and safe for me to make new choices and decisions

I can choose to take one path at a time

I easily discover that which 'sparks' or inspires me – and follow that which lays within my heart and Soul

I welcome New realms, New ideas and insights, new pathways and new highways in line with my Soul's plan

I now welcome New choices that align with my true Soul Purpose and Destiny

This Chakra now holds and anchors with the new Grid and Nadi system safely and appropriately

This upgrade is completing perfectly, safely and elegantly

I fully move into Co-Creation, and Co-operation on a Unity level a

I now connect safely and appropriately on a Soul-Group consciousness level

We now operate from a place of KingShip / Queenship, and not just KinShip...

I now fully embrace my New Gridding System opportunities

This Chakra is now 100% Clear and Whole

This Chakra is now 100% ready for initiation and activation

This Chakra is now 100% initiated and activated

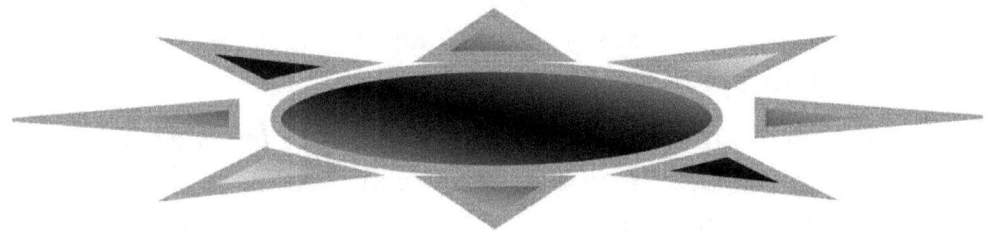

Eleventh Earthing Chakra

Utopia /Dystopia Polarity Exploded. Reconnection back to and liberation of the Female Energy and Principle. Balancing of the Female with the Male, the demise of the patriarchy. The heartbreak and wounding through separation and disrespect of the Divine Feminine is also ready to heal and to move beyond. Ancient weeping that has held the Soul back or in fear is now dissolved, and illusion and allusion is replaced with a positive reality possibility.

The separation of connectedness within the self that results in false or mistaken beliefs in the Illusion of Utopia is exploded. So too is the fear of Dystopia, the opposite of the 'Perfect'. Utopia is the imaginary picture or state of the perfect place, governing system or situation. The dream and sometimes the implementation of a society possessing highly desirable and near perfect qualities. This may appear to be excellent but often in current humanity's horizon somewhat impractical, idealistic and not realistic. Dystopia, its opposite or polarity, is a nightmare society; dehumanising, and sometimes the result of a driving force to create a Utopia – resulting in the polarisation of energies and governing matters and attitudes or agendas. These are old models, and models that have been often used as offerings and excuses for controlling 'the masses', but which in reality only favour a few elite and exempt personages. This energy and polarity has been influencing the Planet for hundreds of years, and its time is now drawing to a close as exposure and transparency reveals the strings and investments behind false promises.

This then gives way to new understandings, where the humanity of humanity and its inherent spirituality are allowed to develop and advance in less harmful ways. The liberation of the feminine principle being a major influence and resource for these changes on the Higher levels. When one feels valued, there is less likelihood to seek or wreak revenge as recompense.

This shift then gives way to new creatorship, new co-operations, new group connections and new pathways.

Located about 5 feet below the Tenth Earthing Chakra, or thirty-two to thirty-seven feet or ten to over eleven metres. There is often some variation with these more advanced Chakras, depending on the positions of its predecessor. As long as the Chakras are directly below each other and possess the correct spin etc after balancing, then they are in the perfect position.

Keywords / Main Purpose

Divine Gender sorrow and wounding is addressed for healing. Spiritual comfort. Replacement of the Old; with New Highways and Gridding Pathways being set up, constructed and operational. Following one's own Spirit. New Group Connections being instigated. Move into Co-Creatorship. Duality and Polarity issues revealed for reconciliation and resolution.

It can bring a sense of safety; oneness with the Planet in a safe and protected way. Meditation on this Chakra can bring one closer to the amazing vistas, horizons, valleys and timeless features of the Planet. In fact, it can bring a sense of timelessness and awareness to the body and the being. It has a very deep healing ability.

Main Keyword; Liberation of the Feminine. Realistic Equality. Spiritual connectedness and comfort.

Initial Action of 11th Earthing Chakra

There is a series of progressions as the full functions of this Chakra activate and become more clearly defined.

Chakra Actions / Function –

- Gridding System Anchor
- Lots of gridding lines connecting to it, like a Net
- Very high frequency / sound / pitch
- 5' Below 10th Earthing Chakra

Connections

Connect or reconnect to:

- The Heart
- The Heart Gridding System
- Open to New Group Connections

Chakra Clues

When examining and exploring this Chakra, be aware of:

- Ability to download and receive information more readily available to the common 'man' should he chose to tune in to the higher frequencies in neutrality or ethical readiness

- Light Bringers choosing to continue to heal Planet Earth or others now emanating energy from a different place, to support others without their own individual loss of light
- Light Bringers able to transduce Earth and Light frequencies for the common 'man', place and realms
- Build up of transformational energies for the next stage in Humanity's evolution

In appearance, it is usually rotary-like, and may possibly have an outer edge of Platinum or metal. Silvery-grey, with an inner void-like appearance of Royal Blue or Azurite Blue, it may feel as though it has a hollow centre which is spinning and draining off negative frequencies. It can have a Vortex, Worm-Hole or a Stargate appearance. Or it may appear as a spinning circle of Symbols or Geometric Shapes. If it has flanges or fins along its upper surface, these may well reveal an outer edge like Iron. It can also appear as a kind of screw top with wings or baffles on its horizontal surfaces. There may also be threads of Light emanating upwards from its surface that create shifting connections with the Tenth Earthing Chakra, allowing for creative communication.

KEY CHAKRA CODES STATEMENTS

Statements that can reveal, diagnose, initiate and activate include:

I Follow my Heart.

My Soul and Spirit is in Charge

I have ceased Weeping Spiritually

I now Engage

Further Action Support Statements:

This Chakra now easily and safely connects with and anchors the New Grid and Nadi system

This upgrade is now complete

I now easily and safely move into co-creation and co-operation on a unity level, Soul-group consciousness level and intergalactic level without harm

I allow new realms that support my Soul and Spirit to beckon. New ideas and insights, new pathways and highways now appear

I embrace, allow and enhance the Feminine Energy

I align with appropriate and supportive Soul Group members

With my new found freedoms, I manage my new choices and options

This Chakra is now 100% Clear and Whole

This Chakra is now 100% ready for initiation and activation

This Chakra is now 100% initiated and activated

11TH AND 12TH CHAKRAS NOW ESTABLISHED

For some, the 11th and 12th Earthing Chakras began initiating and revealing themselves with new 2012 incoming energies, establishing these advanced Chakras into current reality. In my 2010 workshop, there were only a couple of people in the class who had reached this level. Since then numbers are increasing fast especially amongst the Light Bringers.

In 2008 my own Eleventh Earthing Chakra had to 'kick' into action – there was a series of whirring sounds, and 'stop-start's until I focused on it intentionally asking it to align.

Initially I felt headachy as I could feel the energies trying to engage, then a build up of energies attempting to 'drive' it or engage. Then a chugging sensation until it activated. Using the energy vibration of Iron on it assisted to make this process easier.

I saw a series of flanges, like the fins on the tail end of a plane, unevenly space, not yet fully set. It had a metallic feeling, and needed Iron (again) to stabilise it. This sometimes meant seeking sources of Iron to quench that need, for which I turned to nutritional Iron Supplementation. Then a series of other substances, essences and metals were required. I also used Star Energies as these were needed for this particular alignment in my energy system.

The Twelfth Earthing Chakra is a stage in itself, and this is now fully available for those who are developed and ready to engage to this level. More on this in its section.

12: THE FUTURE

The Opportunity to Redesign a Better World.

This particular Chakra is a Stage or Module in itself.

For many, it appears as a bud once the Tenth Chakra has been activated, maturing through a vague dodecahedron shape into one or other more distinct geometric shape. This than acts on the previous Chakras, pulling some into more geometrically shaped formations.

Now that old implanted propaganda, unfulfilled choices and pathways, and claims of servitude are cleared, we address the ancient warped Stargate horizon that was instigated to lead us off the path of true Ascension.

At this point, we can deactivate and delete Old Reptilian Stargates that were set in place to recycle Souls as fodder on the Hamster wheel of human life. Old data collections and dictations can be cleared in order to establish this Twelfth Chakra as one's new Stargate.

When correctly cleared, balanced, aligned and activated, the New Gridding System Connections and Nadis linkings commence. These bring one into new choices of purpose. New possibilities of creation and contribution.

We reclaim our own personal Automony, our Authenticity and our Rights.

This is a major stage for anchoring in the energies required for full Ascension.

Higher Future Functions are Revealed, Initiated and Activated at this level. Soul Purpose is Redefined, Soul Connections are Reviewed, Soul Healing related to Other Incarnations, Experiences, Species, Dimensions and Realities are Activated.

Stargate; 'Future'

This important Chakra acts as a Stargate and links into the Earth MerKaBa and Our Solar System MerKaBa. These links and connections must be done in a way that supports us and that will not keep us 'locked-in, or allied with another's particular Karma and Trauma history. Our connection MUST be fully conscious at this level, or we will wear and process the harms, labels, ills, defeats and sometimes despair that our Planet and Solar System have experienced eon after eon. This does not benefit our own Soul or its own evolution. And this is not what loving or supporting the Planet is about, in any way.

But this has been used against us in times past. This story has been warped, and dysfunction has been recycled, utilised by intelligences that wish only to thieve, rule, control, drain and destroy. They have succeeded in past lives and incarnations, but this is our (and Her) opportunity to create a new and different outcome. And a different Future!

Be assured that as we ascend, to whatever and wherever that may mean for each Soul, the Planet herself is assisted in her own ascension, her own ability to prevent her destruction and annihilation at the hands of her antagonists and plunderers. Our energy and consciousness can support her. *Our* success can assist in *her* success.

Twelfth Earthing Chakra

StarGate Anchor and Transducer. Reclamation and move into co-Creatorship. Creating the Future.

For some beings, this Chakra is still maturing, and so it may still appear like a bud. Activation of the previous Chakras appears to stimulate and quicken its development. When this occurs, the reaction can cause this Chakra to move into a dodecahedron shape.

As this 12th Earthing Chakra comes into activation and initiation, its new energy and functionality brings another shift which may again redefine these Chakras in a different way.

The response to this activation in the 12th is a further response that creates shift and change in the whole of the Chakra assemblage, causing a new sense of structure to emerge. As this Chakra aligns and anchors, it creates a shift and change in the whole of the Chakra assemblage, causing a new sense of structure to emerge that initiates some of the previous Earthing Chakras to also redefine and to further shape-shift.

The Recalibration and Platform Chakras in particular may begin moving into icosahedron, pyramidal, dodecahedron or other more distinct geometric shapes and combinations, even strings or halos of assorted geometries or symbols.

This is because it takes on the Earth Light Codes at a different point in time-space, which allows a 'hidden' light code or frequency to resonate throughout the entire Earthing Chakra Matrix. The effect of being free from past influences on a Planetary, Global, energetic and vibratory level, with its associated strangle-hold on free consciousness, now pulses in waves through the Chakra, establishing new tones and new enhanced settings.

In short, they are affected and advanced by this Future Chakra. Their codings may spin like the ring around Saturn or a series of strung out moons in the same orbit, closely spaced together.

The 12th Earthing may eventually evolve into a light or flame; or starburst of energy. Possibly some may show violet within this flame, others magenta-reds, others may show aquamarine. Or it may remain in its geometric or symbolic form.

The same kind of subatomic sub-quark energetic and etheric chain reaction could be said for the 5th Earthing and the 8th Earthing, as well as the 9th Earthing, but it is much more pronounced and particularly significant at this point of the Earthing Matrix with this 12th Earthing Chakra.

In 2012 we were at the exact mid-way point of this 30-36 year transition period (surrounding this point in the 26,000 year long cycle). 2012 was the median-centre, the mid-point switch over from one era to another, from one cycle to another. We are already well into the New Era Incoming Energies, and engaged in the process of anchoring, aligning and refining them.

We are now able to anchor in at a much deeper level. This is necessary as we move through Cosmic and Galactic Space connecting with the Photon Belt of the Milky Way Equator - and Beyond - more and more every day, and as the ancient pathways that worked against human freedom are being revealed or triggered again.

There is a growing need or impulse to be fully present in the physical to enable 'right' action and thought from the spiritual level to be captured and processed in physicality, action and 3D reality as well as 4th Dimensional level and the associated relevant inter-dimensional levels. We are mid-point in the switch over from one era to another, from one cycle to another. We are already in these energies, and anchoring, aligning and refining them.

This may be seen by some as a move to more of 'Heaven On Earth'.

Location - Generally found at about thirty-nine to forty-two feet or twelve to thirteen metres below the feet.

Keywords / Main Purpose

Converts and Anchors Higher Frequency Earth Light-Codes and connects one with Star-Codes. The future is now being handed back to us. There is now no external power, but the reclamation of the Innate-God-Power within. We are becoming our own authority, and our own conscience. We now have the opportunity to redesign a better world. This heralds the move into Creator and co-Creator-Ship.

Establishes more Light holding ability on a Galactic Gridding Level.

Correct and appropriate safe connection to the Planet and the Solar System without harm or detriment to our own journey and future.

Main Keyword – The New Future Stargate, Anchor and Transducer. Link to the Earth MerKaBa and our Solar System MerKaBa.

CONNECTIONS

Connects to All Chakra System Matrixes.

Access to the deepest aspects for healing.

The Future is now being handed back to us. There is now no external power, but the Reclamation of the innate god-power within. We are becoming our own authority and our own conscience.

CHAKRA CLUES

When examining and exploring this Chakra, one may see the Chakra as a Star or as a cluster of mini Cosmic Clouds, or even as a Cluster of brilliant Stars. It may be a shape, symbol or geometric shape. It may shapeshift. It may cause the other Chakras to change.

It is what it is. Simply allow the connections to begin. Allow the light to grow

CONNECTIONS

- 8th and 5th Earthing Chakras (Module Anchors and Transducers)
- The Heart Chakra
- Link Star Chakra
- and the Upper Spiritual Chakras where appropriate

This Chakra now Anchors the New Grid and Nadi Systems being formulated and refined by those Light Beings that support the Planet and its evolution.

KEY CHAKRA CODES STATEMENTS

Statements that can reveal, diagnose, initiate and activate include:

I Know Who I Am. I Know Who We Are. I Take My Rightful Place

I Own Myself

I Am Created, I Am Creator; I Am Self-Created

I Give Myself Permission to Create and to Co-Create

I Accept My Transformation

I Accept My Ascension in Timely fashion

I Develop and safely Hold My Light

Further Action Support Statements:

I Allow that I Am of Heaven

I Allow that I Am of Earth

I Accept Heaven On Earth

I Create Heaven On Earth

I Am my Own Heaven on Earth

As Above, So Below -   So Be It So, So Be It So, So Be It So'

This Chakra is now 100% Clear and Whole

This Chakra is now 100% ready for initiation and activation

This Chakra is now 100% initiated and activated

THE NEW EARTHING CHAKRAS ASSEMBLY TO TWELFTH EARTHING

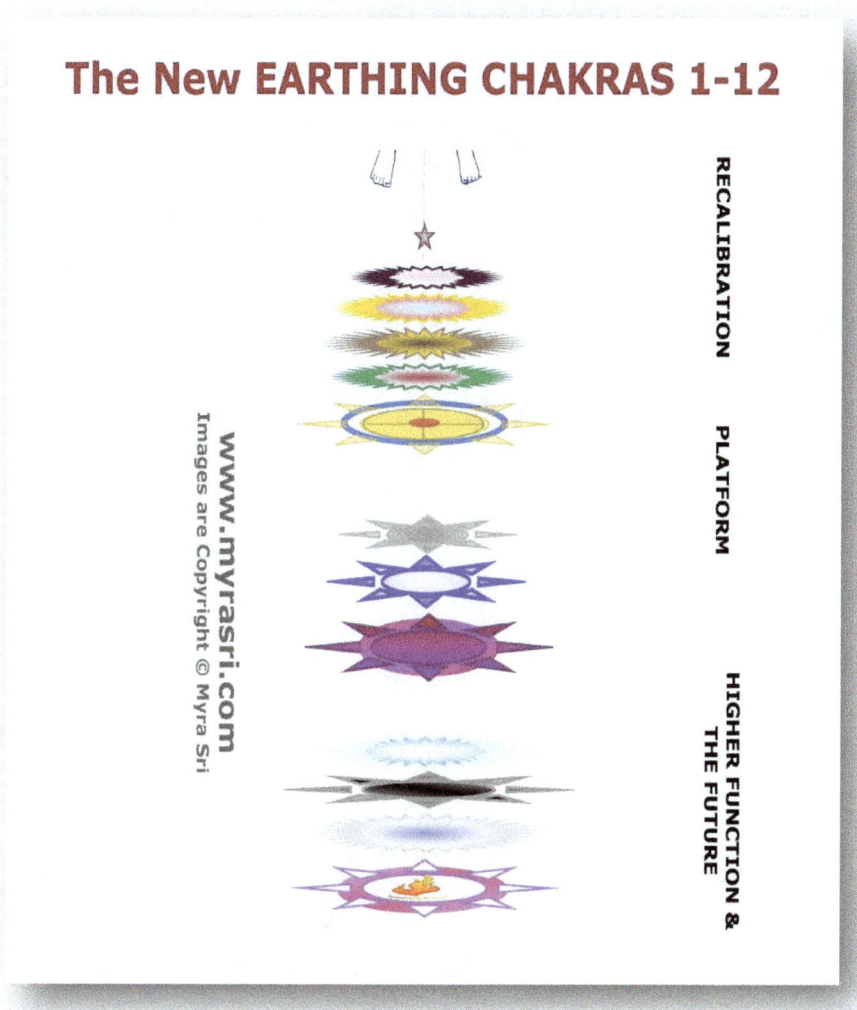

THE HIGHER AND EARTHING CHAKRAS

Now that we have the activated all of the Earthing Chakras, the Higher and Earthing Chakra Assembly now looks like this:

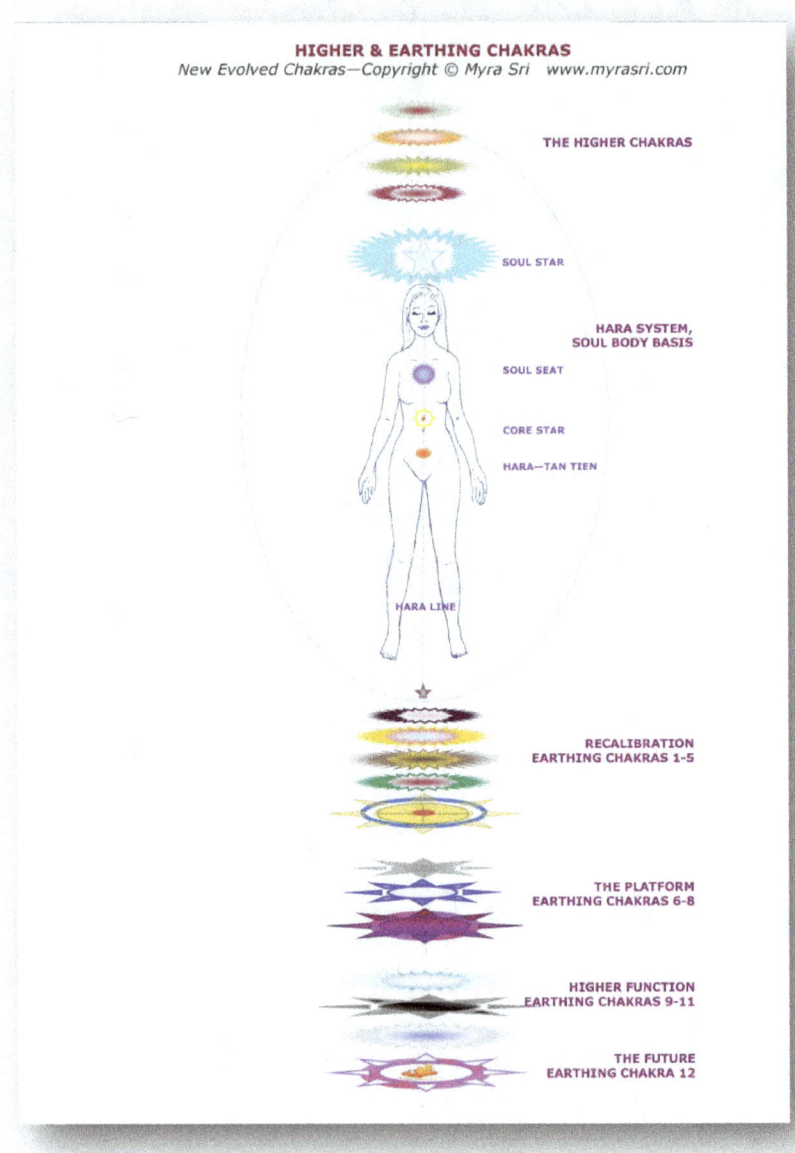

A Word on our Earth / Gaia

Our Earth is an Intelligence, an Entity. Her companion, the Moon, emits a vibration that can remind us of or trigger our shadow sides, and of the cycles necessary for human life.

Gaie (or Gaia as she is more commonly called) resides on the outskirts of the Milky Way. She is viewed by some as an experimental project, though one not caught up in the full Solar Central Winds. Some consider her a colony for waywards, some consider her a borstal camp for the unethical. Others consider her a coaching college for Soul development. Others know that she is a training ground for Mastery… And a gathering place for Souls from other Star systems. Some see her as a Heroine taking her last valiant stand against detrimental powers determined to use, abuse, pillage and again to totally destroy her.

Whatever we consider is our reason to find ourselves here, we are dependent is many ways upon her, and some of us work to assist her. She is supported by hordes of Light Beings, continually ministering and monitoring her progress and well-being. As we move through the full Stellar, Cosmic and Galactic alignment of this period and enter a new energy vibration, there are many things we can leave behind us.

Our Earth is wonderfully and powerfully made – her hot raw heart of molten lava, continually renews itself and refashions her outer garments, having its own resonance and heartbeat. Our bodies are tuning in to a different sound and vibration as it emanates from her heart.

As cultures and ages past have always seen The Sun as the life-giver and The GOD behind The Gods, now we are each of us being given the opportunity to awaken to our own True Divine Source, right here, right now. Our 'God' is closer than we have every known – no longer seen and experienced as external, we are learning that our own unique True Divine Source can encompass the dimensional activity of the planet and yet go way beyond this planet and the Galaxy we find ourselves residing in - just as we embody Spirit, we also partially embody The Earth and need to be mindful of navigating these terrestrial energies.

THE NEW PSYCHIC CHAKRAS AND ANATOMY

SECTION AGENDA:

~ Background Information to the Discoveries of the New Evolved Psychic Chakra System.

~ Current Psychic Anatomy Understanding

~ Foundations for the New Psychic Chakra Anatomy

~ Head Psychic Chakras

~ Master Psychic Chakras

~ Psychic Chakras in the Body

~ How to Calibrate the Chakras

The New Evolved Psychic Anatomy

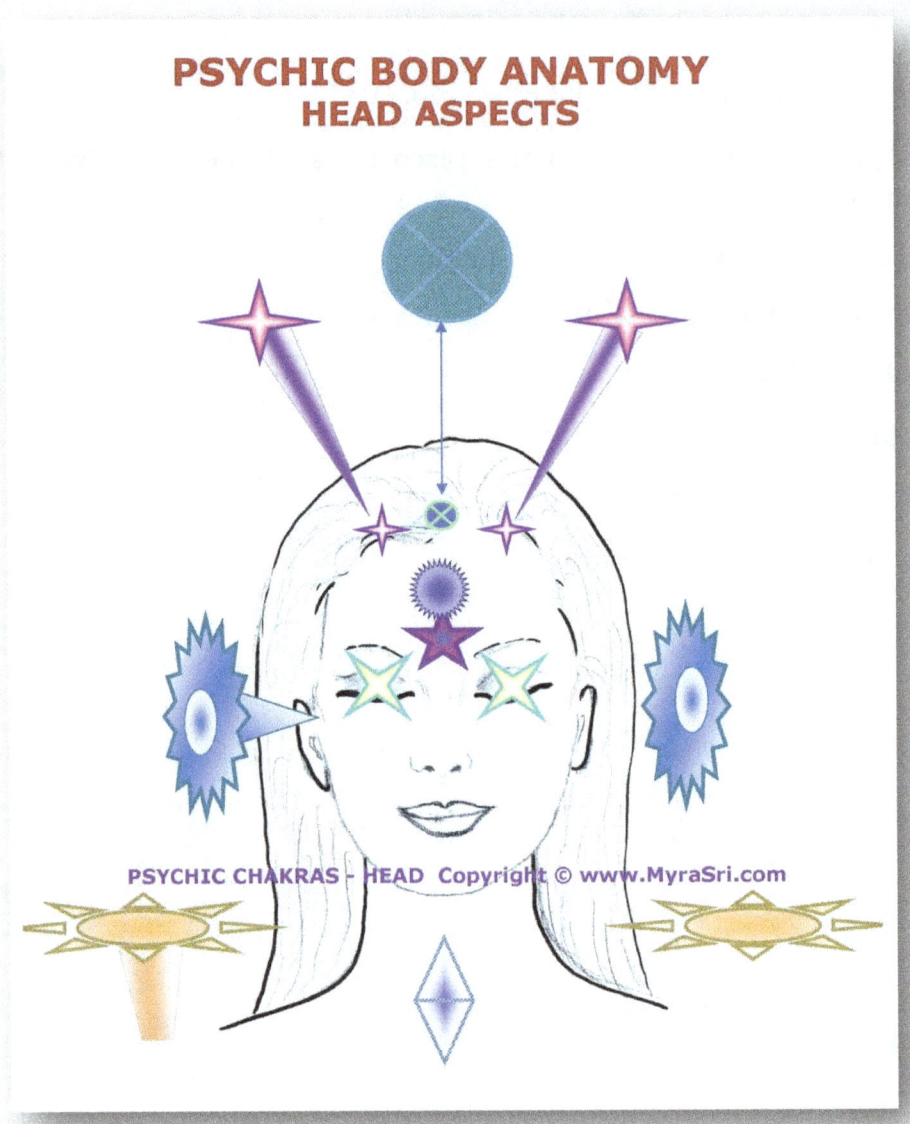

The above image illustrates a section of the Psychic Chakras and anatomy.

Who would have thought that there could be so much activity, so much Chakra formation, so much outer accoutrements of Psychic structure around the head? Certainly not I. Not until I began my own journey into why I missed messages and why I misread signs, and why I allowed others to get the better of me, even though I had sensed that this was not the path I should be going along…

The journey with the Psychic Chakras began initially for me around fifteen years ago. The answers started to make sense around 2002.

Discovering the frontal lobe attachments, the 'Psychic Horns' as I call them, was the beginning of the clearing of my psychic channels. Early on in my kinesiology and energy healing trainings I had tried to clear the psychic channels for greater enhancement. This was not necessarily a purely selfish thing, as I had also wanted better abilities for understanding the nature of client's issues. I tried many which ways, but still seemed to be limited to only what my eyes could see. Though I began to realise that I heard things – phrases, a word, a statement – and when I pursued these things, more often than not they meant something and were very relevant. Later I realised that I had some measure of clairaudience, and that it was *not* just 'my imagination'…

As I cleared more, I discovered more Chakras, as I reclaimed these and listened more, more was revealed.

Sensitive Trap

However, I also fell into the trap of continually 'looking' for answers, of continually having my mind, energy and intellect seeking the answers I was so bent on hearing. This is not a good place to be.

Being a Sensitive left me wide open to not only what I was seeking, but also whatever I encountered along the way. I see this with many Sensitives, and have been able to learn my own lessons from all this and to pass these lessons along. Discovering and researching about the Earthing Chakras at the same time was a major benefit to the reclaiming of my own identity, abilities and place, for they assisted me in staying grounded and in processing the positive changes and enhancements.

Each Psychic Chakra I encountered, each issue I dealt with that pointed to another Connection Point in answer to my desire to deal with whatever issue it was attached to, each step along the way brought me more information, more confirmation, more revelation. And more assurance.

I began to realise that these Chakras were not just a few addendums, a mere glossing and frosting on the energetic anatomy. But this took some years of discovery and again I had to be reminded not to be consumed with seeking answers.

Patience was challenged, and I gained ground and understanding.

At the point of knowing most of the Psychic Chakras, I found that my psychic sensing was so open energetically that I was picking up other's thoughts about me to the extent of passing someone in the street and being energetically 'slapped' with their judgements. I had long learned not to seek to know what was going on in other's lives unless they requested a session with me, and had long practised stopping judgement as much as is possible on what I do not fully know, nor yet have been invited to investigate – Mind My Own Business…!

Indeed I did not yet fully trust my 'psychic abilities' to the degree that it could read strangers, and I had already realised that others could only probably see a small percentage of what was actually going on in my life anyway.

But this picking up of what other's felt about me, what they thought about me, it was ridiculously debilitating. I had trained my psychic awareness too much maybe? Maybe – and maybe not… What I still had to learn was the level of lack of Boundaries that I had. Protective lines of limits, borders of the being – these had been torn down by not only childhood events, abuse and experiences, but also by attempts at destroying the brave light within me by those that preferred the dark. Fortunately at this time, I also began to discover some of the Survival Chakras, as I initially called them. Chakras that were indicated when addressing any issues to do with Survival, issues that pushed one into 'Survival Mode', issues that affected one's energy reserves and ability to hold onto peace. These were being discovered and revealed to me in connection with some of the debilitating issues I had still had that were linked with self-worth, self-empowerment and self-autonomy. *Sensitive* had been only one part of the equation – unsupported and abused had been another part. The boundaries of a Sensitive can be difficult to maintain on occasion, and to have them destroyed does take some rebuilding and reclamation. But first has to come the energetic recognition.

So dealing with old shock resonances that signalled Survival issues led me to work with the Signal-Survival Chakras. Rebuilding, indeed even recognising where a Boundary should be, became very important for the continued journey and also for my improved functioning.

Lacking boundaries meant that I could be influenced by others, without even knowing that this was happening.

On a conscious level, one knew where the boundaries were, what was appropriate and what was not, what was fair and what was not. One knew what not to do to others, and subsequently expected the same treatment by others, the same considerations and respect. So then why was this happening to me, why were or had others treating me so badly?

I had much to learn about the way energetics worked compared to rational reasoning and conscious intention – and how the subconscious could affect the actual energetic intent of a person.

As an Indigo (ultra) Sensitive, I had to learn that others could place labels on me that swamped my psychic anatomy; that certain others would try to take from me that which I knew and had worked hard to learn. This was usually through using their own psychic abilities to attempt to drain mine; others through ill intent cocaused through envy, inadequacy, laziness or greed could try and put a stop, a claim or a drain on my abilities. I learned about this. And I learned to find where these things were held, and to clear them!

Someone may succeed for a short time in negatively affecting another, but when one knows what to check to ensure that there is no lingering attachment, no debilitating intent or device, no clouding or false data, then that same one can claim the final victory. And do so with a clear and ethical standing.

Not only people, but also events can cloud our energetic anatomies. Much is happening in the world, and to those around us. Psychic Antennae and Chakras can pick up much that is going on around one – training them *not* to be so 'alert' and to be able to recognise that which we need to pay attention to, and that which we need to simply note and release is *life-changing*.

Knowing my Psychic Chakras and anatomy now allows me to monitor them, to recognise when they have been compromised, where I need to clear them, what needs repairing or rebalancing.

I trust this knowledge helps you too.

SHIFTS AND CHANGES

We are in the midst of a whole influx and sometimes storm of energies, vibrations, resonances, frequencies, messages, influences, inter-dimensional communications and more. Some are riding it well, others are not doing too badly though they may well be feeling the chaos and sometimes the confusion, and yet others, particularly the sensitive, are very confused, or feeling quite battered and bruised energetically. Where possibly meditation used to help, or astral travel, or certain types of energy healing, much seems to have changed, and the old ways are no longer serving us quite as they once did.

In fact, whereas I once used to do some *Astral Travelling*, I no longer venture willingly or quickly into these regions, fraught as they currently are with a whole multitude of dangers. In these times of huge shifts and changes with past historic resonances also up for review, and karmic resolutions and lessons being faced by many, it is too easy and too common to encounter any one of the host of disharmonious beings and entities presently flooding the astral realms seeking resolution or revenge; or a free ride at someone else's expense. It is currently not a safe place or space to be, though this may change in the next twenty or thirty years as we emerge from and overcome the many issues being dealt with as a planet and a species, as well as a consciousness.

Even the usual vibrational remedies have changed. For instance Essential Oils energies have shifted some of their frequencies, and their previous uses. I have found that the etheric codes and unseen colours of Essential Oils have also evolved and support newer applications and actions, and I have documented some of these in '*Secrets Beyond Aromatherapy*' at the insistence of students. We can use these codes for a variety of chakras, meridians and the new anatomy which is coming into more widespread distribution and use in the evolution of humanity.

I can share with you that recently all of my Crystals had to be totally reactivated in a different way as they had gone into a kind of sleep and weren't working as before. I discovered that the 'old' energies were no longer as effective as they had been and that the crystals had to be reprogrammed with the new incoming energies. They are all quite happy and active again, and I marvel at their new infusion of energies now that they have been aligned with the new light and healing frequencies.

So if our usual crystalline vibrational Rescuers have met a brick wall so to speak, is it possible that they are also presenting a mirror to us that our own Auric system needs to be addressed and upgraded?

Yes, I certainly think and feel so. Or I wouldn't be writing this book.

Navigating With New Tools

To move forward with the New Era Energies, to utilise them better, to 'go with the flow' if you like, of the potentialities for the positive with these new energies, then we not only have to upgrade and reactivate our existing anatomy and functionality, we also have to recognise, include, connect and activate the new anatomy.

Which is mind-blowingly beautiful!

It is imperative that we recognize the existing and new systems in order to better monitor, sort, clean and maintain them for optimal function. To identify one's own particular energy pathways of input and higher energy information is vital to maintaining their full functionality and clarity; and a clearer ability to navigate the huge energy shifts that we are currently experiencing. And will be doing so for some time to come.

When our psychic anatomy or chakras are clogged, then information can no longer be relied on to be clear, and can no longer be interpreted as accurate, or reliable. Psychic 'madness', psychosis or 'Stupidity' may be an extreme experience, but these may be caused by toxic build-up or over-stimulation. It may also be caused by damage through as an inappropriate or a forced 'Shakti-Pat' energy initiation or energetic transference (a Kundalini explosion / activation also has the potential to blow the psychic circuits wide-open); or some other form of Psychic Interference, Bullying or Enlistment to another's agenda. One can become 'punch-drunk' with energy - 'energetically-drunk' - as they find themselves unable to correctly process or integrate the incoming information or to relate accurately to the reality they need to in order to function in present time living and participation. And one can consequently make entirely erroneous choices or decisions.

You know, it really is an exciting time. The old limiting ways are being challenged and the existing beliefs and controls are being reviewed and changed.

We have more personal responsibility than ever before, and we also have more personal Soul opportunities as well. And maybe for some, that is the very reason why they are here at this time in this place on this planet...

Old School Psychic Structure Information

The Psychic Body structure or Psychic Centres in the body are often based on the older versions and understandings of the esoteric and energetic information past on by the early pioneers in the realms of esotericism, theosophy, psychism, mediumship, shamanism and channelling. During earlier times these were discovered, explored, documented and handed down through the ages by skilled or worthy ones.

The Secret Mystery Schools of Old such as Temple Mystery Schools of Mithra, the early Mayan Secret Schools and Ancient Egyptian Mystery Trainings of many and diverse secret knowledge and understandings would have been a lot more comprehensive than our current energetic and esoteric subtle body knowledge and information. In the ancient bids for control and through programs run by fear and greed, so much has been destroyed during the ensuing wars, pirating, plundering, government overturnings and religious fanaticism that has left our knowledge base bereft in many areas. And in some cases, knowledge has been deliberately obliterated, perverted or destroyed.

However, information is being revived, re-member-ed and built on.

New windows of information are being opened. If we were to stick purely to the ancient wisdoms and information alone, we might not be prepared fully for the current and future waves of incoming new energies.

THE NEW EVOLVED PSYCHIC ANATOMY

The word Psychic is derived from the Greek word *psychikos* ('of the mind' or 'mental') and refers in part to the human mind or psyche (ex. 'psychic turmoil'). And to some degree, the mind is certainly involved.

Beginning in 2003 the evolving Psychic Body anatomy was revealing itself, or rather, I was recognising it. Since then it has become much more defined and comprehensive. The early model I had been working with, as most other energy workers I knew had, appeared to be centred around the areas that included the head - mainly the Third Eye and Crown Chakras. I then discovered a new connection at the area around or above the Navel which later proved to be the connection with the Soul Body and so this was included. I became more aware of this developing anatomy identifying itself as a new body and system. I drew little diagrams as I discovered each piece and found that working with them made a difference with clients. Over time, the head antennae was included in my diagrams though I was not yet necessarily clear as to how to calibrate them to the new energies.

I also began to realise that there were Psychic centres in the brain. These co-related to certain glands in the brain; the Pineal in particular which I had already been working with and in hindsight was rather obvious. The Vedics had known of these centres in the brain for some time. Further aspects of the Psychic Chakra system became clear as I questioned functionality and application of indicated energy points on and around the body.

As this growing body of Chakras and related connections developed into a cohesive system, it became obvious to me that this was not just a series of Chakras, but a *whole system* or body governing the interpretation of invisible and vibrational information. When balanced, one could feel more of one's own energy, and find it available to the self. When unbalanced, clogged or dormant, it could enable certain difficulties, vulnerabilities or disorientation.

This in particular was very helpful when I worked with Sensitives as it seemed to settle their energy systems and to correct overwhelm resonances.

Through the witnessing of and working through these developments, other parts of the jigsaw became clearer – and this revealed a larger and more comprehensive Psychic Body Anatomy system.

Though in some places it is connected to and interacts with the Astral Body as well as the Soul Body, the Psychic Body has its own identity and functions.

We will be looking at the whole of the Psychic Body Anatomy which includes the Chakras and Connections in the head and in or around the physical body itself. We will also look at the current energy receptors as well as the current evolved Psychic Head Chakras. These can be key areas of neglect, interaction and disharmony.

SPIRITUAL AND PSYCHIC

Most people relate to the Third Eye as the Psychic Centre. Others were and are aware of the psychic centres in the brain, and some also knew of other energy centres that were aligned with the psychic and sensory centres. However, now the assemblage of psychic anatomy has become a cohesive force and body in itself.

Knowing its structure and how it functions is now **vital** for navigating the current and prevailing energies for the foreseeable future.

Everyone has a 'Psychic Body' to some degree or another… and not just those who are called or thought of as Psychic. The difference is that not everyone is aware of it, connected with it or able to fully use it. What is often misunderstood is the *Purpose* of this amazing anatomy…

There is some fear in certain quarters about anything labelled 'psychic' and true psychism (psychic ability) is not necessarily understood. This is understandable to a degree, given that there have been unscrupulous people throughout history who have used their gifts for purely selfish means, regardless of being religious or not. There are also many really spiritual people that I know who are not only spiritual, ethical, moral and gifted who also possess amazing psychic abilities. To discover for myself that I had some psychic abilities, and to accept these, coming from a deeply religious background as I had, did take some time. And I had to see personally for myself how really truly genuine spiritual people could have these gifts and use them correctly for healing and for truth before I could dare to explore these for myself.

Anything that I came across that went against my own innate motto 'Do No Harm' (a typically Christian 'rule') was dismissed and left alone. I had decided long ago that I did not want to play in an energetic playground of fear, doubt or darkness, or dabble in anything connected with spirits, dead relative, mischievous or meddling energies of any kind, and this was my shining torch that brought what I needed to know to me.

Spiritual to me means the realisation that on some level we are all one and that what we do affects others. And that we leave a legacy behind us, and we also take one with us; and what we do returns to us in kind in some way and at some time.

Being sensitive to the pain of others had taught me much. But I had not recognised just how sensitive, empathic or psychic I was until I realised it when certain things I said came to pass, and that what I felt in my body was often what someone close to me was going through. All of these were lessons on life for me, but not necessarily for everyone else. When information came to me because I had asked to know, and this information was confirmed over and over and over, I was eventually able to accept that in some ways I must have some psychic abilities. I already knew that I was spiritual, so this was in interesting development.

One rule I have had for some time, is that I never use my skills unless I am asked to or unless an issue is impacting directly on me. I believe in non-infringement. One clear understanding I gained is this: a person can be spiritual and *not* psychic; a person can be psychic and *not* spiritual; or a person can be both spiritual *and* psychic. What a person says and what a person actually does will help you to decide which and what they are for yourself.

Having said all this, let us come back to what a Psychic Body – and the new evolved Psychic Body in particular - means to the ordinary person, and not just an energy worker or LightBringer...

What this means actually is **Autonomy** – the opportunity to filter and process information accurately in order to navigate the wealth and plethora of energies that are coming our way in these increasingly energetic and often intense times. Without infringing on another and without being infringed on.

Psychic Anatomy

We have acknowledged that there is a current Psychic system we are all familiar with, generally the Third Eye and /or some of the Clair-Skills as listed. However, we now take into account the upgrades that have been occurring, and find we are discovering a relatively new Psychic Body anatomy that is much more than our previous 'dumbed-down' five or more senses (the 'Sixth-sense'). For these senses have served us reasonably well down through the ages.

What is exciting though is what is currently occurring. For we are not only working with a variety of newer frequencies and having our current psychic structures upgraded, we have also been evolving new psychic anatomy for this new era. New frequencies require new technology to better interpret, process, modify and utilise. New technology in this case means new anatomy.

So getting back to the current recognised systems, what *is* relatively new is the understanding that these senses, systems, structures or constructions can suffer over time through use, experiences, toxic build-up, internal pressure, global consciousness input / release and overwhelm to name a few. In short, there has been a shift as to the potential of existing psychic anatomy. Furthermore, there has been an evolution process that has given us a more developed psychic anatomy and functionality, for this is required to navigate through the new frequencies and into the new Era.

The energetic shifts that began around the turn of the century and hit a kind of critical point in 2012 are still ongoing – nothing has yet settled, in fact it seems that more and more 'dust' if you like, is being stirred up, and mankind is actually only a part of the way through this transition from an old and stuck way of being to the path of evolution and 'Ascension' as some label it.

Whichever way one views our individual path to Soul freedom and the ability to follow our own true Soul purpose and destiny, much has changed and is still changing. We are still surrounded by a sort of chaos, as the new energies come through and shift and stir up 'Stuff' for change, and many are busy handling both the culling of the old and the seeding or establishing of the new. And this is probably going to change again, as our Souls gain more purchase and grip with the new energies and its opportunities for growth, contribution, and personal evolution and possibly Ascension.

The New Psychic Chakras and its Subtle Body Anatomy

The discovery that the existing model – based on the Third Eye together with the ultra-senses (usually and generally) being fed through the Main Chakra system is actually only a small part of the ability to pick-up, receive and work with incoming energetic, vibrational and psychic information - was an exciting and enlightening awareness for me.

Most people understand that the Third Eye is a main core psychism engine, together with a connection with the Pineal Gland in the brain. However, the new discoveries have fortunately been revealed at a time when we need it most: in a time when such a lot of subliminal and multi-levelled information and manipulation via media and a variety of other control mechanisms and methods are being used that may upset or override our own knowings, autonomy and identity.

This new energy body differs with our other energy systems or Light Bodies, such as the Emotional Body, the Mental Body and other Auric bodies in that their outer appearance generally seems to be orbital or similar to the shape of an egg. The Psychic Body does not fit into this same Auric Egg mould or shape. It seems to be comprised mainly of receptor sites such as the Connection Points and Chakras, though it also seems to possess a kind of gentle webbing system that flows from point to point external of the body. And this appears to me as a pale-ish green colour, almost Olive Green. The Nadis that emanate and form the greenish sheath are of fine filaments of pale green and pearly light unless they have been burned, damaged or gummed up.

The Psychic Body allows us to make better use of the new energy shifts and frequencies that we are experiencing as we move and spiral our way through the Cosmos. This new system was so large, so comprehensive that I had to call it something, and as I had not read or heard about it from any other source, I named it simply 'The Psychic Body'.

So what *is* the Psychic Body?

And just *what* is its *Purpose*?

Psychic Body And Its Purpose

The Psychic Body is a system of energy receptors that pick up information on an unseen level for inner processing. This is to assist in *our* journey of pursuing our own particular destiny and purpose.

It is *NOT* just for so-called Psychics, and working on enhancing it is *NOT* simply to make someone more psychically powerful!

It is comprised of Chakras and sets of Chakras, and these all relate to an overall system that is its own separate energy body. This means that there are not just Psychic Chakras, but an entire Psychic Body; one which receives and processes information via the major and minor psychic receptors placed in and around the actual physical body. Some psychic points are housed entirely within the body and others are actually contactable outside the body, which is where they receive their impressions, vibrations, incoming frequencies and interactions in the immediate vicinity and also with impressions and emanations via communication. These external receptors connect in with and interact with the in-body receptors and interpreters to give a comprehensive internal symbolic language or image. These can confirm a situation or provide an alert as to contradiction in a given situation. Compromise, trauma damage, gumming-up through overwhelm or arrest in any of form will compromise their function, affecting a faulty interpretation of incoming and understood data and sensory information.

The Psychic Body is an enhanced communication and confirmation system. It is vital to the process of awareness and the understanding of nuances, meaning and genuineness in human and environmental interaction.

But this is not all…

It goes way beyond that, for it has a spiritual purpose, and aligning this vital energy system enhances the Soul and spiritual journey and the quality of life *on* that journey. When correctly cleared, balanced and aligned, a spin-off may be that a person's skills are safe to emerge more fully, thus enhancing their ability to interpret more correctly that which cannot be immediately seen or heard. This enhancement, though, is intended to be in the spirit of non-infringement toward others less aligned and for supporting positive information and change in navigating one's own life.

It is *not* for influencing or manipulating others, it is *not* for perverting to raise up or open to dark energy (and indeed the information given here is for assistance in *clearing* negative energy!), it is *not* for greed or the gathering of the resources of another. It is *not* for interfering in the minds or affairs of others, and indeed any psychic who offers up information you have *not* elicited, requested or solicited does **not** know how to manage their abilities and is causing an infringement. The only exception to this is in a life-or-death situation.

It *is* for understanding the times we live in; it *is* for recognising those things that influence or impedes our own energy, capabilities and resources and addressing these; it *is for* enhancing, complementing, benefiting and improving our path, and the paths of those that we care about or that may come to us for help.

The Psychic Body and its evolved abilities works beyond words, it works beyond what is seen, it works beyond what is heard, and it works beyond emotions. It is, in part, the reclaiming of abilities we all once possessed before language became our main form of communication. And currently it is the enhancement for us to be able to connect more spiritually in a safer and more consciously aware way.

For some people the Psychic Chakras or anatomy are not as evident or as pronounced as for others, who may well often be labelled Sensitive. It is usually more developed in those who work a lot with intuition or a sense of Knowing, or who get flashes or insights that prove to have some truth to them.

Right now, it would appear that many dormant or untrained Psychic Bodies are awakening in some aspect or another. Most people are experiencing some sort of subtle differences over the last few years that they cannot explain. Whether it's some form of occasional and unaccountable dizziness, lob-sidedness, déjà vu or weird imaginings or dreams, most of us have experienced some kind of energy or energetic type interference, which we are currently trying to make sense of through the new evolving Chakra systems, but which we don't necessarily quite yet know how to activate or clear properly.

Only recently I balanced someone who was feeling really sick and nauseas in their stomach, to the point of real anxiety. It was only when the Psychic Chakras were cleaned out and then balanced and their Psychic Body Anatomy aligned that the tense and 'Sicky' feeling went, and they brightened up.

Their awakening anatomy had picked up a lot of energetic information from others, and also some of the toxic debris being energetically released by others, but the person had no way of knowing what was happening, because the very 'radar' that could warn them was so thickly gummed-up and clouded over. So not only did they *carry* other people's detritus, they also couldn't *recognise* that this was what was happening – which meant that they could do nothing about it to help themselves.

Understanding your own Psychic anatomy and being able to tend it and clear it does not necessarily make you a great psychic... but what it does do is help keep your energy systems clean and clear so that you can manage your own life and journey better!

And this ability to navigate better is the very least of its gifts!

FOR LIGHTWORKERS OR JUST FOR 'PSYCHICS'?

For some while I have had a problem with the term 'LightWorker'. Having personally been forced to entertain some reservations about certain 'psychics' who claimed to be LightWorkers, but were actually far from being spiritually ethical, or indeed even working with Light, I could still not get past the true function of the name though I now change my term to Light-*Bringers*, or even Light-*Seekers*, as that is the difference. I have met too many that count themselves as working with the Light, yet are so dark within themselves, or who are unevolved or have a spiritually immature view of the world, and quite often they have personal agendas running their egos and affecting their work – this allows them to bring dark into their work, and they are not always necessarily aware of it – after hearing their grand claims and attending their workshops and courses I saw how they delivered a little of the truth, but also hooked people in to further work with them - so I re-defined them to myself as TwiLight workers; on the edge of the Light - some light, some dark...

Whilst I was working with true Light-Bringers, spiritual seekers, therapists of a high Soul calibre and other Souls of extraordinary qualities, and whilst mapping the information I was receiving about the New Evolved Chakra Systems and the new Psychic Body, I saw them (both clients and their Psychic Chakras) literally bloom in front of my eyes in their new Psychic Body and their increased Psychic Body functioning.

Balancing this new system allowed them so much ease in their other energy bodies, and so much more clarity in interpreting the energetic information being pounded down to us all through The Cosmos as we ride the waves past the Mayan Long Count Calendar and the ensuing Transformational and Ascension energies.

My previous knowledge and understanding had been turned on its head, and it is now my opinion that only by recognizing the shifts, waveform transmissions and the many forms of energetic vibrations can we navigate with clarity, safety and understanding through these changing times.

Psychic Body Basics

Current Psychic Anatomy Understandings

These are the basic senses that enhanced sensory or psychic ability builds on. The normal human senses that allow us to experience the outside world are usually recognised as:

- **Sight** – light input receptors, windows to inner world
- **Hearing** – perception and interpretation of incoming sound tones and frequencies
- **Touch** – interpretation of physical stimulation or proximity, the registering of pressure, vibration, pain, pleasure, temperature
- **Taste** – registering and interpretation of sensory data via the tongue, mouth and back of the throat
- **Smell** - registering and interpretation of sensory data via the nose and olfactory nerves

Whilst the other senses or allied faculties that allow us to understand our physical place within that world are:

- **Proprioception** – whole body sensory receptor for perceptions of movement, balance and direction
- **Communication** – word-power and vocal healing (or negative) vibrations via the voice, eyes and ears

All of these faculties can also be extra sensitive, and have amplified abilities. This is where the degree of amplification makes the difference between the mundane and simply physical, with the empathic and the intuitive, through to the Sensitive and the obviously psychic. Some people can 'taste' fear, some can 'see' tunes, others can feel presences, but this is not necessarily recognised as being psychic, even though the skills may be just that.

So how is this ability to see, hear, feel, smell or sense-beyond the obvious-to-everybody-else happen? Just what is it that can allow this? Let us look at what we know of the Psychic senses and its anatomy to see if this gives us any answers.

Apart from the use of the Third Eye as a tool in psychic practice, and one which has generally been associated with clairvoyance, there are other forms of psychic expertise. There are other forms of ability to pick up or recognize interactions not of a purely 3D or physical experience or reality.

Those who have spent some time in exploring phenomena, atmospherics, frequencies, ambiences, or energetic expressions not explained by the physical or the mundane, will recognize the following to some greater or lesser degree:

- **Clairvoyance** – visual receiving of energetic information or phenomena
- **Clairaudience** – auditory receiving of energetic information or phenomena
- **Clairsentience** – sense reception of energetic information or phenomena
- **Clair Gustatory** – taste sensations of energetic information or phenomena
- **Clair Olfactory** – smell sensations of energetic information or phenomena
- **Auric Reception** – Astral body exploration and interpretation
- Sundry: **Chakra** input gathered through the hands, feet or main chakras; picking up of energetic information, vibrations or phenomena and the interpretation or use of vibrational stimulation and frequencies
- **Synaesthesia** – a rare and unusual mixing of the senses where one of the above triggers another; the ability to smell colour or sound, or to hear smell…

On the physical level each special sense or faculty may be thought to have a dedicated nervous system pathway. The special afferent nerves specifically related to taste and smell are the olfactory, facial, glossopharyngeal, and vagus nerves; the optic nerve is responsible for the special sense of vision while the vestibulocochlear nerve is responsible for hearing and balance.

We can see from the list above that we can take in information on the physical and also the invisible levels – we can engage the Inner Third Eye, the Chakra Third Eye, the ears, the senses of touch, taste and smell, and the nervous system messages conveyed via the existing Main Chakra system. The physical anatomy has its own meta-mirror image that corresponds to the Psychic Anatomy.

Discovering that the Psychic body connected with other energetic systems made sense. Linking and interacting with the Amygdala, the Psychic Body has third-party connection to the Earthing Chakras (particularly 5th and 8th Earthing chakras) and the Signal Chakras. We also include here the energy system housed through the Hara System to the Soul Body.

Because this is an easily recognised energetic structure working on the Soul / Spiritual level through access to Divine Source and Earth Harmonising Energies, it will naturally register frequencies in a way not directly connected with the Senses. And the Hara Line structure echoes the central Channel of the Psychic Core. But our main focus here is on a more common understanding of what is meant by the term Psychic Body and the energy anatomy that supports these abilities and sense-ings.

Psychic Body Foundation – Middle Pillar / Core

First things first. As mentioned earlier, let's look at getting the foundations right. In my workshops on these Chakras, I guide my students through a process to ensure that their Central Core Chanel is clear and activated before proceeding to diagnose and balance these Chakras or its system. This exercise is important and wise for both client or practitioner or simply self balance. It will ensure correct connection to one's true Spiritual Source which aids to reduce error, ensure neutrality, and allow the highest results.

The exercise that I use to clear and strengthen the Central Channel is the **Psychic Toner Exercise**. This exercise is included in my book *'Secrets Behind Energy Fields'* and is part of the **New Evolved Chakras Workbook series**. It is also available as a Guided Meditation.

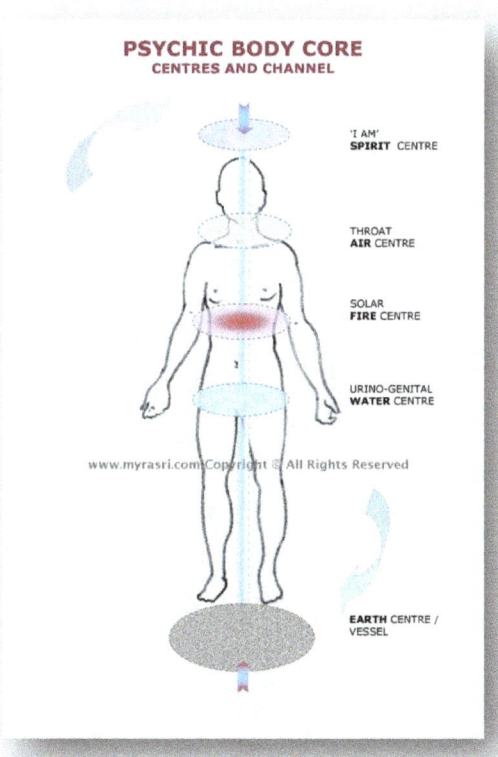

Once this core aspect of the body is strengthened and cleared, we can assess the new Evolved Psychic Chakra structures.

The Psychic Body Toner Exercise looks like this:

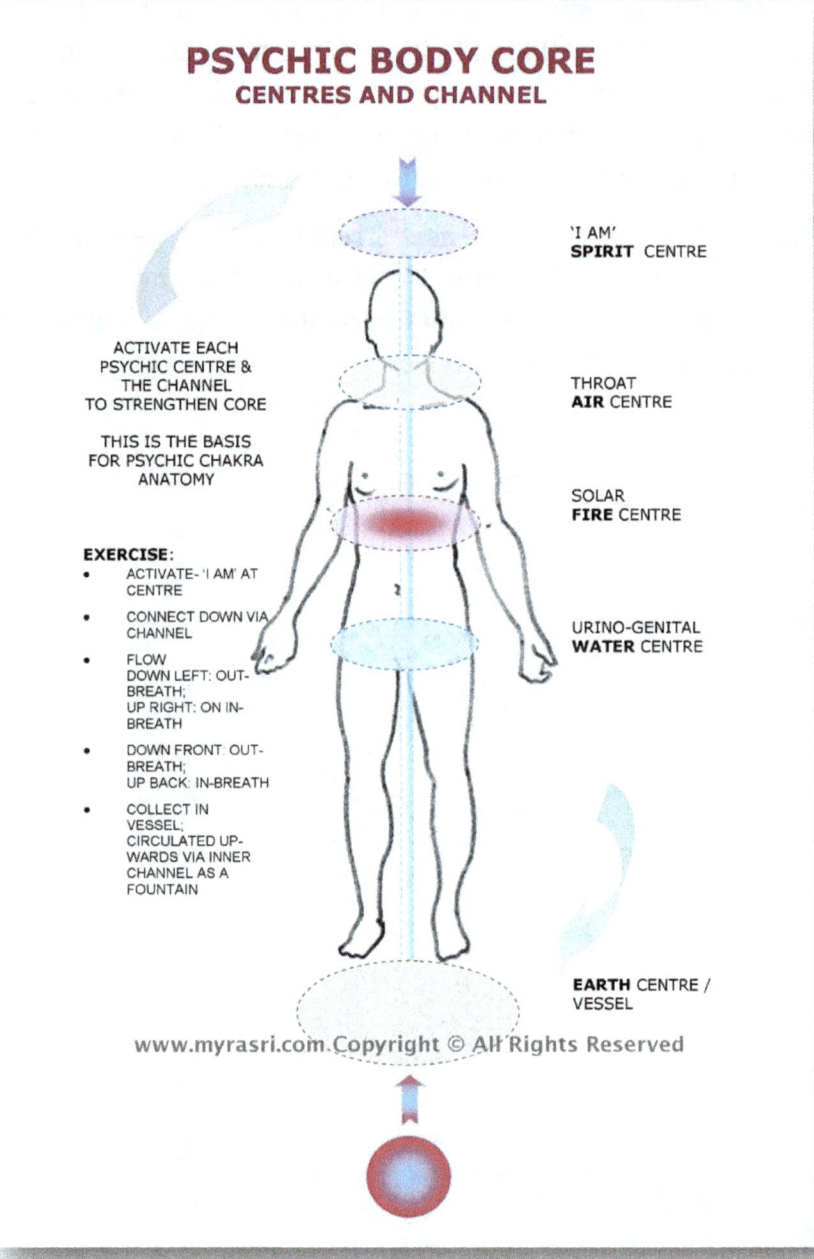

PSYCHIC BODY ANATOMY – THE HEAD

So just what are the Psychic Head Chakras if not just the Crown Chakra and Third Eye Chakra?

We will attempt to approach them from the head down and from within the inside of the body outwards.

Looking first at the Psychic Chakras connected with this extra-ordinary system of perception that have Access / Contact Points that are external to the Head we have quite a collection in the head area.

Viewing them clairvoyantly, psychically or scanning them etherically external to the body we will discover these amazing outer Chakra points.

Having learned of the Transpersonal Chakra many years ago, I was already aware of the 'Unicorn' effect of this Chakra. I then discovered that it worked with the Psychic Chakras and was also part of that system.

Then I discovered something new and unexpected to me.

Two etheric antennae that look like 'horns' appear to emerge from the frontal lobes either side of the hairline.

I was amazed when I first felt these on a psychic person who made her living helping others but who was suffering a great deal of pain herself.

On further examination it was clear that one of these antennae was actually stuck or glued in place at a distance of approximately 8" (20cms) external to the body; it had been caused through picking up too much negative gunk from others. And this had caused it to be continually 'On' or attempting to function. The other Chakra was still able to retract, but had also been affected by the malfunction of the other.

Many people do not have this problem as their 'horns' are poorly developed so they may remain constricted within the head, like the nubs of antlers on a young deer. But those who have been using their antennae – whether knowingly or not – run the risk of picking up everything in the atmosphere, both energetic and emotional. Learning how to care for and retract this important energetic anatomy can be important for the survival of some Sensitives.

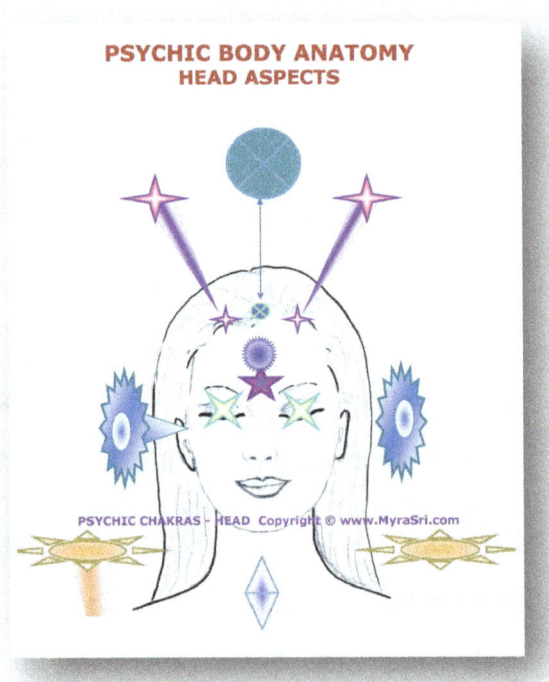

The Antennae, 'Psychic Horns' or Horn Antennae

There are several names for this particular anatomy, as they are all descriptive of their function.

As you can see there is an energetic protrusion on each side of the Frontal Lobes extending up and out in a similar manner to 'horns' and these are approximately positioned just inside the hair line or scalp.

A famous picture of *Moses* by Jose De Ribera shows his Psychic Antennae or 'Rays of Light' as they are claimed to be called – they can be seen quite clearly and he has *never* been called demonic. Not that I am aware of anyway.

In ancient times, these same 'Horns' were included in pictures and sculptures, demonstrating not a demonic or devilish image, but the image of a wise sage.

His statue by Michelangelo in the Library of Congress also show these two protrusions from his head.

They are an interpretation of the 'horn like rays' emitted from Moses at these points. And this is precisely what the antennae are in highly developed psychics.

Their function is to act as receivers of energetic information, picking up frequencies, and channelling these incoming frequencies into the brain centres and inner Psychic Chakras for interpretation and action.

Many people are now not only growing these but also further developing them. I have noted them in a lot of my clients though they were not always present in everyone when I first started working with these Chakras some time ago.

Main problems usually are a 'rusting'-in-place with psychics who have never closed them down, or turned them off. Or they have become badly gunked or gummed and stuck in sensitive types who have not fully recognised their abilities but been prone to input overwhelm or attack from others.

One psychic I know went a bit mental because she never, ever closed them down or retracted them in. Her energetic information systems were continually on alert, always picking up information, and these ever changing vibrations were, in part, running her life. She was also in the habit of interfering with people she picked up information about, whether or not it was her business or not. This is not only unethical but also unhealthy. Besides which, no one should be subjected to a psychic approaching them uninvited with whatever story interpretation they have and wish to impress upon them. If one is going through a series of energetic changes, and is part way through a 'story' or chapter in their healing process then a snapshot of issues by any casual psychic observation can be totally way off, for they have not seen the progression to this point, nor has the client yet reached the end point of this integration. What is actually a releasing and a resolving of a symptom may be erroneously interpreted as an actual issue on its own – and consequently handled incorrectly. Sometimes something has to emerge to be releases, not simply subdued back down again...

When this person interfered with my own clients, I had to put a stop to it, and rather than her recognising that she may have been a bit off-beam about things, she became very dark and nasty. Her own antennae were so overwhelmed with information that she was not always correct on her interpretations, and she was psychically exhausted by all of the psychic activity and information.

If she learned to retract her horns antennae regularly, and to give her senses a chance to rest and rebalance and clear, she would have been less energetically excitable and over-reactive. Other clients of mine have been taught this and were so relieved to be able to find the rest they needed from continually attempting to 'be on alert' and to 'be ready to read' the energies.

This continual psychic alertness is not necessary and is possibly self destructive.

These chakras can be cleaned up and retracted back into the skull again, and re-educated to retraction when they are not required.

To do so, they need to be 'oiled' or to have the 'rust' or 'gunk' removed which has jamming them into a partially or fully 'On' position. Gentle manipulation by the practitioner can un-jam these, as the Etheric frequencies from the indicated Essential Oil (on a tissue) can also assist in both cleaning and oiling. Gently and very carefully working these antennae Chakras in extension and contraction can allow them to remember their options and functions.

Access / Contact Point

The Contact Points are located approximately 12 – 20 cms (5 – 8 inches) out above the temples at an angle similar to a pair of horns. If one cannot feel their presence until they are found close to or on the skull, then it is usually because that they have either not been activated, cannot be activated or have been retracted at some point and have remained there through being 'glued' in place with psychic gunk.

TRANSPERSONAL CHAKRA

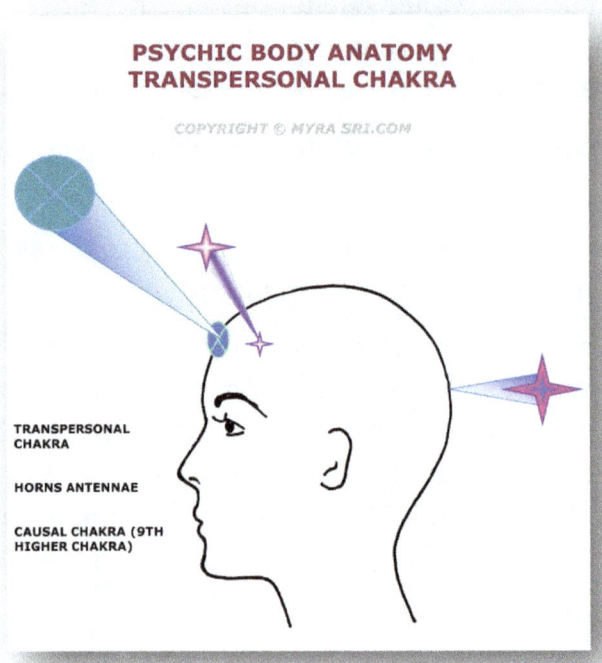

The Transpersonal Chakra is sometimes known as the **Frontal Chakra.** The functions of the Transpersonal Chakra affects and interacts with the Pineal, the Temporal lobes in the Brain, and associated Psychic Brain Centres. This Chakra and the frontal brain lobes are involved with not only communication, but also with its interpretation. They filter information and dialogue then instigate the results and input back to other physiological aspects, affecting physical and emotional output and behavior. Differences in each other's perceptions can be registered here, which can contribute to the resulting dialogue.

Avoidance in direct communication willingly or otherwise can result in a Transpersonal Chakra that is bent or leaning downward or to one side, often the result of trauma, depression or direct attack or bullying from a more forceful mind. As its name implies, it is about one's persona as well as one's personal views, which can be transferred or can be communicated to others or can become or create cross-contamination. Transferring implies the putting upon another whether appropriate or not, whilst communication implies the ability to both give and receive information and views. Cross contamination is the picking-up of someone else's 'stuff', being personally infected with it and also possibly passing it on to another,.

Someone who has been continually controlled or antagonised may well find it hard to accept another viewpoint from someone else. Particularly if the person that has affected their Transpersonal has a strong mind and is psychically forceful and lacking in integrity.

Access / Contact Point

The Chakra emerges from the psychic centres in the brain to protrude out at about a 45 degree angle diagonally at the hairline, appearing like a Unicorn horn. Usually it is about 30 to 50 centimetres in length, and governs direct communication with others. It often overlaps or connects with others when close to them or in communication with them. Thus non-verbal communication takes place here.

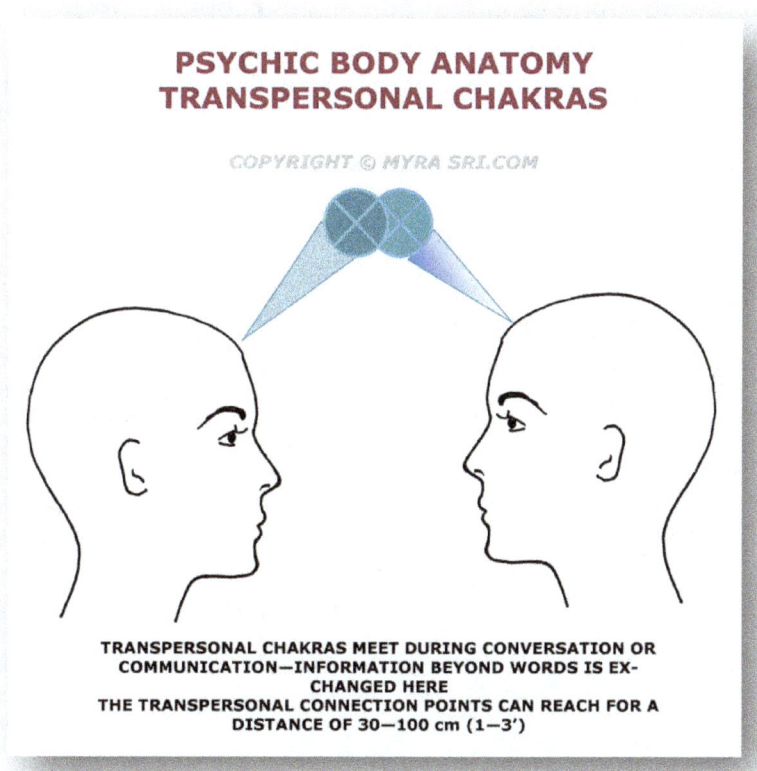

Third Eye-s Chakra

Most usually think of only one Third Eye Chakra placed approximately between the eyebrows and part of the Main Chakra System. When open and working, this is able to function whilst the eyes are open, providing visual information on Auras, frequencies and in some cases beings or entities not normally visible to the naked eye.

There is another psychic eye and this is the Inner Eye. This is placed slightly lower down and is available when the eyes are closed. It allows us access information within our own head and mind, where we can visualise and view from there.

Importantly it can also provide us with a clear space or inner screen on which to see external frequencies that our normal vision cannot access. As Neo in 'The Matrix' with his blindfold on did, when we clear and train this area we can see things normally unavailable to us. Both of these psychic eyes interact with the Pineal Gland and the Ajna Chakra, and can also connect to the Guru Chakra and the Transpersonal Chakra.

Access / Contact Point

Approximately 5 cm or 2" from the mid-brow area.

Eye Chakras

These are external access points to the Eye Chakras, which are approximately 4-7 cm external to the closed eye. The external aspect of these Chakras connect in through the eyes and are connected to the brain via the optical nerves which pass through and loop at the back of the brain. The real origin of both Eye Chakras are actually inside the head where the optical nerves meet to cross-over, sitting in the place of interpretation of incoming information. The Connection Points external to the eyes contact this entire energetic optical system.

These Chakras can become clouded by another person attempting to occupy or 'See' into someone's mind, or to 'See' through their eyes. The clouding can cause us to blink often or to feel like we have a film across our eyes. Caused by psychic gunk or disresonance from the other's visioning, this can prevent easy vision. The eyes can also cloud up like this when we attempt to see into a situation that is not appropriate for us to 'read' at this time, or that has harmful, negative, incompatible or toxic frequencies to one's own.

The simplest method to clear is to wipe the external Chakra point itself with a (selected) Essential Oil on a tissue, taking care not to touch the eyes or the eyelids. Wipe in front of the eyes and also at the back of the head at a similar distance. One can draw the Essential Oil energy into the visual areas with imagination, my breathe technique (my *Secrets Beyond Aromatherapy* book) or by intention, in order to clean and clear along the entire optical nerve system. Dispose of any used tissues safely and hygienically as the tissue will have gathered toxic or negative etheric phlegm or psychic plasma.

Access / Contact Point

Approximately 4-7 cm (1 ½" to 3") external to the closed eye.

Ear Chakras

The Inner point for the Ear Chakra is about 2-5 cm internal and the Outer Ear Chakra position is approximately 5-15 cm (2"-6") external to the body.

The Ears generally function and collaborate with other Psychic head Chakras, in particular the Transpersonal, the Horn Antennae, Third Eye and the Cerebral Psychic Chakras in the Brain. Interestingly they operate separately to the Eye Chakras, though they may well collate their incoming information within the Master Centres in the Brain through the Psychic Centres. The ears often have protective filters and these need to be cleaned occasionally or as needed.

Access / Contact Point

The Outer Ear Chakra position is approximately 5-15 cm horizontally external to the body.

Ear Filters

Enlisting and instructing client to clean their own filters energetically empowers them. The use of colour to clean and strengthen in the following sequence is considered very helpful:

- Gentle removal of filters; bathe to clean off gunk in etheric soapy water
- Rinse and repair in one of the indicated: turquoise / aqua marine / light aqua / or spectrum blue-aqua
- Follow with rinse and an infusion of one of the following colour frequencies as indicated: gold / turquoise / royal blue / silver / platinum
- Before replacing, ask your client to clean behind and inside the inner ear with choice of: soap, shower, spray, any color or method they choose
- Gently replace filter
- Recheck ear Chakras and filters after clearing
- Recheck tone of the Psychic Body anatomy again for confirmation of positive change
- Always dispose of all cleaning waters and receptacles as you go

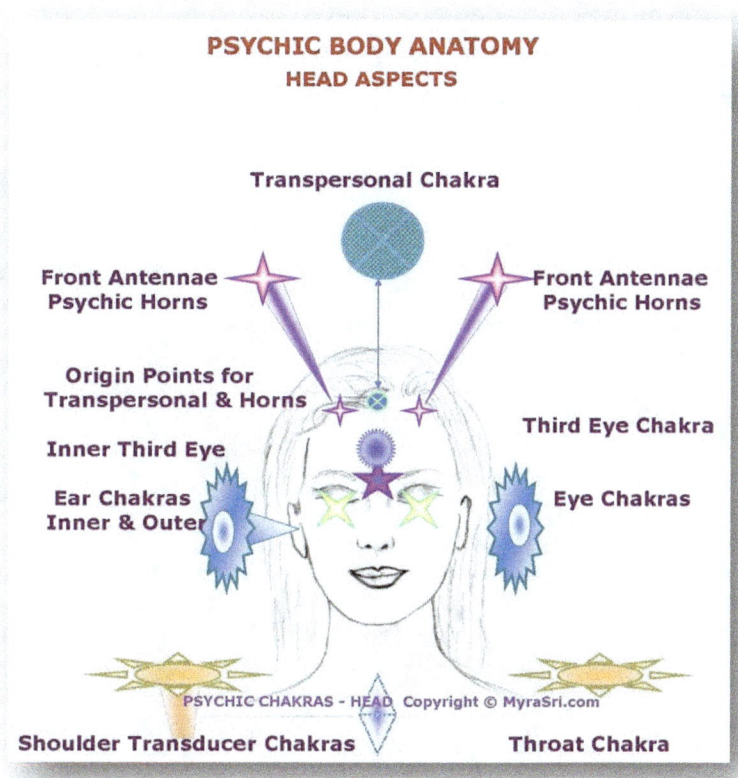

Nose and Mouth Chakras

These Chakras are more upgraded than newly evolved, for these have been in effect for some time. With the inflow of the new energies, some may find that these senses are either more enhanced or more inhibited when they assess them.

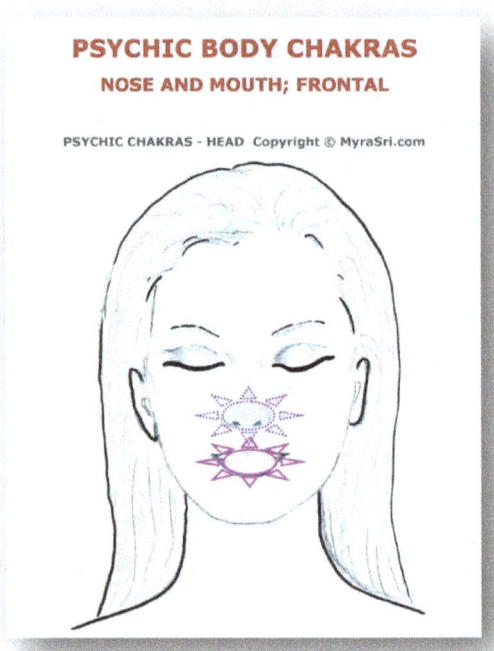

Nose Chakra

Connected to our Inner Knowing in the ordinary person this Chakra is often undeveloped, underdeveloped or covered with psychic phlegm or gunk. Coughs and continual colds may indicate some sort of energetic overlay from another more energetically or psychically stronger or incompatible person. It may also or alternatively indicate a tight restriction on trusting what one knows, or it may be connected with a lack of self-trust. As humans, many of us have learned 'to comply' in order to maintain harmony or safety, which has meant a quarantine on following our own knowing; until we mature or learn differently!

Access / Contact Point

Best location is approximately 5cms (2") from the nose.

Mouth Chakra

This Psychic Chakra is the only one besides the Eyes that engages with giving out as well as receiving information. It actually starts at the back of the tongue, though the Chakra range is about 3 inches or 10 cms external to the mouth and can be accessed at this point.

It is capable of harnessing inner power and psychic abilities, bringing healing or condemnation (depending on the spiritual development of the being) to the recipient.

It may be influenced by the Amygdala unless this becomes more evolved.

Access / Contact Point

Contact Point is best located about 5-10cms from the mouth.

Throat Chakra

The Throat Chakra in the Psychic Body system governs self expression, one's own truth and the holding back of words and thoughts. It is usually not considered as part of the Psychic Body, but its power with language, truth and prophesying must not be underestimated. Because of its connection with the Mouth Chakra it has been included as part of the Psychic Body anatomy. It may be affected by intent to control what one says by another, or where there is conflict regarding what one says being heard.

Access / Contact Point

Anywhere along a trajectory of approximately 3-15cms from the body.

Shoulder Transducer Chakras

These particular Chakras are Master Gateway Chakras and are covered in the *Gateway Chakras* section.

Master Chakras

There are Key points in the Psychic Body which act as Control Centres. Checking these first can give us an overall view. Ensuring that these are re-checked at the end of any Psychic Chakra correction can confirm a fully or correctly functioning Psychic Body. If one of these Control or Master Chakras is out, then checking each individual Psychic Chakra can further clarify the issue involved. Some of the Master Chakras act as Gateway Chakras and are covered more fully later.

The Master Psychic Chakras are:

- Psychic Centres in the Brain
- Shoulder Transducers (Gateway Chakra)
- Spatial Chakras (Gateway Chakra)

Psychic Head Chakras

Let us explore the head anatomy and Psychic Centres in the brain...

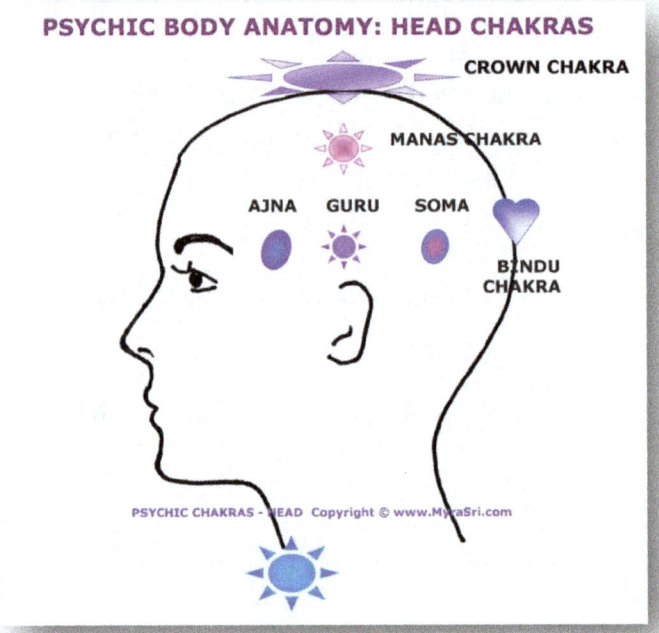

This illustration indicates the positions of possible present or active Chakras in the head.

Not everyone may have these, and indeed not everyone may *need* these, though most people will have one or more in some form or another, even if it is only a partly operative Ajna, which is closely equated to the Third Eye. The indicated names are from the Vedic system.

The associated cerebral centres in the brain that work with the psychic senses and Psychic Chakras are considered to be Master Psychic Centres. They are roughly located in the Lateral Ventricle in the Brain. Here there is a lot of fluid, and it provides a conducive and conductive energy sphere for energetic information, electrical and nerve or neuro-transmitter processing. Fluid itself is highly conducive to lightning-fast communication and aids the ease of sharing impressions, vibrations and consciousness. Areas in the brain involved with actual thinking link in with psychic data and impressions to create a sense perception, picture or internal image for interpretation. These thinking centres can be generally evolution-dictated (usually through the family line) but an expanded consciousness and a higher Soul purpose can override an inhibited awareness and also further enhance its existing function, usually in a spiritual way rather than a psychic-egoic way. Major family or social restrictions can serve to inhibit function, though with a higher calibre Soul, the being will eventually overcome some of any resultant debilities.

Interactions on a physical level are with the Pituitary (via the Crown), the Hypothalamus, the Amygdala and on a psychic level with the Pineal via the Third Eye and other related centres in the Brain.

Channelling of psychic energy is usually via these centres, though not necessarily always. **Importance** must be placed on working only with the correct compatible vibrational initiations or activations, as some have been known to experience Psychic Aberrations, Psychic Shock, Psychotic Episodes or Psychosis and even Psychic Madness when a vibration or frequency is too strong, too alien, has a string of darkness attached, holds hidden agendas or is driven by force or ego.

A past life historic experience of Psychic Madness can well leave an imprint in these psychic centres, and it is important to heal this and remove all related past resonances for a healthier current life function in order to navigate the everyday occurrences as well as extra-ordinary vibrations that we currently find ourselves living in.

CROWN PSYCHIC FUNCTION

The Crown Chakra besides being important in the Main Chakra system is also a Psychic Centre point. It receives spiritual information on one level, and it also communicates etherically on another level. The Access / Contact Point can be directly on the head to approximately 4-12 cms above it. Its Psychic function is through its ability to interact with the Manas and Guru Chakras.

One of the main energy points is the **Pituitary Gland** which governs hormonal output and regulation. Imbalance here may affect sensory perception or interpretation. It is usually related to the Guru Chakra and interacts with it.

In the head, the gland associated with the **Third Eye** is the **Pineal Gland** and both are associated with the **Ajna Chakra**. This generally emerges from the near the centre of the brain through the front of the forehead and out between the eyebrows, showing as the **Third Eye Chakra**. There is a corresponding position at the rear of the head, which some refer to as the **Download Point**, and is the **Bindu** Chakra. This can also be associated with the Causal Chakra which sits external and angled up somewhat from the Bindu at the back of the head – see 9th Higher Chakra.

PSYCHIC CENTRES IN THE BRAIN

Some of this anatomy has remained unchanged for centuries, however, there have been upgrades and changes, and I present my current understandings here.

These are the inner centres within the head that govern or relate to psychic function.

The Crown (Sahasrara) Chakra is a comprehensive Chakra and emerges above the head. It also sits in the Crown of the head itself and the underside faces downward directly over the Manas and Guru Chakras, interacting directly with them. The information from the coronal or Crown Chakra is related to one's own personal understanding, and this impacts on the interpretations of the sensory and energetic information and impressions.

As the Manas and Guru Chakras are energetically related directly to the Crown Chakra, information from the Crown merges into the Manas with the Guru facing upward.

The Ajna is also energetically related to the Amygdala.

The Soma is energetically related to the Bindu Chakra which sits on the back of the head.

The Bindu Chakra is located at rear of head, sometimes called The 'Download' Point.

Notes:

'**Gu**' means darkness and '**ru**' means light. Guru is the light that dispels the darkness of ignorance.

The **Bindu** Chakra lies beneath the cowlick that most people have at the **back of their head.** Anatomically it is located where the bones of the back and sides of the skull meet (the occiput and the parietal).

SPATIAL CHAKRAS

These are Gateway Chakras and are covered in the section on these.

Psychic Chakras in the Body

Whichever way we approach the Psychic Chakras, it remains that all components of the human energy system are somehow and in many ways interrelated to each other, and these parts or aspects communicate with each other. However, the Out-of Body connections that have been observed are usually at Junction or *Connection Points* that give rise to their own individual energy centre or Chakra point or points at those junction positions.

Here is how the Psychic Body anatomy looked in 2009. These were all that I could track at that time and they appeared to be linked or superimposed in the same locations as existing in-body (internal) Chakras:

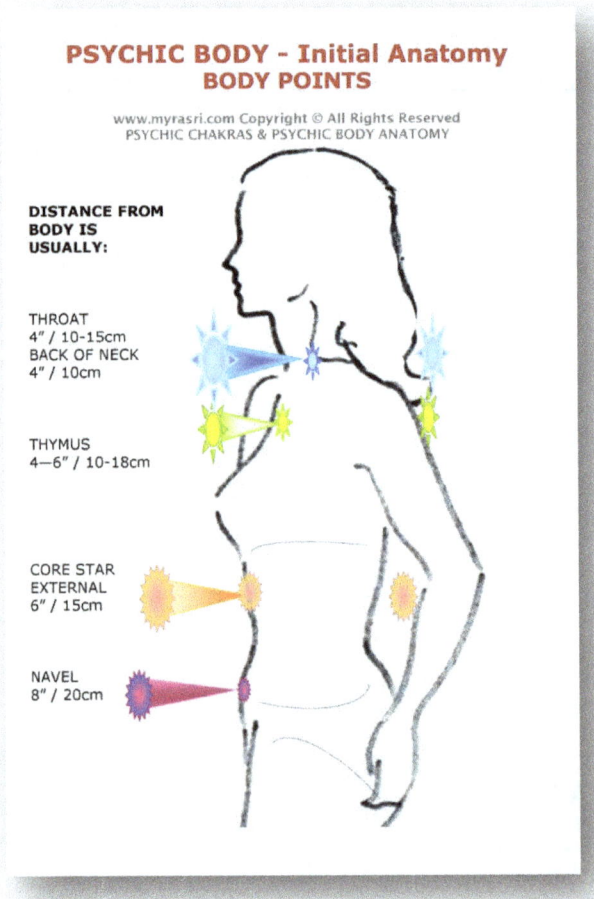

There may be invisible lines of connections and some intereaction to the In-Body Chakras from these external Access / Contact Points, but the point of Power or Balance would actually be in the external Points that have been identified here.

When these Chakras emerge from the body in this manner, they are easily and best accessed via their external position – one does not need to touch the actual body that aligns along its pathway – the Contact Point will contact and connect with the whole of the particular Chakra, including its bio-locational origin and its full projection position.

Though some of these Chakras may appear to occupy positions similar to the Main Chakras, or even part of the Hara system - do not assume that they are indeed the same Chakra. They just happen to occupy similar space positions but usually and often on different levels, dimensions or energy bodies. However, some Chakras are Key Chakras (or Master Chakras) and act as important links or connection points.

To Summarise; Chakras from other systems can co-exist, but they have their own particular purposes and functions; the Psychic Body Chakras and the Main Chakras and the Signal Chakras have separate tasks.

As we have already looked at the head and brain Chakras, let us consider the Chakras that make up the Psychic Chakra body on or around the body which include:

- The Throat Connection Point
- Back of the Neck Connection Point
- Core Star Connection Point, front and rear
- The Navel Connection Point

THE THROAT CONNECTION POINT

The Throat Chakra is related to the ability to communicate, and in the psychic sense, this is related to the ability to give language to one's sensory perceptions and understandings. Psychic control from another can also inhibit this area. The Connection Point can indicate balanced communication with other areas of the Psychic Body.

BACK OF THE NECK CONNECTION POINT

There is a point on the spine at the base of the neck that sits parallel to the shoulder line and is viewed by some as a Psychic Protection Point.

It is located close to the back of the Throat Chakra and is sometimes confused with or labelled as the 4 ½ Chakra though I consider there has been some confusion as to its proper function. It is a Psychic Body Point.

This vital point has sometimes been used as an 'escape' hatch by one or more of the energy bodies, the Soul itself or part of one's spirit; this 'escaping' usually having occurred due to some trauma, horror or terror early in childhood, in the womb, or around conception. It is usually accompanied by a desire to leave the body and escape to a happier or safer place, usually back to one's Soul Home. See *'Some Considerations'*.

If the client has escaped this way in the past, there may be a weakening in this area or an established tendency to use this point when highly stressed and this too may need addressing. This may also cause it to be susceptible to negative attack.

There may be some clouding with this point, if hidden, so if there is a need to work with it, approach it gently and be mindful to send love and safety for access and for permission to attend to this sensitive spot.

TO HEAL: When used for escape by the Soul I would suggest the following: Seal by closing down the Gateway or Lotus Chakra here, seal with Circle of Light and Cross (X or +) of Matter. Ask the client's Soul to undertake not to habitually do this again (check for real agreement). Heal any old Trauma wherever it lies on whatever level, dimension, lifetime or body. Affirm that this Gateway is available for important information, but not for habitual escape, or easy access or invasion by others. Check both Front and Back Points for correct 'In' / 'Out' energy settings and finally re-establish harmony with the other Gateway Chakras (Spatial Chakras).

Access / Contact Point

Contact can be directly on the skin. The best contact position to test I have found to be 8-15cms away from the back of the neck.

Core Star Connection Point, Front and Rear

The Core Star Chakra is linked in with the Soul Body and interacts with the Psychic Body. It acts as an integration point for psychic information, data, experiences and conflict. Rebalancing this so that one may better access one's own Core energy and resources without overlays or impact from others (and their psychic intents) helps to maintain its integrity. Old, buried or unresolved issues may impact or progress through to the back of the Core Star Chakra, affecting the middle or small of the back.

Keywords are: *Soul Expression, Integration, Integrity*

The Navel Connection Point

The Navel is a Major Connection Point with other Energetic systems. Past psychic experiences or connections may be accessed here, and new psychic connections may be created here. Identity and dependency issues may be located here, which can compromise our ability to correctly discern and disseminate incoming data and information.

Unresolved or buried issues may affect the lower spine and one's sense of foundations, as this point is also a connection point for the Soul Body.

Its keywords are: *Knowing, Nurturing*

Gateway Chakras

The Gateway Chakras were the last Psychic Chakras that I discovered. The following Chakras are vital Chakras in the Psychic Chakra Anatomy. They are all externalised Contact Point Chakras – they may or may not be connected to another internal Chakra but similar to the others, they exist in their own right and have a separate function.

- Shoulder Transducer Chakras
- Spatial Chakras
- Mid-Shins Chakra

This is because they are major energetic gateways to other energy fields and a variety of energies, vibrations, memories, records, data, realms and dimensions. There are other Master Gateway Chakras, but these are only present in a few people as yet, and the information will be released when there are sufficient Souls requiring this advanced information.

On a more day-to-day level, these Gateways act as governing Centres that are Out-of-Body, and are actually vital to its health and function, helping to keep the psychic functions centred and free to operate.

The first set to be discovered were the **Shoulder Chakras**. The second set are called the **Spatial** Chakras. These are **Gateway Chakras**, along with the Psychic Point (Back of the Neck) and the Master or Psychic Centres in the Brain.

The New Evolved Chakras

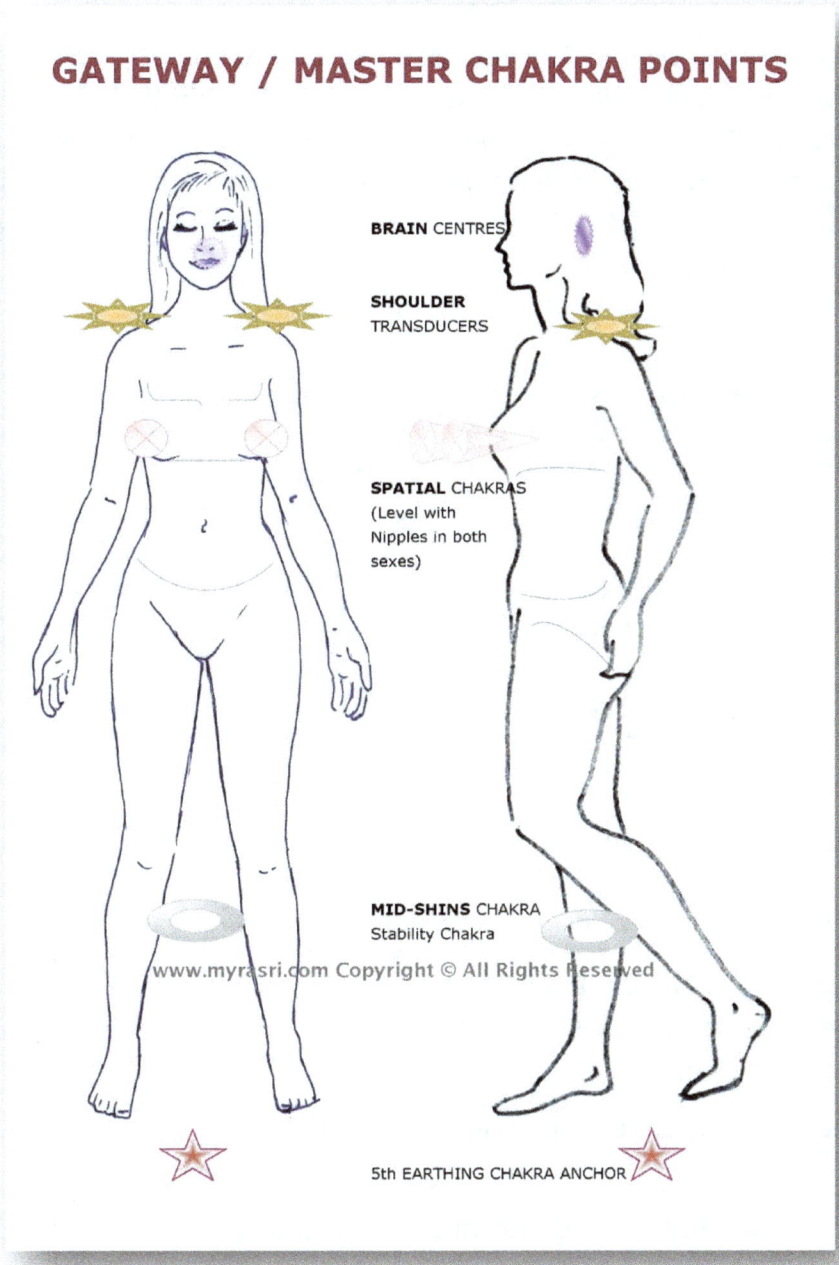

SHOULDER TRANSDUCERS CHAKRAS

Hovering approximately 2' – 5' (5-10cm) above each shoulder, these Connection Chakra Points are major factors in balancing the Psychic Body. These act as Outer-Filters and **Transducers** of energy and information. They are important Portals as they link to the Psychic Chakra System, the Higher Chakras and the Auric Bodies. They are the first to receive galactic information or other vibrational broadcasts.

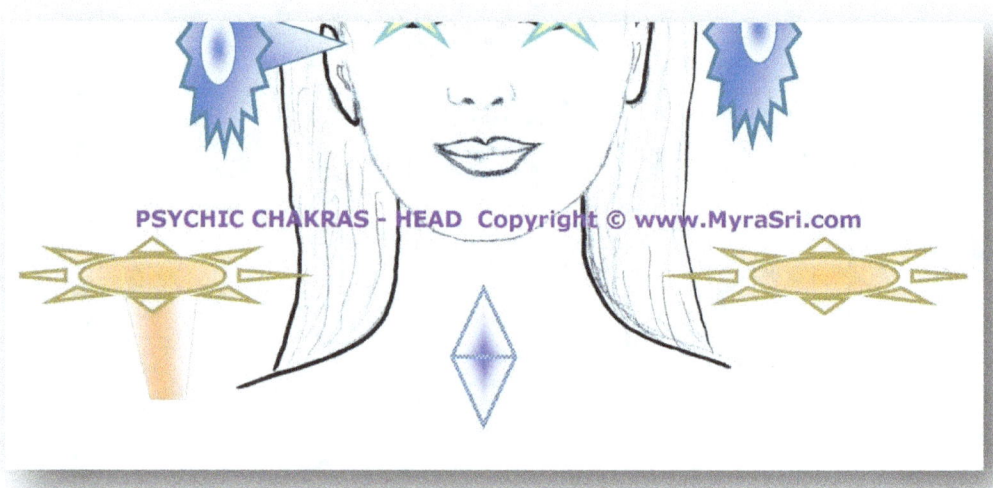

Their key words are: *Transducing, Channeling, Receiving*

Once cleared, centred again and balanced, they seem to assist in clearing many of the other psychic channels to provide a clearer and easier flow of energy input and information.

Always check these important positions when looking at balancing the Psychic Anatomy.

The spin on these Chakras was not initially easy to track. However, they are found to generally be like spinning orbs on a horizontal axis; similar to seeing miniature Saturns with her rings sitting horizontally above each shoulder.

The energy is connected via a sort of channel that emerges from each of the shoulders themselves.

Balancing Possibilities

To balance them these are the methods I have found effective:

- Use of an indicated Essential Oil (via kinesiology, intuition, reference or pendulum) in a sweeping, wiping or clearing motion. If working with a particular issue, for further understanding of the choice of Essential Oil, refer to '*Secrets Beyond Aromatherapy*'.
- Emission of Essential Oil Etherics from a static hand held in the Chakra space
- Holding of energy together with another Psychic Body Chakra (often the stomach / Navel or a another Psychic Chakra)
- Performing Figure 8 movements in different directions are effective when overwhelm or stagnation is present; most effective are horizontal movements
- Use of sound (tuning forks, cymbals etc) to 'break up' congestion in and around the Chakras, also finger clicking if none of these are available
- Check the ears and their filters after clearing the shoulder Chakras

Access / Contact Point

Positioned horizontally approximately 2"– 5" (5-10cm) above each shoulder.

SPATIAL CHAKRAS

Keyword: *'In/Out'*

Position: At approximately breast or chest nipple height and at an angle of approximately 20° away from the midline, and about 30-50 cm distance and in line with the nipples (in both men and women) there are two Chakras concerned with a variety of functions.

These have been one of the most recent Chakras to find and identify on the Psychic Body. Their concern is to work in concert with the Aura. They have a variety of tasks, and they not only take in information, energy and stimulus into the energy fields, Psychic Body and physical body, they also release over-produced Psychic energy from within and further assist in assigning Psychic energy correctly within the Psychic body and its components.

These are **Regulator** Chakras and they have a major function with growth and development. Each Chakra is a major Psychic Gateway. They may also link and connect with the back of the neck Psychic Point.

The Spatial Chakras also can connect to Past Life Karma and issues as they feed into the Soul Body and Causal Body and back again as part of their duties with communication and interpretation.

These Master Chakras link to the Emotional and Etheric Bodies.

Access / Contact Point

About 30-50 cm away from the breasts or nipples, angled at 20° from centre.

Mid-Shins Chakra

I have also labelled this Chakra as the **Stability** Chakra.

Keyword: *Stability, Direction*

This is the Psychic Chakra for **Stability**. It helps to hold the Psychic Body steady and unwavering when an influx of energies may unbalance it. You might view it as a kind of anchor point, and it aids to connect the Psychic Body to the Soul Body and Astral Body. Its Keyword is Direction and it is also concerned with Stability issues. This Chakra is multi-directional.

Position: It is located between and just slightly to the front of the middle of the Shins.

Psychic Body Chakra Links

Psychic Body Anatomy is an energetic body, with various unique and specific Connection Points located at various positions related to the areas and functions that they are connected with. I discovered various sensitive points along the surface or the Psychic Body and when these are indicated as requiring attention, they can signal a related function to the area involved.

The illustration shows various Light Body Connection Points as minor Psychic Chakras.

These are responsible for signalling and transmitting information (to a lesser degree than the Master Psychic Chakras) to the Psychic Body.

These can be affected, un-balanced, impacted or misplaced through trauma, negative energies or accident, and this can have an affect on the overall functioning, though to a lesser degree than the other more major Chakras. However, they are important in that they help to keep the body aligned and in the right space location. This prevents a form of disorientation which tends to distort perceptions and may result in faulty readouts of incoming information.

They may also be seen to be points along the perimeter of the Psychic Body, if there was a real Psychic Energy Field boundary in the sense of the word. What has shown up is that when they are imbalanced, they affect function, twist it or allow interference that taints it.

If all else shows clear, but there is an issue in the Psychic Body, then it is worth checking these points out. Sometimes it's as simple as a message about a person or place that is inharmonious in frequency. Other times, it may simply be an elemental energy that has become caught up in the psychic anatomy in some way.

You will see by the Psychic Body Chakra List that there are issues that can cause imbalance in the system that are not necessarily from an obvious or dramatic cause.

Access / Contact Points

These points vary depending on their position and on their current state though a general rule is that they are contactable on the body to a distance of about 4" or 10cm. Some points are safe to access by touch directly on the body (usually over clothing if present) such as the hands and feet, which can be accessed by touching the soles and palms. The side points – knees, ankles, elbows etc – can range from body surface to as far as 10cms or more away from the body.

The Contact Points for the Throat, Thymus, Back of the Neck Point, Core Star, and Navel may radiate from between 10-20 cms out from the body.

The keywords and functions for these are included in the Psychic Chakra List that follows in the next chapter.

The Mid-Shins Chakra is included in the Gateway Chakras and the Contact Point is between and just slightly to the front of the middle of the Shins.

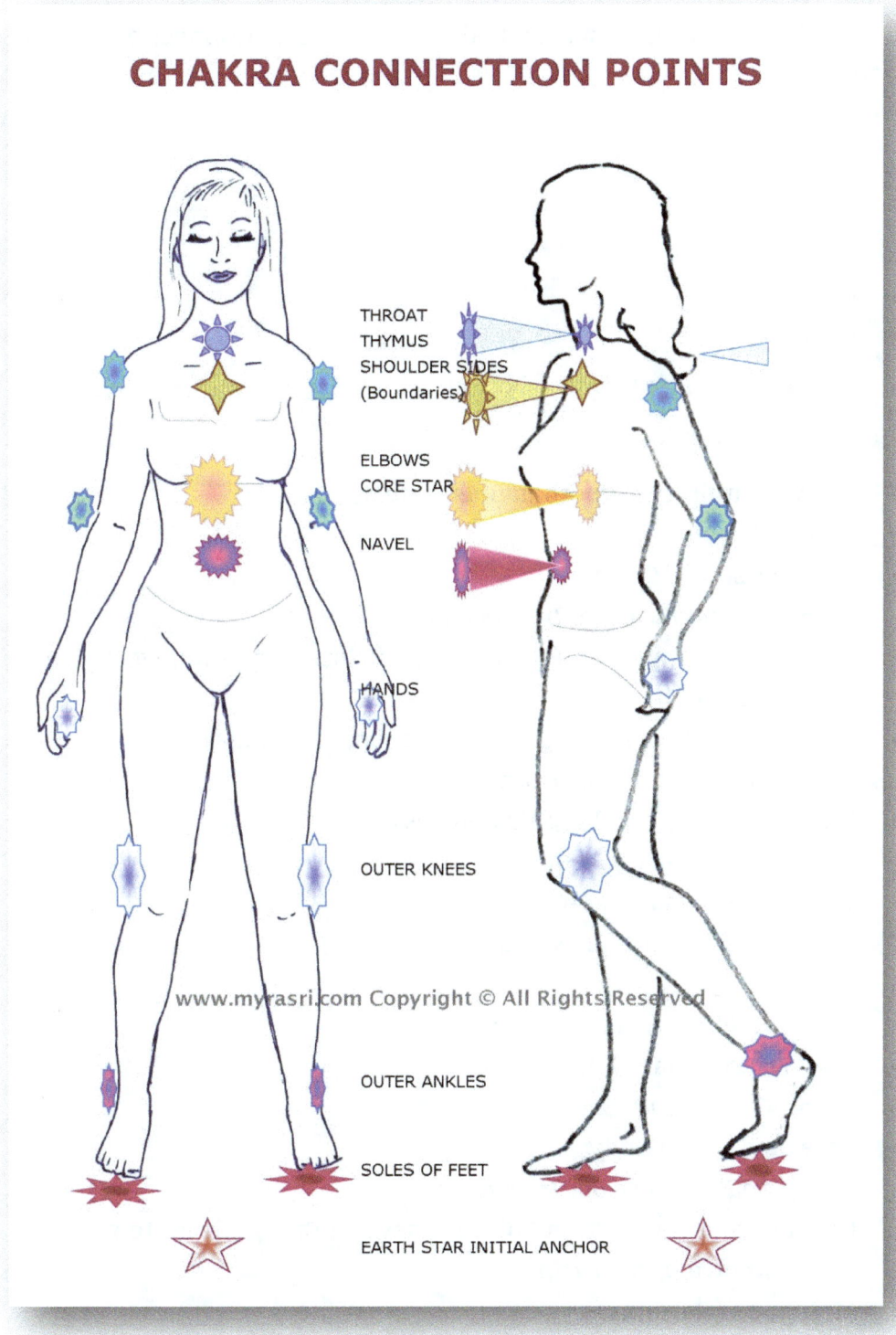

SUMMARY - PSYCHIC BODY CHAKRA LIST

Here is a listing of the Psychic Body Chakras and Connections for ease of reference:

Psychic Centres In Brain

- Guru
- Ajna
- Soma
- Manas
- Bindu – Download point - Occiput

Centre / Mid Line; Front

- Crown (Pituitary/Hypothalamus/Pineal)
    - *Channeling*
- Transpersonal (Pineal)
    - *Communicating, Interpreting*
- Third Eye / s (Inner and Outer) (Pineal/Pituitary, Kidneys, Spleen)
    - *Visioning*
- Mouth (Link To Throat, Nervous System, Amygdala)
    - *Prophesying, Affirming*
- Nose (Olfactory and Psychic Centres)
    - *Sniffing-Out, Knowing*
- Throat (Nervous System, Throat);
    - *Prophesying, Language*
- Thymus
    - *Healing, Safety, Self Love,*
- High Heart, Solar Plexus
    - *Channeling, Love*
- Core Star – Soul Body
    - *Soul Expression, Integration*
- Navel (Major Connection Point for several Energetic systems)
    - *Knowing, Nurturing*
- Mid-Shins (Gateway)
    - *Direction, Stability*

- Earth Star, Earthing Chakras
  - *Grounding, Anchoring, Reality*

Centre Line; Back

- Causal Chakra – 9th Upper Chakra
  - *Connection Point to Soul and Mind*
- Psychic Point / Back Neck
  - *Access and Escape Point, Healing, Autonomy*
- Heart
  - *Access Point, Back Entry*

Side

- 'Horns' Left and Right (Link To Throat, Heart, Stomach)
  - *Accessing*
- Eyes (Link To Heart and Throat - and Lungs)
  - *Visioning*
- Ears and Inner Ear Filters (Link To Heart, Throat and Solar Plexus)
  - *Input*
- **Shoulder** / Neck Outer Filters **Transducer** / Portals (Gateway) : Links To Chakra System, Higher Chakras and Auric Bodies)- First To Receive Galactic Or Other Broadcasts
  - *Transducing, Channeling, Receiving*

Out-of-Body Chakras; Pairs

Generally related to Boundaries, our personal Space, our ability to relate to others and to life.

- Top of Arm / Side Shoulder – *Teamwork, Shared Goals or Values*
- Outer Elbow – *Boundaries, Safety, Guarding*
- Hands – *Major sensors and interpreters in touch and energy*
- Outer Knees – *Strength and humility in direction and movement*
- Outer Ankles – *Flexibility in direction and movement*
- Soles of Feet – *Standing our ground, Walking our path, Earth empathy*
- SPATIAL Chakras (Gateway) – *Breasts – In/Out, Governing, Feedback, Release*

HEALING THE PSYCHIC CHAKRAS

BALANCE AND CALIBRATE THE PSYCHIC BODY

I have found that a variety of methods can be used to clear, balance or align these Chakras.

Activation of these Chakras may begin for some people as soon as they see a picture of them... Those that are somewhat more advanced or energetically evolved may find that looking at one of the pictures can trigger an action (or reaction) in a Chakra; and this may simply be because the Chakra requires this visual symbological input of information.

Part of us is always wanting to heal itself, and a visual message can be sufficient to begin the process, particularly for the Psychic body which has direct input into the visual and sensory mechanisms, for it acknowledges in a more observable concrete or viewable form that which should be, and the energy systems then set about sorting this out through its desire to be whole again.

To work with the Psychic anatomy, first start off with familiarising oneself with one's Core – the Psychic Toner Exercise assists in this. Using the Connection Points and pictures in the order they are presented makes for a Psychic Chakras were cleaned out and then balanced and their Psychic Body Anatomy aligned

Clean up the Chakra Connection Points using any of the methods in *Balancing Techniques and Tools*. I find that the most effective healing tool is to track back in time.

The Most Effective Methods:

Tracking back to the original time and source of the problem that caused the imbalance; find and clear the cause energetically.

Settle, clear or clean up the Connection Point or Chakra; use energy work, the breath, essential oils, affirmations and support.

Feel for a smooth flow in the energies, clearing, aligning and recalibrating as you go. Reconnect to the appropriate links as suggested. Once the Psychic Body and Chakras have been balanced and aligned totally, and the Shoulder Transducers set, together with attention paid to the other Master Psychic

Chakras, it is a much easier matter for the next balancing session. For having aligned all of the Psychic anatomy, the next occasion that there appears to be a possible problem or issue, one can go straight to the Master Chakras to check for an indication that the issue lies in the Psychic body.

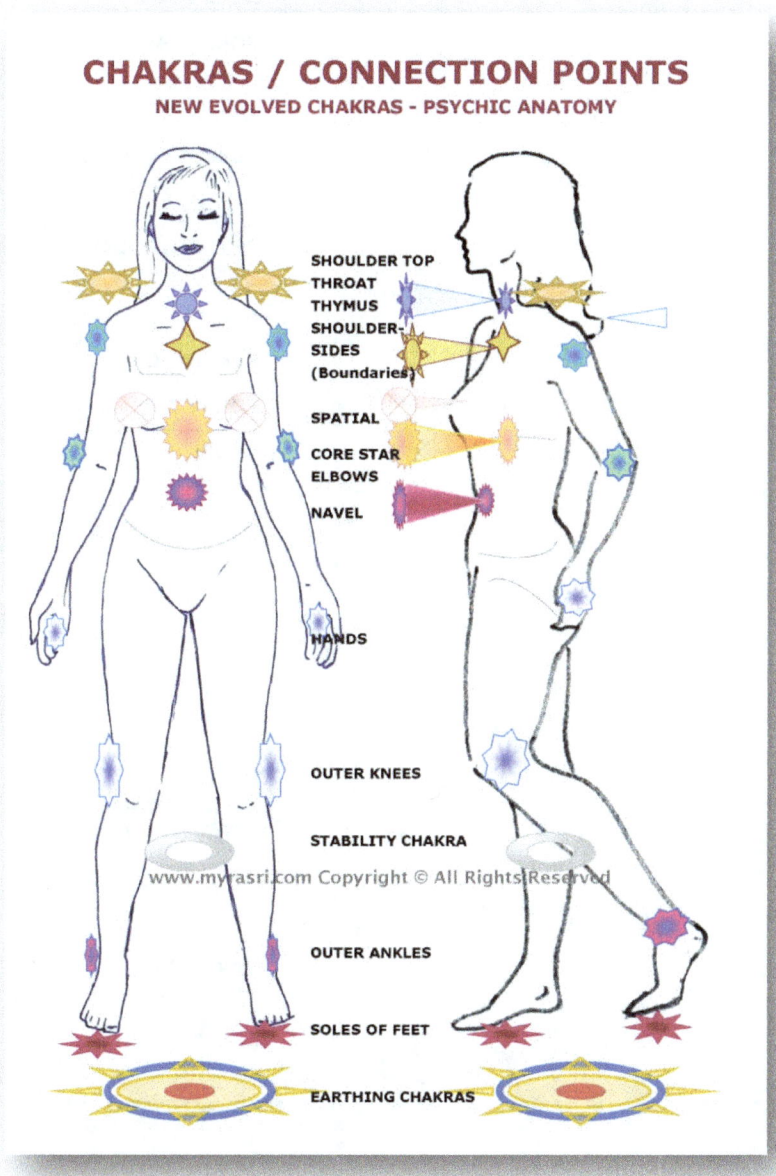

Psychic Body Connections; Astral and Soul Bodies

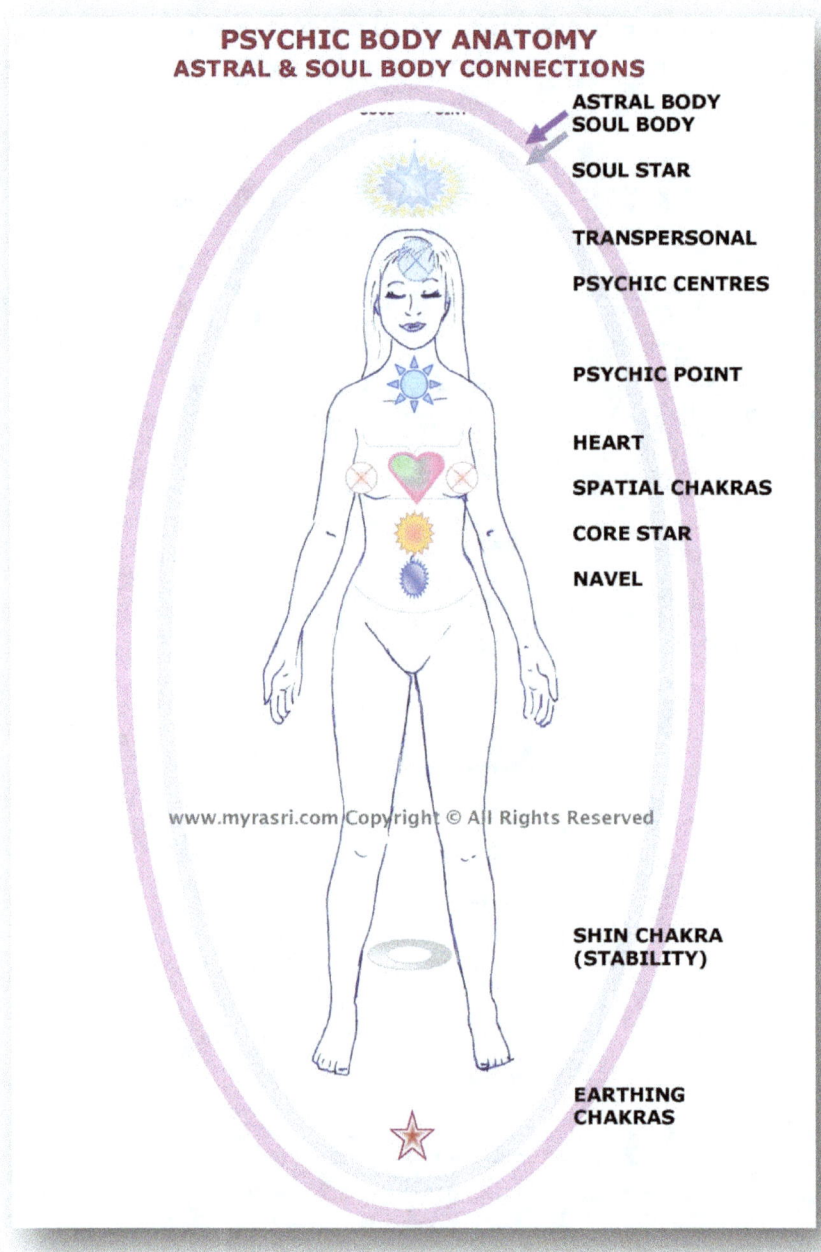

This diagram indicates the Connection Points that connect and link the Psychic Body, the Astral Body, Earthing Chakras and the Soul Body.

The Astral Body is like a malleable component of the Psychic anatomy in that it reaches out and explores places and spaces, sometimes a great distance away.

It is multi-coloured, flexible, continually moving, auditing, interpreting and relating.

This provides feedback which further supports the innate sensing and psychic abilities via other Chakras and connections. It can stray, explore, react and 'stick' if not monitored. The Astral bodies of others can do likewise.

The Astral Body can also assess the potential of possible relationships with others whether we are conscious of its actions or not. It is intrinsically linked with the Psychic Body via the Mid-Shins Stability Chakra.

The Soul Body has access to Soul Records and for some gifted people this means that they can access Past Lives or previous incarnations in order to give meaning to current life lessons for others. Or for themselves.

The Soul Body connects in at the Heart, Back of Neck (Psychic Point), Core Star, Navel, Mid-Shins, Earth Star or Earthing Chakras and Master Psychic Centres in the Brain.

Finish off any balance with registering the healing in the Soul Star Chakra.

The Mid-Shins Chakra or Stability Chakra aids to connect the Psychic Body to the Soul Body and Astral Body. Its Keyword is Direction and it is also concerned with Stability issues.

The **Earthing Chakras** help to anchor the Soul Body through the Transpersonal, Navel, Link and Soul Star Chakras.

SOME CONSIDERATIONS;

Excerpts and Lessons from Case Histories.

Understanding how past incarnations affect the Psychic Body...

Usually consideration is given to rest, consolidation and future planning between life-times, though at times in history this is not always possible, with some Souls working busily from one life time to the next, foregoing rest until certain aspects of their purpose have been achieved, or certain obstacles have been overcome. In this case, disillusionment can be an issue for that particular Soul.

Further considerations are:

- Planetary Planning, Cosmic Timing all come into this choice of present time incarnation.

- When timing is important for an incarnation – the window of opportunity presenting may be small, and the choices of and appropriate family to incarnate into may be limited:

- During times of upheaval or war not all events can be 'managed' due to the varying nature of Souls 'getting lessons' (or not) and the impact of their choices on outcomes: 'loose' plans are laid – and have to be adapted as events unfold. Nothing is set in concrete, despite hopes for destiny.

- So if timing is important, a certain Plan 'A' is a specific family / individual / place / culture, and a Plan 'B' is also set up as fall-back in case the Soul has begun their preparation for journey into the womb/world, and unforeseen death has occurred in whatever form to the fetus or to the mother: the Soul may have to switch quickly to Plan 'B' (Family 'B') rather than hang around the same family for another opportunity. This may cause its own type of scarring even before this incarnation;
    - If the incarnation is quick from one life time to the next, with little chance for full de-briefing, support, convalesce and resting for the Soul, the Soul may be struggling somewhat, but their mission /purpose usually helps keep them on 'here' or on-track.

- - If the Soul has been counseled or 'instructed' for a greater good to return quickly.
  - If a Soul needs to meet another Soul, and Soul has had to incarnate quickly.
  - If a mission has been aborted through unexpected death of self or host (chosen parent or fetal body / child's body).
  - Remember, plans can change as global consciousness 'gets' some things that are necessary for fulfillment of a particular purpose, but may also not 'get' something that is crucial, so another purpose is chosen, plans are shelved, or events are 'waited-out'.
- The Psychic Point can be invaded by others so check this for 'in' / 'out' energy settings, or whether there is a need to 'seal' this area from inadvertent escapes.
- Inter-dimensional damage may affect the leg (Knee, Ankle, Mid-shins Chakra) function – possibly a Past Life memory triggered. Also check the Spatial Chakras as well as other Master Centres.

THE NEW SIGNAL CHAKRAS AND ANATOMY

Signal / Survival Chakra System Overview

DEALING WITH SURVIVAL, SHOCK AND 'IN-CRISIS' FREQUENCIES:

RECOGNITION and ANCHORING OF BEING and ANATOMY

SHOCK INDICATOR

COLOR FREQUENCIES

BALANCE POSITIONS

SKELETAL REGISTRY

SENSORY RECOGNITION SURVIVAL SYSTEM

LINK CHAKRA

Survival Chakras

When I first discovered this system and its Chakras, I referred to it initially as 'The Survival Chakras'; this was because I had discovered that they acted as a kind of fast-track indication of where Shock or Trauma was being held in the body, and also of where and how to rebalance the body again.

The Survival or Signal System and its related Chakras are a kind of Gridding System –I call it the Signal System (or New Signal Chakra System) – that which indicates or signals that there is an issue that has not yet been dealt with that may hinder our journey or thrust us into 'Survival Mode' on some level. Until these are cleared, it can be difficult to have or to maintain peace in the body.

This set of Chakras has the ability to act as Warning Signals for shock in the body, and also to indicate when the body is in crisis or Survival Mode at some level, hence its name. The system is useful for not only diagnosis, but also for direction of the best healing energy placement.

Shock and Survival

Shock can be held at various levels in the body. Over time, if these are not alleviated, renovated, removed or mended, they become absorbed into the body at ever deeper levels. Sinking below skin level, below muscle memory, past the Nervous System network, they settle into the very bones – and they remain at a Skeletal level, thrumming at some repressed frequency which ultimately causes an instability tremor or frequency within the being.

For me, this was a major breakthrough in my understanding regarding the healing of the body and the being. If your home was continually experiencing shudders or tremors of any kind, one just may possibly get used to it over time. But would one really feel able to be at complete rest? I think not. If shock vibrations are continually being played out at some level, can one really feel safe enough to be able to recover one's energy; and to then herald all of one's resources towards building good health again? I doubt it. Part of the being's energy is always elicited to maintain and attempt to control the tremor in order to continue to function in other areas.

So the benefit of the awareness of this system is to be able to identify quickly if there is, or remains, any shock frequencies still inhibiting the body or being on any level. And to locate quickly the most effective form of energetic application to resolve shock frequencies and to bring stability and deep level calmness back the body.

The points and Chakras illustrated here give indication as to the most appropriate place for energetic application, as well as possible starting points (or points of blockage or housed tremors) for tracking initial or original causes of these effects.

DEALING WITH SURVIVAL, SHOCK AND 'IN-CRISIS' FREQUENCIES

The Signal Chakras and Anatomy System is a System of identification, diagnosis, balance and healing that connects the physical, energetic and mental systems. The Signal Chakra System is now timely, relevant, easily accessed and extremely informative for speedier diagnosis of overwhelm, shock, survival, crisis and toxic penetration and related family, cultural, relationships and geographic location issues.

Shock can throw the body or being into Survival Mode. As 'Survival' issues can cover a whole variety of problems, concerns, matters or subjects, a quick reference system is often very useful to give fast focus for shock or trauma issues of any kind.

Sometimes dealing with the cause of a Survival Issue doesn't necessarily mean that the associated shock that was or is resonating through the system has been completely addressed or settled. I can confirm that after being involved in many thousands of energetic balances, shock and trauma can still remain in the energy bodies for ages without being addressed, even though the 'issue' has been dealt with. Until these resonances and vibrations are addressed and settled, true healing may not be able to become real or completely hold.

If the client or practitioner cannot or do not recognise that some form of shock is still present, even though they may have cleared some of the levels of shock that were present, then they cannot possibly clear it; you cannot fix what you don't know. So having a way of testing for shock - of any form; whether it's residual, recent, past, hidden, buried, absorbed etc – can be of immense importance in securing a foundation for physical well-being as well as for energetic and emotional health.

When the Shock Test proves positive, then be prepared to handle wherever it may lead you, and do so as gently and kindly as possible.

REPEAT SHOCK

When an injury has occurred and the shock has not been completely dealt with, it can re-occur when a further injury takes place at the same position or site on the body. I know from personal experience that abuse or violent physical attacks that have registered like this in the body can re-emerge as part of the current injury, and may cause confusion as to the length of healing required because of the compounding effect of past hurt on top of present hurt. A broken rib that was from an abusive partner may yield prolonged bruising when the same rib is broken or bruised from a fall in later years. In the case of a broken shoulder, it took well over 5 months for bruising to begin to abate as past unresolved and associated hurts held in the body came up for healing. The person had been subjected to much abuse as a child and as a sensitive person they had simply absorbed these beatings in order to get past the intense physical, mental and emotional hurt that had been caused. The new injury allowed the body to release these old held-in shock frequencies completely. A long recovery, yes, but a freeing up occurred throughout all of the associated physiology as well as an understanding on a mental and emotional level that this was an opportunity to release these old frequencies in a way that normal energy healing had not been able to reach. Good physiotherapy and Bowen post Signal Chakra work also contributed to a much freer body and mind.

SHOCK ALERTS, SIGNALS AND ALARMS

The body is always trying to maintain balance and healing within itself, as are the energy fields, Aura and Soul and spirit of a person. To be able to reveal certain aspects that are out of balance within, we need a safe space to be able to open up that incorporates not just a sense of safety, but also a sense of competence or knowledge and understanding from the person we are opening up to. Someone who has a serious liver problem may not be able to give a full vote of confidence to a well meaning friend who has no real knowledge of the problem, no matter how caring that friend may be.

The body holds many messages and keys within itself, and tries to speak to us in gentle whispers. When we are unable to hear these whispers, or do not recognize what is going on, we may suddenly wake up to its shouts. In this case, survival issues, shock and the alerts and alarms that we cannot see or hear will affect our Nervous System in the demand for peace and healing.

Shock from trauma of any kind, or from sustained or intense crisis will resonate in the energy systems until dealt with. It is possible for them to be kind of 'held under control' to a degree, though this usually means that intense pressure on any random occasion can cause a 'meltdown' or 'explosion' until the repression is not only dealt with, but also the need to keep it under control is addressed.

Tribal and Culture Resonances

When we think of shock or trauma, we generally tend to think of current day situations, or of the last huge argument we had, or of a car accident, or possibly even way back to the shock of one's birth if that was traumatic in any way. This is a limited point of view. Though we don't always realize it, we bear and wear the energy imprints of our ancestry, our cultural or tribal heritage, and along with this can go any trauma that has been unresolved. This can continue until we deal with the trauma whether it impacts on us from within, or reflects in that which we attract to us.

Some of this can be labelled 'karmic', some of it can just be collateral, and some of this may simply be passed on. Whatever the cause, tribal and cultural resonances that are still giving off shockwaves within any part of our body or being need to be resolved, settled and healed.

We are in an age where we have not only the responsibility to do so, but also the right to do so. Within the New Earthing Chakras, there can be a holding of Shock resonances due to inter-dimensional or past incarnation-al experiences that can only be released when other aspects of the being are stabilized – and when it is a safe place to recognize this occurrence and to let it go. So too with the Signal or Survival Chakras do we need a safe space to deal with the heavy and accumulated energies of our mass of culture and tribal identities and resonances which still register shock within our system, particularly if much trauma has been accrued and gathered.

Recognition and Anchoring of Being and Anatomy

The main shock identification system, called the 'Skeleton' system, holds major shock resonances that have permeated right through to the very 'bones' of our body… the skeleton is that which is the toughest part of our anatomy, that takes the longest to be replaced, that holds our greatest 'mass' or 'matter' on this earth plane.

When shock or trauma registers here, it is literally buried in the body at its deepest point. It may be layers of accumulated small shocks, it may be a major shock that was not dealt with for a variety of reasons, it may be a shock that hit us in a less than obvious way but which was registered in our nervous system and subsequently resonated and filtered down to our bones. The skeleton is the last place it can hide… And because shock is energetic, it silently ripples and trembles away, creating instability or dysfunction – until discharged. Clearing from this part of our anatomy can create a lot of inner peace, and assist with the other lighter side of healing the associated traumas or issues.

Metaphysically, when we work with this level of the body, we can relate it to the aspect of the Soul in that it is the framework, if you like, of this incarnation, or our identity in this incarnation. Any tremors at our identity level, at our Soul level, will indeed make life not only difficult, but unstable, fraught with wobbles and unsteadiness, unpredictability and insecurity until this is sorted and settled.

To re-anchor the body back to itself at a Skeletal level, and then to build upon this at the other signal or chakra levels, will give the body confidence and recognition that it is now able to be stable and to maintain this new equilibrium free from past internal dis-resonances.

Healing the Signal Chakras

To assist in rebalancing the body from shock, we can use a variety of methods. I don't think that Reiki or Ki-Force or EFT or Pranic Healing or any other form of energy healing application is the *only* way for any one person, as we all vibrate at different frequencies. Even though I am trained in a variety of energies, I prefer to use a natural energy that does not have an attached name to it, and that comes from Divine Source and is acceptable on a Soul level with my client.

Use Compatible Energy

Before you rush to 'correct' any imbalance by automatically using Reiki or whatever, please, *please* first check – and without any personal investment or need to prove that it 'works' – that it is *appropriate* for your client right now, and in *this* instance. Using the wrong energy application and piling shock frequency on top of shock frequency through incompatibility whilst attempting to release past shock frequencies *may* make you appear to look good (or busy) –

for the moment – but it *won't* help your client. This is true of any energy healing frequency if it is the wrong one!

Clients with incompatibilities with Reiki that have been negatively affected by it simply because it was not harmonious with their own constitutional frequencies can suffer from a variety of resulting energy and Chakra problems, and I have had to put quite a few people back together again after them encountering it and even after going through the various trainings. This is not a condemnation, just an important point to note that just because something works for you doesn't automatically mean that it works for *everybody*!

A Reiki Master had serious health problems, and when we worked out where the energy imbalance was, it stemmed directly back to the Reiki energy, and was also connected with the energy of the person passing on the Master Reiki energy... Not everyone has compatible energy with our own, and not every energy healing system is the right one for one and all. After clearing the resulting shock of these incompatible frequencies, and deciding to leave using Reiki alone for a while so as to settle the energy systems again, his health immediately began to improve, and his whole emotional and mental tone lifted.

USING THE SIGNAL INFORMATION TO REBALANCE.

The first step is to acquaint oneself with the Shock Tap Test. This follows shortly.

Learning or using the illustrated hand positions to track where shock is held and where to place one's hands if energy work is required is the next step. I find that actual hand connection on the key points is extremely beneficial and effective. Due to the nature of shock resonances, this provides a gentle and nurturing approach for the client.

Understanding or acknowledging the type of shock you are dealing with can also be valuable. Making use of any of the listed Keywords or associated information will also contribute to a more profound healing experience. There may be layers of the shock, and gathering in as much or as many of these layers of cause as you can will ensure cleaner and deeper releases.

Refer to the Healing Procedure section for more information.

FORMS AND TYPES OF SHOCK

There are many types of shock that can be experienced by anyone at any time, depending on the circumstances and the constitution and reaction or response of the person involved.

We are more fully aware of a recent shock, and if given the opportunity and safe space to process it, we can recover reasonably quickly.

During the Second World War, many soldiers experienced PTSD, though it was called being 'Shell-Shocked' back then. When they returned home, those that were injured were nursed back to health, and generally they all received several months in a care home by the sea, experiencing peace, stability, comfort, support, peace and quiet; the components required to help them to heal from their wounds, and to repair the damage done by injury and war. Things have since changed, and this is not always the case for the wounded now.

Not everybody has this essential support in order to release and recover, and many of us push down the associated feelings in order to rise to the challenges of life…

Shock Keywords

Keywords, as explained previously in this book, can be powerful in triggering and in collecting the associated energies to an issue.

Recognizing the type of shock can be of further assistance in allowing the body to understand and to cooperate with the body-mind-spirit aspect.

The types of shock that can be left unattended to can include:

- Residual
- Past
- Hidden
- Buried
- Absorbed
- Crisis Shock
- Survival
- Trauma
- Overwhelm

- Survival
- Toxic Penetration
- Cultural Shock
- Relationship Shock
- Geographic Re-location
- Extended Alertness
- Major Energetic Incompatibility
- Sudden Alarm
- Accident
- Operation
- Attack
- Birth Trauma
- Forced Energy Frequency

Causes of Shock that can be handed down or not be consciously experienced:

- Energy Imprints from One's Ancestry
- One's Cultural or Tribal Heritage
- Tribal and Cultural Resonance
- Cellular Memory
- Genetic Memory
- Physical Memory
- ElectroMagnetic Input
- Aura Destabilisation

These can be related to any item or issue on the previous list.

RESONANCES OF SHOCK

Shock is held or locked-down *Energy* in the body.

Energy just simply does not disappear; it needs to be transformed. In order for the locked energy to be transformed and released completely, on its journey *out* of the body it often creates shifts and change *in* the body, and these can be experienced in a variety of ways.

The movement of shock energy creates a resonance; a vibration that continues to repeat itself and maintains itself as it is running at a frequency that cannot be simply just stopped or arrested by another energy. Shock resonance is often difficult to clear, for it needs certain types of frequencies to clear it, or the correct space to allow it to free itself from the body.

The body is amazing in its ability to absorb shock frequencies and to continue to function – we have probably all experienced some form of shock and eventually gotten over it – but it does take some time, and the right support for us to pass through it (or for it to pass through us) easily, safely and quickly. There are many problems today that can be traced back to hidden shock in the body, and not just in the mind or emotions. In order for us to heal from shock, we often re-experience some of the associated memories or the sensations AS we heal – the body does a kind of house-keeping of these sensations and feelings, almost as though it is examining them to understand or to decide before letting them go… and our part in this is to decide to release them and *to truly let them go*, together *with* the associated issue. And one of the clues here is that if we *haven't* resolved the issue, it may be really hard to let the shock go! Difficult as it may sometimes be in releasing issues at this level, there can well be accompanying feelings or pictures that we wouldn't welcome at any other time; but if they come up as part of your process, then NOW is the time to finally release these issues, memories, associated feelings, resentments, fears or whatever it is that has helped to keep it in place. There is nothing to fear when you have the right place and support set up around you.

There is nothing wrong with feeling any of the following, for these can often actually be *positive* signs that the energy is now emerging for release and resolution:

- Trembling
- Heat

- Cold or Shivers
- Rolling Sensation
- Tears
- Pain or discomfort that moves around
- Feeling heavy
- Feeling restless or wanting to leave the space
- Tears
- Shaking
- Waves of Energy

When you are assured that the shock itself has been cleared, it is also recommended that any possible resonances, say something that was a similar experience or event or situation, be tracked so that there are no further allied or similar resonances from other times left outstanding.

MERIDIANS

Some of the Chakras or connection points in the Signal / Survival Matrix can be related to Meridian points, and Stress can be held in these points. Acupuncture and Acupressure points can also hold stress.

These points usually register as 'sore' points on the body when pressed. They may also register as 'very itchy' and the 'itch' is the body's message that there is an energy blockage which needs attention.

The Meridians don't necessarily register shock in the body, but may indicate blocked energy flow caused through shock. They can also be used as 'Alarm' signals for shock if you have that knowledge.

SHOCK LAW

THE BODY and being usually only deals with what it is *prepared* to deal with, what it is *ready* to deal with, what it has sufficient *energy* to deal with, and in a space that allows it full reign and *no demands* in order to explore and resolve. There must be no personal or ego investment by the practitioner as this is counterproductive. If the person cannot or will not yet deal with an issue, sometimes simply putting the body on notice that there IS shock present, can begin a process of self investigation that *will* allow a resolution. If you test for 'Shock' and it shows up, but will not yet fully reveal itself, just see this as part of a preparation process, one that will allow the whole of the being to become involved, and to begin to be ready to release this burden. Use one of the affirmations to find out just *how* willing or ready the person or body is right now. Make another appointment in order to follow this up.

AFFIRMATIONS

Using an affirmation or statement can often help to trigger frequencies, and here are some for ideas that can be tweaked or refined to the current situation. Please feel free to experiment or reorganise until you find the statements that feel just right. You can relate it to a known issue or do a general check.

It is now 100% safe for me to acknowledge that there is shock still held in my body or being at some level regarding ……. (the issue if known)

It is now 100% safe for me to release – gently - any shock that is held in my body and being regarding ….

I am 100% ready to begin to heal any shock that is held in my body and being regarding ….

It is now 100% safe to deal with old hurts, old traumas, old crises in a positive manner

I am now 100% ready to deal with old hurts, old traumas, old crises in a positive manner

I am ready, willing and able to recover from past hurts and alerts

I am 100% ready, willing and able to recover from past hurts and alerts

Healing Procedure

Identify Shock

The 'Shock Tap' or 'Shoulder Tap' test will indicate immediately if there is any buried or hidden shock to be dealt with. There may be layers to deal with, for imagine if all of the shocks one had in a lifetime were revisited at the same time, one may well collapse under it all. So when performing this test, more than likely the body is indicating that it is now ready to process this particular stress and trusts you to help it to do so.

The only time that shock is present and this test will not show it as being so, is when the body is *very* locked-down AND / OR doesn't feel the current situation is safe enough for it to deal with right now. There may be an incompatibility issue, there may be a trust issue on behalf of the client, there may be other factors that are considered a priority right now; If one has a major interview the following morning, or some other project of importance to attend to that requires focus and energy, it is possible that it will choose not to deal with it yet. Accept the body's decision, and work with it. Set aside time to recheck the situation at a later date. We are currently living in a society that believes that we must force the body to comply with us, even though we may not give it all of the things that it requires in order to do so easily; nutrition, time, recovery etc.

When we have a 'Shock Tap' Test indication as indicated below, and we are ready and prepared to deal with it, we can further ascertain what parts of the body it is currently held or locked in.

Always be prepared to deal with what arises *immediately*, as things will often begin to unravel very quickly when the body recognises that you are aware of what it has been holding onto so desperately in order to keep itself together.

The best sequence is to go through the points indicated in the Skeletal Registry illustrations to ascertain which points are relevant.

Having established the initial area of imbalance, and always being mindful of tracing back through all relevant shocks or traumas to the original first causal issue, one can now progress through all relevant information and positions as indicated.

SHOCK INDICATION — THE TEST

Only perform this test if you are *prepared* for the consequences. This is a very simple yet powerful test, and can go underneath many masks, any avoidance patterns and a lot of self-sabotage or psychological denials. This can be in regard to a particular relationship, person, event or a long-standing issue.

The '**Shock Tap**' on the shoulder - and the body's response - is the Indicator of Shock present or resident in the body.

To perform this test, I use the left shoulder, with the right arm extended for muscle testing purposes. With the flat or palm of my other hand I sharply tap the top of the upper arm – not hit to hurt, but enough energy for the body to feel it. We generally need the energy to go through layers of clothing, and this is what we are doing; sending out an energy signal, like a sonic vibration, seeking a response from the body – the mental intention being; '**Is there any Shock present?**'.

When using this method of testing if Shock is present then the other outstretched arm will simply drop immediately. If it doesn't drop – or 'switch off' - then there is no shock to attend to at this present time, or, and more happily, there are no further layers of shock to deal with.

The body can respond to both verbal and non-verbal communication, and when it witnesses – as in kinesiology – the visual and visceral response by a 'switched-off' indicator muscle, the whole body, nervous system, mind and awareness is immediately engaged. This can begin a chain reaction that can allow hidden issues to begin to emerge; if it is a safe space to do so.

The '*Shock Tap*' or '*Shoulder Tap*' seems to access this deep level stress, repressed tremors or frozen shock *immediately*!

Reading the alerts, alarms, signals and emerging survival messages can be of great help in assuring the body (and being) that it is being heard, and that what is has to say is being acknowledged, and to show it that help is on the way. This creates a readiness to explore, reveal and to heal that amplifies any healing aid that the facilitator, therapist or healer can provide. It is important to listen to anything the sufferer has to say as it is being experienced or revealed. As shock tremors often begin to unlock themselves almost immediately, always be prepared to deal with whatever lies underneath the issues, and to provide a safe space for exploration, excavation and revelation.

Using the Skeletal Registry, the application of energy at the indicated positions can very quickly realign and redistribute energy to the appropriate energy levels and physical components. These are done in the order of from the shoulders downwards and horizontally, then along each side of the body vertically. After this, the points are again connected energetically from the shoulders down in diagonal alignments. Finally, the crown of the head and the shoulders are connected energetically to form a sealing-in of the process.

The Sensory Signal areas can be energetically balanced just out from the body, but I suggest that using an essence or oil as indicated would work well.

S*HOULDER* 'S*HOCK* T*AP*' P*OSITION*

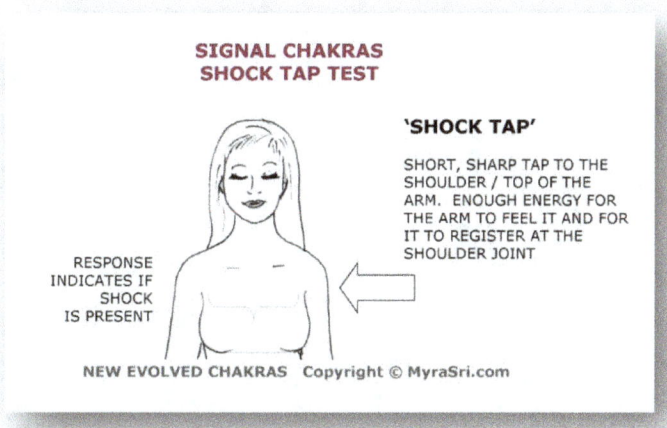

C*OLOUR* F*REQUENCIES*

Channelling or focusing on certain Colours can greatly assist the movement of the unwanted tremors out of its locked-in point or registration point towards movement out of the body.

The most appropriate colours that I have found to best work are included for each position or point.

SKELETAL REGISTRY - Shock Points
Front of Body

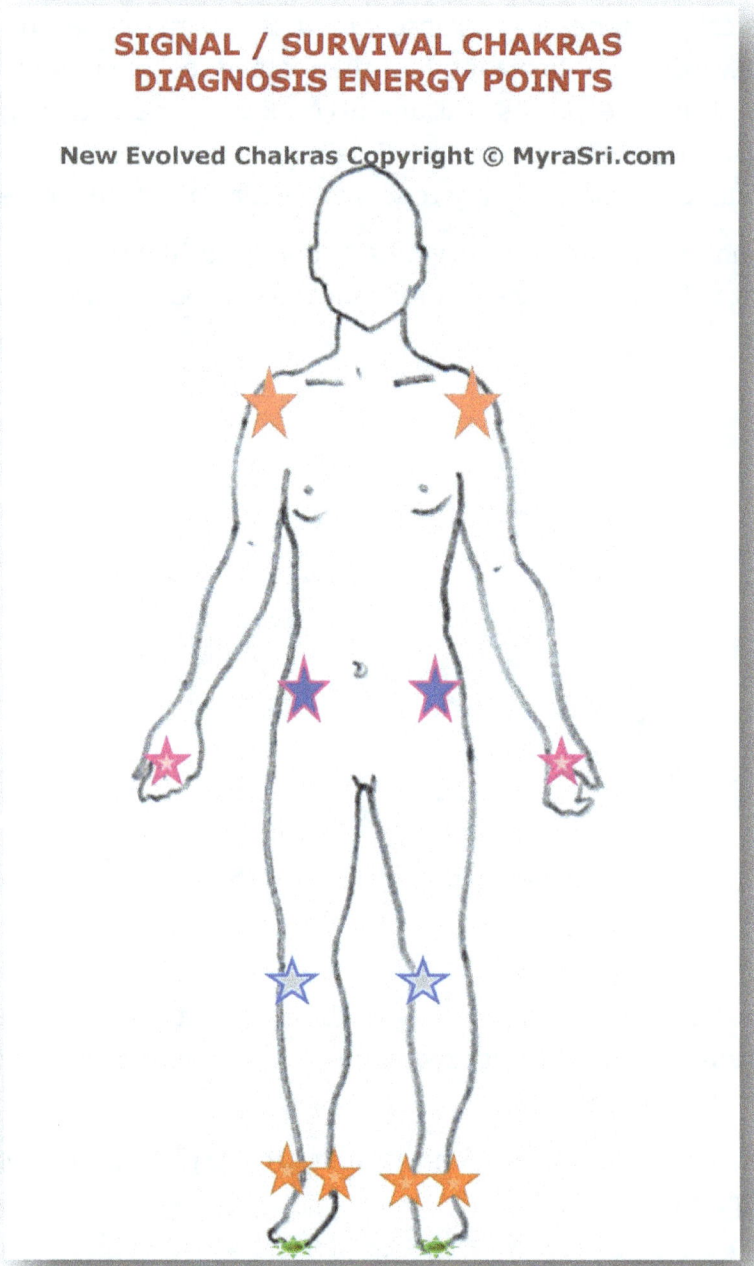

These points assist in identifying where shock is held or present in the body.

They all connect to some part of the skeletal system and Chakra points.

They also indicate the placement for healing support or energy, and the positions that require attention in order for direct application. Sometimes simply holding the indicated positions can allow the shock tremors and frequencies to move out of the body. Skilled facilitators will be aware of how to avoid taking on these exit-ing energies personally and safely.

If you are unsure, seek skills and information to assist you with this. (I have seen many practitioners succumb to the detrimental effects of issues and energies they have inadvertently taken on from their clients.) Or you might like to attend one of my workshops on *Spiritual Cleansing-and Protection; HygienEthics*.

Process, Purpose and Intention

The application of the hand positions and colour energies has a purpose above and beyond the body simply feeling supported or receiving a boost in healing energy.

Maintaining focus on the correct colour frequency, and using the imagination to draw and rejoin the energetic lines of connection, fix intent to:

- First: Move the shock waves or resonances down and out of the body
- Second: Re-establish energy flow throughout the basic skeletal structure
- Third: Reconnect the various parts of the body back to itself
- Fourth: Energise and recharge with appropriate colour where the joints, skeleton or body was once frozen, depleted or in shock

Order sequence

Again, the procedure is as follows:

These are done in the order of from the shoulders downwards and horizontally, then along each side of the body vertically.

After this, the points are again connected energetically from the shoulders down in diagonal alignments.

Finally, the crown of the head and the shoulders are connected energetically to form a sealing-in of the process.

Energise And Reconnect

These positions also indicate the positions to energize or align the body energy systems. This is usually the first healing approach to settle the Shock waves affecting or caught in the energy body and physical body systems.

There is an Order to the application of energy here, for the purpose is not simply or only to energise, but also to reconnect vibrationally each major corner or joint of the body.

Reconnection

When shock is present, there can be a scrambling of nerve impulses on the physical level and also on the etheric level. These need to be re-established. Using the indicated colours and the positions outlined here will reconnect all joints and major bones etherically and energetically.

This is of vital importance, and ensures that down each side of the body, across both sides of the body, and diagonally to each position on the body, reconnection is made, flow is re-established and there is a rebalance and new awareness in the body consciousness regarding all of these Connection Points. This corrects any imbalances of flow of energy that has been caused by Shock Disruption and promotes healthy functionality at the skeletal and bone foundation structure level.

This then creates a firmer basis for supporting progressive positive change in the body, emotions, nervous system and subsequently, in mental and spiritual outlook.

SHOCK 'SKELETAL' POSITIONS AND LEVELS

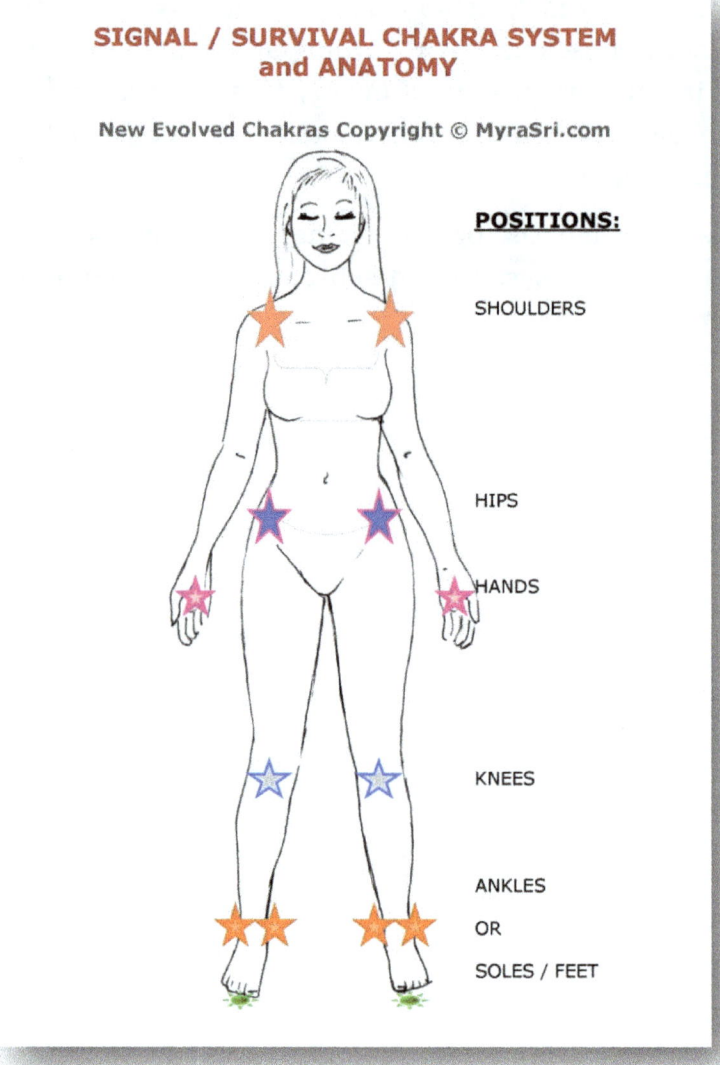

- SHOULDERS   MAJOR
- HIPS   MAJOR
- HANDS   MID - MAJOR
- KNEES   MID - MAJOR
- ANKLES / FEET   MID – MAJOR

These positions give us vital information. They can tell us the level of shock held in the body overall, as well as the best positions for energetic rectification.

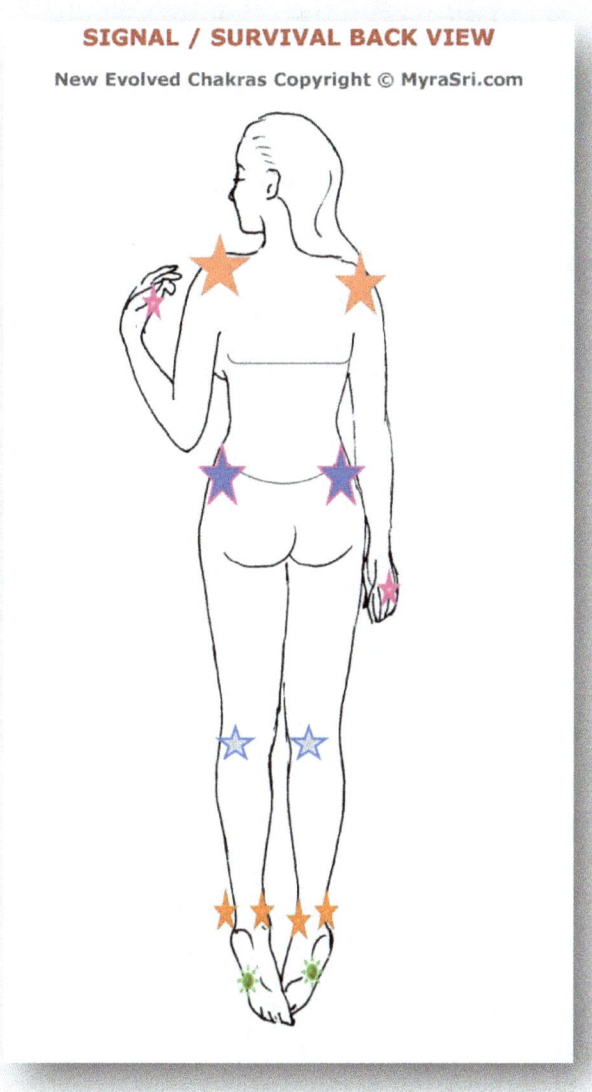

Colour Frequency Chart
Skeletal Registry Colours

Now let us look at Keywords and the required Colour Vibrations.

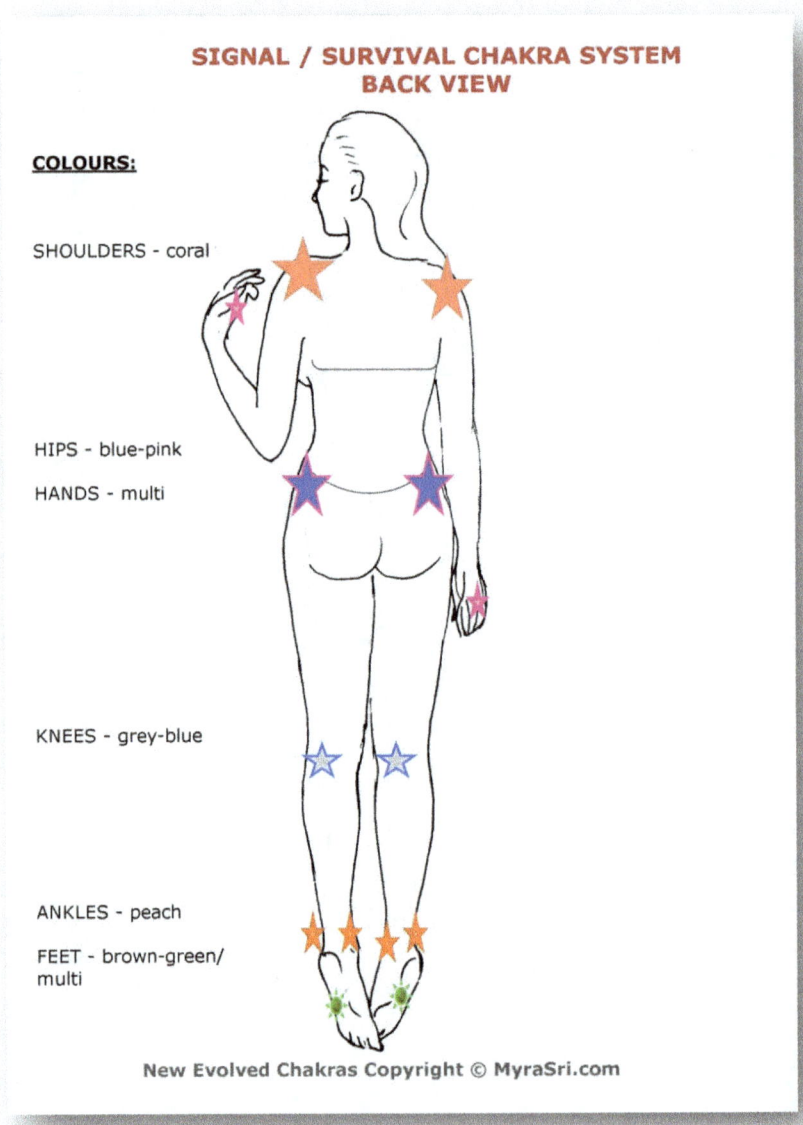

Positions plus Overall Keyword or Tone

- SHOULDERS   SHOCK (Major Point)   CORAL
- HIPS   SHOCK (Major Point)   BLUE-PINK
- HANDS   GIVE / TAKE   VARIOUS
- KNEES   CAUSES / MOVEMENT   GREY-BLUE
- ANKLES / FEET   STABILITY / ANCHORING   PEACH, Brown/Green

Colour, Keywords and Meanings Behind 'Shock'

SHOULDERS
- **Coral**
- SHOCK
- Owning / Ownership
- Identity / Individuality
- Responsibility
- Competition
- Boundaries
- Injustice
- Separation / Family

HIPS
- **Blue-Pink**
- SHOCK
- Security / Physical Threats
- Tribal / Cultural Issues
- Comfort
- Mobility
- Balance and Poise

HANDS
- **Pink / Green Spectrums**, or **Violets / Blues**
- Giving / Receiving
- Holding / Grasping
- Creating

KNEES
- **Grey-Blue**
- Causes—Others
- Causes / Agendas—Own
- Past Life Unresolved

ANKLES / FEET
- **Peach**
- Stability Issues
- Adaptability
- Intuition Grounder
- Direction / Spontaneity

FRONT OR BACK

The positions shown for colour infusion and energy balancing can be done on the front of the body or the back. As the work is actually being done on the skeleton, it usually doesn't matter which side of the body one is working on. The guidelines are; the client's comfort, and whether you can ascertain if one side is more effective than another.

The exceptions are the front of the thighs (Quadriceps) and the face which includes the chin, eyes, ears, nose and mouth. This is because the head is mainly related to sensory shock. And the thigh muscles (the largest muscle group in the body) can carry a lot of withheld energy; fear, shock, anger, frozen emotions or the desire to run or escape.

Hand Position Combinations Sequences

The recommended order of holding (or supporting) hand positions for assisting to clear shock and rebalance of the body are indicated below. Go through each one, feeling or sensing your way, and provide a longer period of Colour Frequency to those areas that feel like they need it.

Generally the pattern of positions is; the body downwards and outwards.

Working from the shoulders down, and from the body outward to the limbs, follow this sequence for the best release and alignment results.

Initial Sweep

In order to encourage the release of Shock from the body, it is recommended to place one palm at the base of the spine (gently and lightly) at approximately sacrum level, and with the other hand move the flow of energy up from the lower spine and along it, up over the head to the top of the head. Repeat for three sweeps, flicking the moving hand at the end of each sweep to release any energy picked up from the spine. Then gently hold the top of the head for a few minutes, keeping the other hand still in place, to settle the energy along there before proceeding as indicated below.

Shock Balance Positions

- Shoulder to shoulder   Coral
- Hip to hip   Blue-Pink
- Hand to hand   Various: Pink/Greens, Violet/Blues
- Knee to knee   Grey-Blue
- Ankle to ankle   Peach
- Foot to foot   Brown/Green

Use the shoulder colours when working on the shoulders, but when working vertically, say shoulders to hips etc, use that which feels or tests as the priority.

As previously mentioned, allow the shock tremors to move out of the body, then reconnect all parts to one another again, and create a clear energetic flow and colour recharge.

SEQUENCE 1

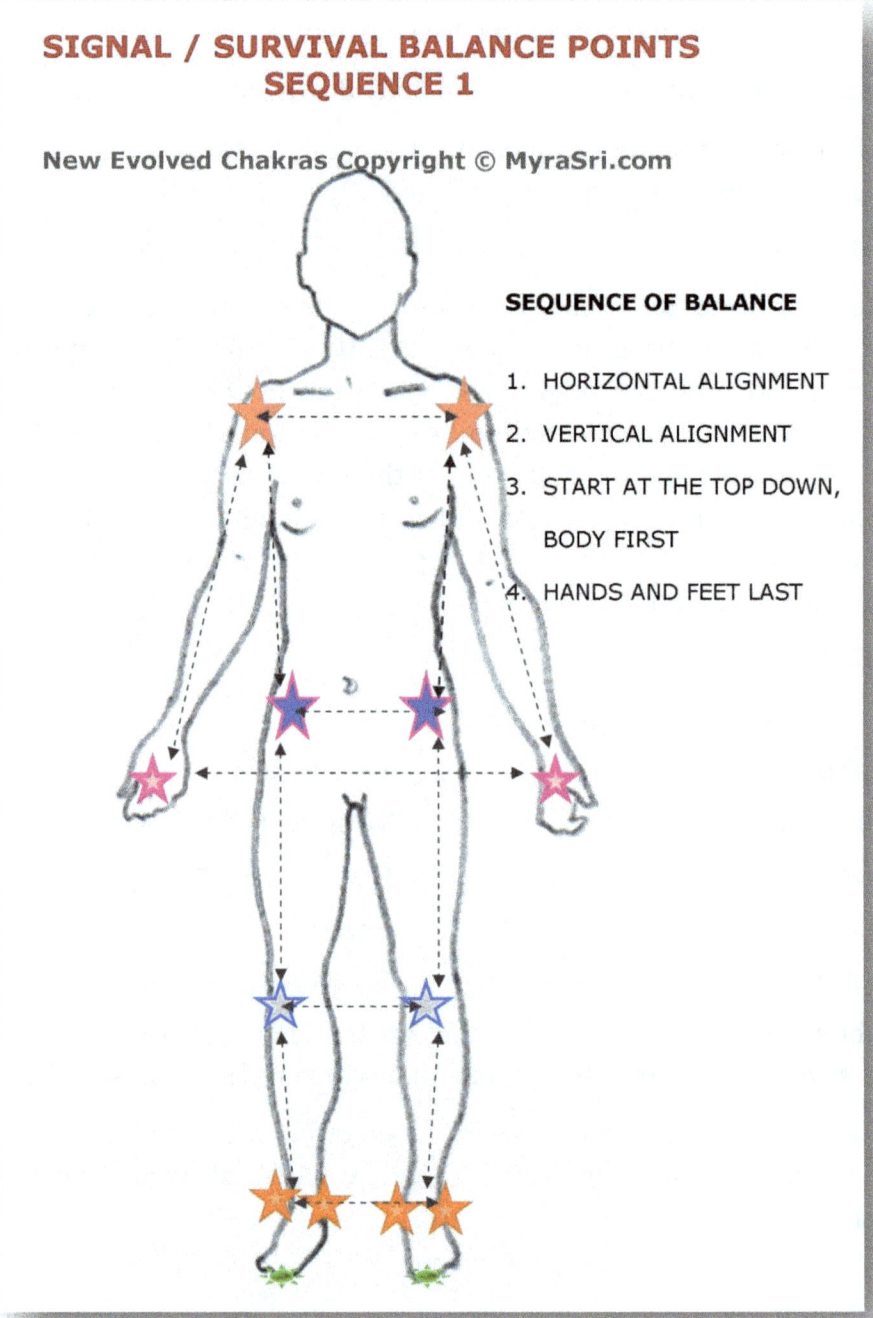

Secondary Balance Positions

- Shoulder to hip – these are all along the same side as each other
- Hip to knee
- Knee to ankle / foot
- Shoulder to hand
- Hand to foot
- Down one side at a time

Other Positions

- Shoulder to opposite hip
- Hip to opposite knee
- Knee to opposite ankle / foot
- Shoulder to opposite hand
- Hand to opposite foot
- Any other combination

Final Position

Finish off sequence of the reconnections with focus on the shoulders and the top of the Head, or the Crown Chakra.

This completes all sequences.

Sequence 2

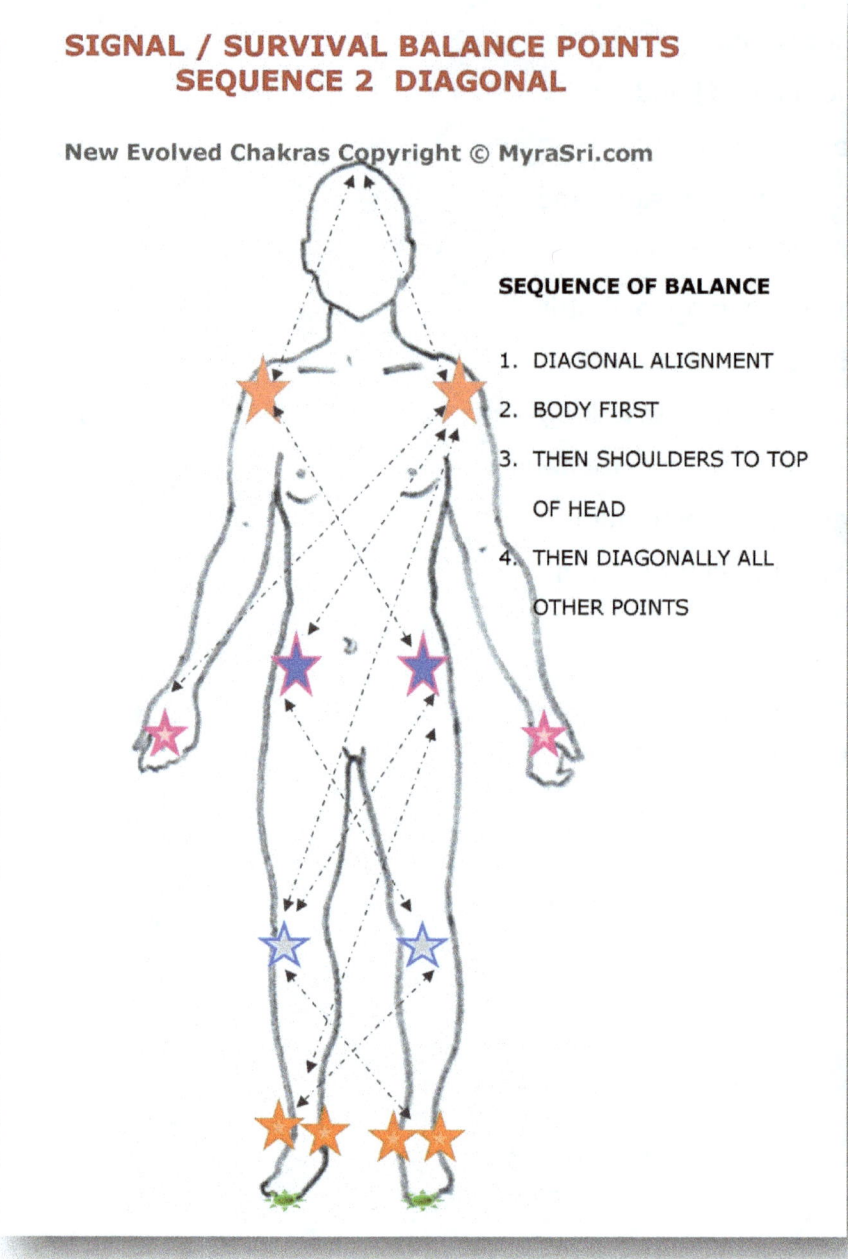

OTHER BALANCE SUPPORT

Sometimes the client may require further support. Here are some suggestions;

- Essential Oils
- Essences
- Mandalas
- Meditation
- Yoga Nidra
- Shake the Body
- Diamond Clearing Exercise* (Guided Meditation)
- Sound
- Affirmation/s

*Guided Meditations available at; http://www.myrasri.com/new-healing-store.

THE CROWN POINT

The final holding position is the Shoulder positions with the top of the head, namely the Crown or 'Hundred Point Meeting Place' (the meeting of certain essential meridians in TCM). This assists cohesion within the physical, energetic and meridian systems and helps to Anchor the new energies.

It also Seals in the energies, letting the brain know that there is a new frequency deep in the body and allowing it to make the connection energetically.

SENSORY AND RECOGNITION SURVIVAL SYSTEM

Though these following Chakra positions aren't labelled as 'Shock' positions as such, they can still indicate some kind of stress, trauma, crisis or challenge that has unsettled or destabilised the being or body. You may consider them as Secondary Shock alerts or alarms.

FACE ASPECTS

Some of the positions involved are echoed in Chakra Systems, such as the Psychic Chakras or Minor Chakras Systems. This can simply mean that these Chakras fulfil several functions. Or that there is some form of shock or alarm still held in these positions. The Colour indicated is considered the best frequency for the particular function.

NOSE

- **Silver / Mauves**
- Knowledge withheld or 'stolen'
- Betrayal, Deception
- Trust Issues
- Leadership Issues
- Self Belief / Inner Knowing

MOUTH

- **Silver**
- Forced to Speak or to Be Silent
- Speech or Silence, Said / Not Said

EYES

- **Lavender**
- Perceptions
- Reality vs. Idealism
- Left: Inner Perceptions
- Right: Outer Perceptions

EARS

- **Blue/s**
- Beliefs
- Conflicts
- Overload / Overwhelm
- Outer Voice louder than INNER Voice
- Frozen Filters

CHIN

- **Deep or Rich Blue**
- Courage / Risk
- Acceptance
- Dedication / Loyalty

Sensory Chakras Positions / Keywords:

- EYES   PERCEPTIONS   LAVENDER
- EARS   BELIEFS   BLUES
- NOSE   TRUST / KNOWING   SILVER-MAUVES
- MOUTH   SPEECH   SILVER
- CHIN   COURAGE   DEEP / RICH BLUE

Other Balance Support

Though the primary balancer is colour and touch, when working around the nose, ears and mouth, these areas often really appreciate the use of essences or oils. (Do not use oils directly on the skin – refer to my Essential Oil Healing Techniques in *Secrets Beyond Aromatherapy*.)

When working energetically with the hands to focus colour into the area, one can position the palm of the hand out several centimetres to several inches to rebalance and clear any shock residue or resonance. Other supports include:

- Essential Oils
- Energise the Chakra or Point (as mentioned)
- Essences; Shell, Gem, Flower…
- Mandalas
- Spray
- Shake the Body or Head
- Diamond Clearing Exercise (http://www.myrasri.com/new-healing-store)
- Intention
- Sound / An Affirmation

Sensory Considerations

The Recognition of how and where life issues affect us can be suppressed, denied or set aside whilst we deal with and cope with immediate concerns.

When we don't have an answer for something, when we do not know how to solve something or when we fear the results of inspecting something too closely, we may choose to set it aside to get on with more pressing or manageable concerns in living.

This action or choice will affect our energetic functioning in some way of another.

The various levels of Signal or Survival Chakra indications can allow progression through to the source or cause for resolution.

Sometimes, simply clearing the Shock that is registering can be sufficient. But if it is not enough, these chakras / indicators will enable us to get to the underlying cause of the Shock. Various levels of clearing through these Chakras may be necessary or experienced in order to settle the shock waves or interference vibrations and frequencies that are thus caught up in the energy fields.

- Consider if the Source of Trauma / Imbalance is on Soul Level. If this is so, be aware that the issue may go way back in time, and can also have a profound effect on the energy systems of the body. If this is a Soul issue, also be aware that by revealing the problem at this level, it indicates that the Soul is ready to deal with the issue, which usually signifies that this is the final layer of this particular problematic aspect.

- Consider if there are also issues with any of the other Chakra Systems that the Chakra may be connected or related to, and whether this system also needs any attention or work in regard to the issue.

- For Kinesiologists: You may also find that correcting the Priority position or Chakra may change the readout or rating of the initial imbalance. This simply gives feedback as to where the balance is at. Check Chakras until all the Chakras are 'in balance'.

- Always ensure that a 'Clear' reading shows at the end of your healing session, to ensure that all of these signal indicators or Chakras are now balanced.

Secondary Signal / Survival Chakras

Other Indicator/Signal Chakras are also important in identifying and balancing Issues.

- ELBOWS — TIME / SPACE
- MID INNER THIGH — GEO-LOCATION VIBES
- CENTER SHINS / CALVES — CULTURE and ANCESTRY
- FRONT MID THIGHS / QUADS — CHANGE

MID –INNER THIGH / LINK CHAKRA
- **Silvery Icy Blue, Crystalline, Etheric, Silvery Pearl**
- Often holds issues from 3 Yrs of age onwards
- Doing versus Being
- Geo-Location Issues
- Vibrational Transducer re Culture / Nutritional aspects
- Registers birth and 'in-Utero' frequencies: longitude, latitude, environment, chemical compositions

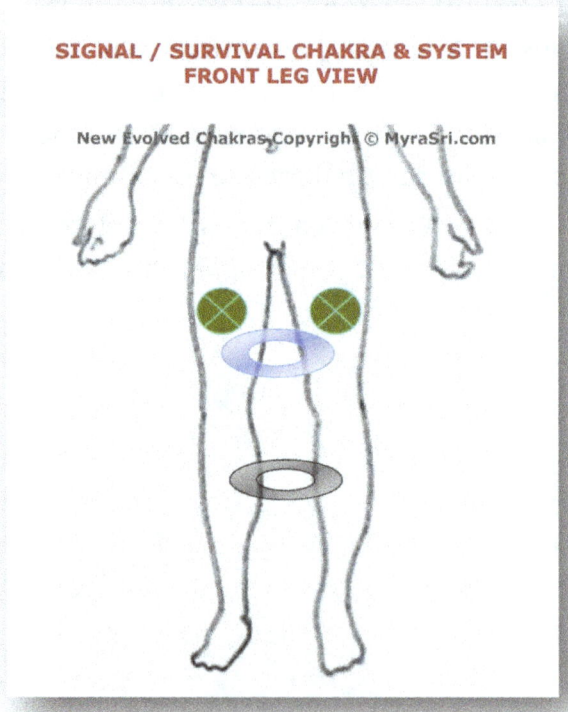

FRONT MID-THIGHS / QUADRICEPS

- **Olive / Lime Green**
- Change / Courage
- Adaptation
- Anger
- Strength
- Conviction

CENTER or MID-SHIN (Stability Chakra)

- **Brown-Maroon, Russet, Silver Birch**
- Issues from 4 Yrs of age Onward
- Family Beliefs and Programs
- Cultural Beliefs and Programs
- Notes Ancestral 'Yin' and Chi
- This point may also rule the knees

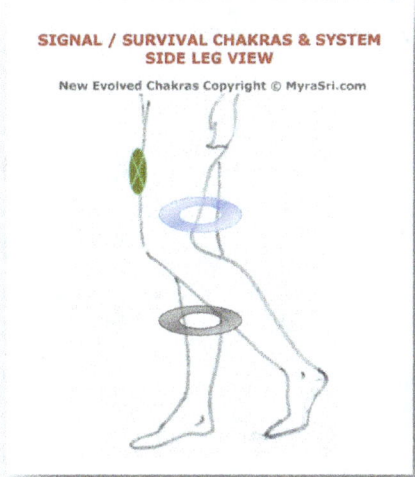

ELBOWS

- **Yellow-Green**
- Personal Points – Boundaries
- Time (Present) - Right
- Space (Present) – Left
- Associated with Sacral Chakra

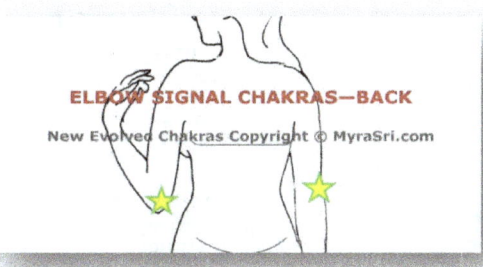

SECONDARY CHAKRA CONSIDERATIONS

As with the other Signal Chakras, in order to clear and balance, trace the issues back to their original Cause using available tracking methods; through from this life time, as well as genetic or past history. The information may also provide further insights for conscious resolution of the issues, lessons or imbalance.

The chakras at Shin and Thigh positions may also be connected to Base Chakra issues, but not necessarily always to every Earthing Chakra or their issues, though this is obviously a possibility.

Signal Chakras Quick Reference Charts

Front

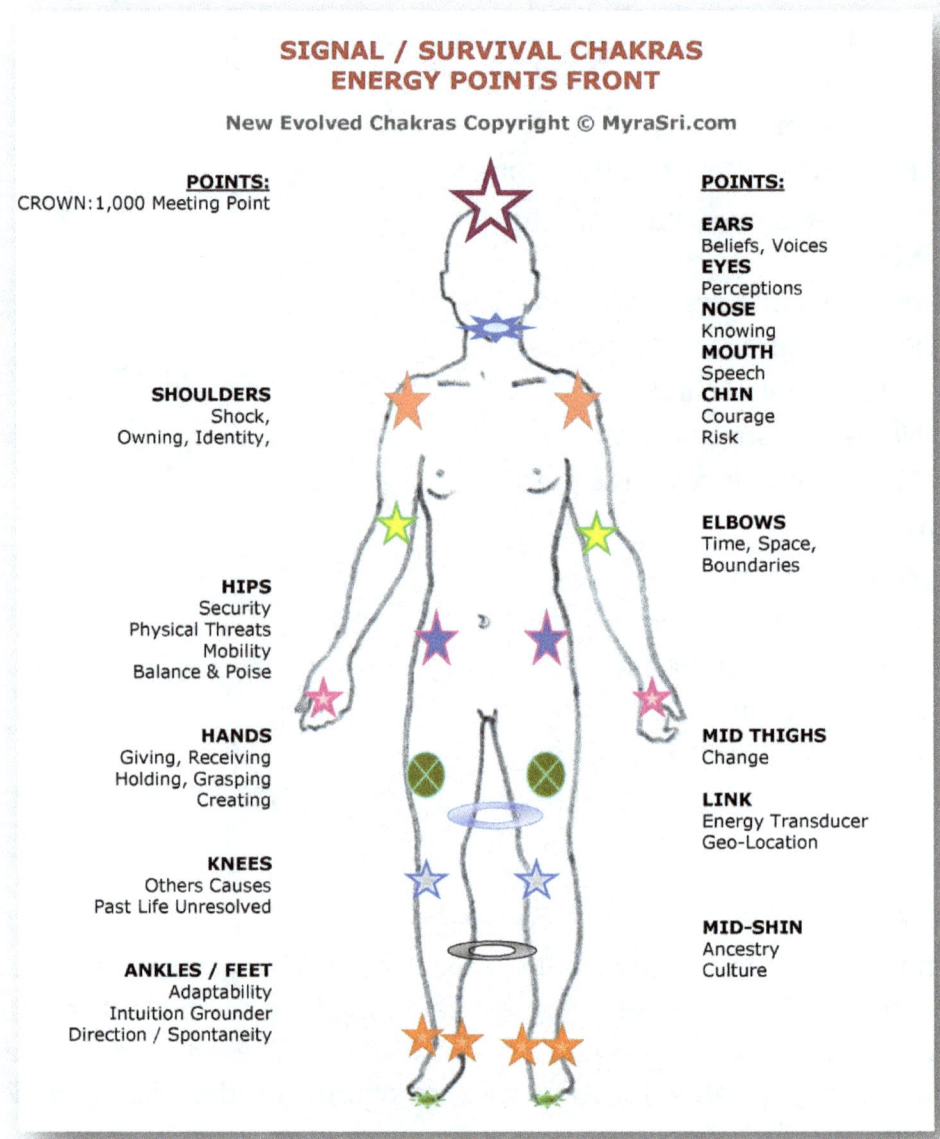

Colours and Major Keywords.

The New Evolved Chakras

BACK

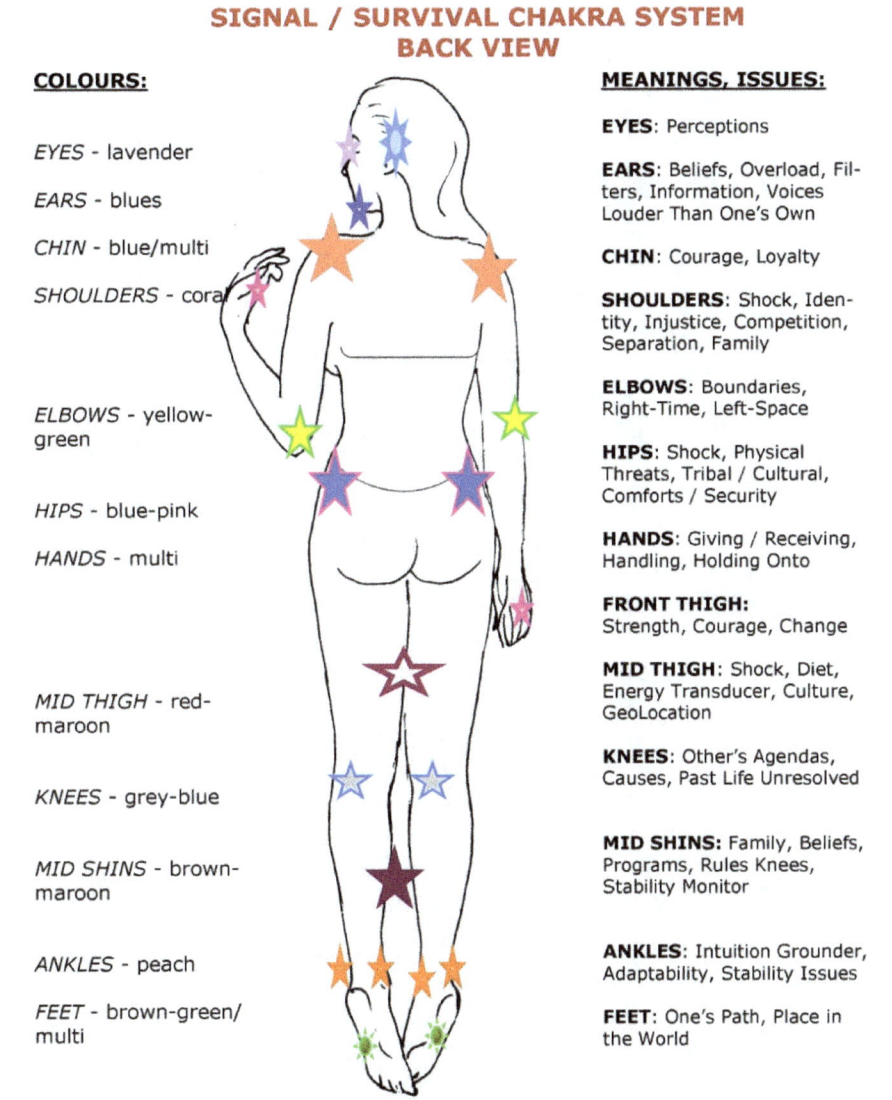

SENSORY ASPECTS

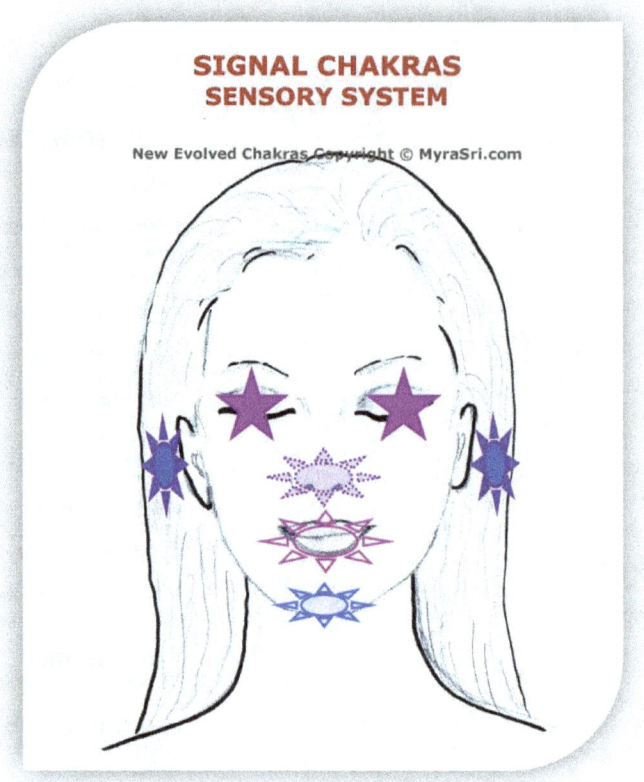

AFFIRMATION IDEAS...

It is now 100% safe for me to acknowledge that there is shock still held in my body or being at some level

It is now 100% safe for me to release any shock that is held in my body and being

I am 100% ready to begin to heal any shock that is held in my body and being

It is now 100% safe to deal with old hurts, old traumas, old crises in a positive manner

I am now 100% ready to deal with old hurts, old traumas, old crises in a positive manner

I am ready, willing and able to recover from past hurts and alerts

I am 100% ready, willing and able to recover from past hurts and alerts

It is safe to ...

It is easy to ...

It is fun to ...

I am ready to ...

I give myself permission to ...

...Learn from the past, to live in the present, and to plan for the future

THE NEW ADVANCED SOUL BODY ANATOMY

The basic Hara system has evolved to provide a fuller Soul Body Anatomy. We have already viewed the Hara System, now this is built upon and enhanced.

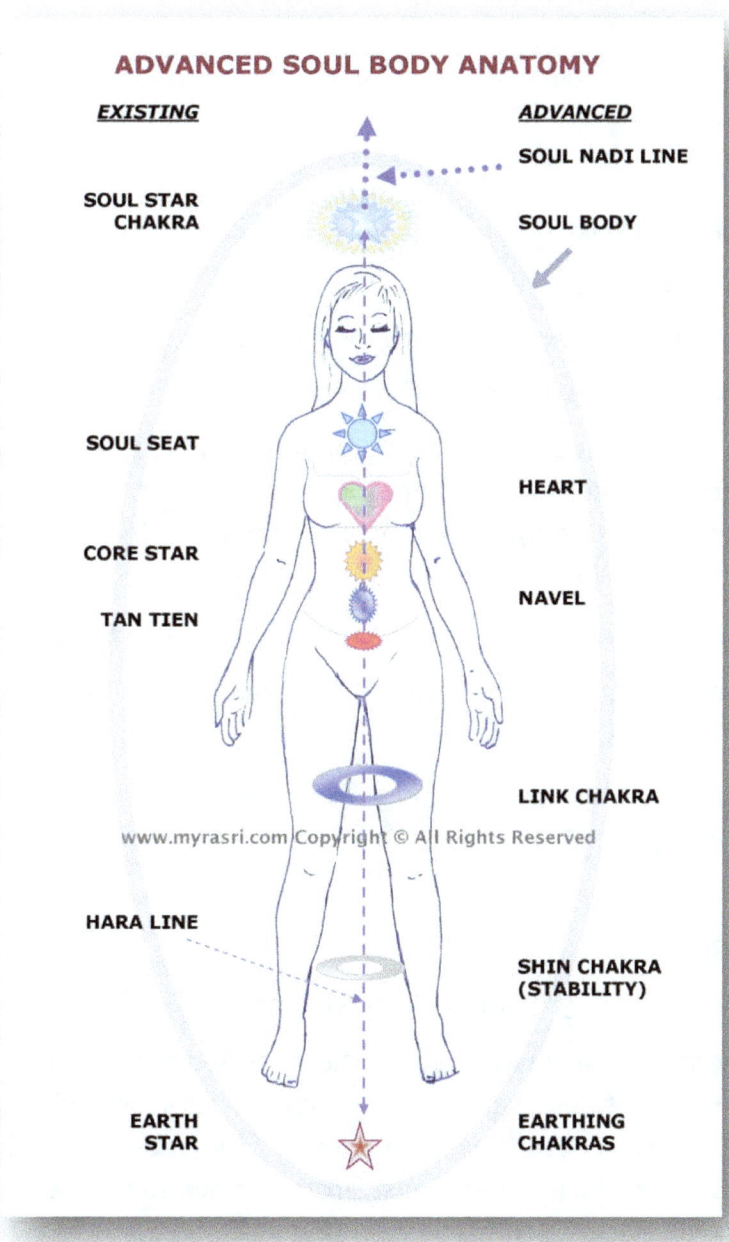

The composition of the advanced Soul Body now looks like this:

- Soul Star Chakra / I.D. Point
- Soul Seat Chakra
- Heart
- Core Star Chakra
- Navel Chakra
- Tan Tien
- Link Chakra
- Shin Stability Chakra
- Earthing Chakras Connection
- Hara Line and Soul Nadi Line to One's Own Divine Source
- Surrounding Inter-connective Soul Body

The Soul Body surrounding the physical body is similar to other energy bodies in that it generally tends to the shape of an Auric Egg. This is a Silvery or Pearlised energy field. Codings or records are held within the Soul Seat Chakra that relate to the Soul's journey and history.

It interacts with the Astral Body, the Psychic Body and the Earthing Chakras.

Further additions to the Advanced Soul Body system and its Chakras are these interactive Chakras or Connection Points:

- Transpersonal Chakra
- Psychic Centres
- Psychic Point
- Spatial Chakras
- Earthing Chakras (5th and 8th in particular)

There is much that can be written about the Soul Body and its functions, but as there are so many possible variations, journeys, choices and lessons, that, I feel, is for another book. Here we have covered the *anatomy* of the Soul Body; Healing at the Soul level can be the most profound healing there is.

Soul Registration

A primary consideration is that at the end of all healings, or major junctures in healing, is this:

All healings should be locked-in or registered at the Soul level

The Soul Body is now involved with the healing process; this is to ensure that the essence of the client's *totality* of being has *acknowledged* the positive changes and *registers* them in order to *integrate* the healing; and to further align and support the Soul's ongoing journey.

This is usually done via the Soul Star Chakra, which is the Soul's Individuation point.

This also allows the aspects of the issue that impinged upon or negatively affected the Soul in any way prior to the balance or healing can flow through to assist to heal the Soul Body. As the Soul is that part of the Being which registers and continues the journey and travels of *all* of its incarnations, it is fitting that the Soul is considered and assured with each healing.

Soul Records can then be re-ordered and what has been dealt with and no longer requires further processing can be 'taken off the table'. Other priorities can now be re-considered if necessary and other choices or options can be presented.

If there is difficulty in completing this registration, then it may indicate that there are still other allied issues involved that require attention or clearing so that the Soul can fully register the change.

My Soul, body and being now 100% accepts this balance and healing, easily and safely.

I now 100% integrate and retain ALL of the benefits of this balance for my Highest Good and in alignment with my own True Soul Purpose and Destiny.

NADIS AND THEIR FUNCTIONS

What Are Nadis?

The literal meaning of Nadi is 'flow' and they are thought to carry a life force energy often called *prana* in Sanskrit, or *qi* in Chinese. In physiology, a Nadi may be translated as *nerve* in English, though they are not actual nerves, more like energetic nerves. In Yogic references a Nadi is thought of as a channel.

Nadis are fine, thread like lines of energy and light that stream forth continually from Chakras. These filaments of light pick up and decipher energetic information whilst all the time connecting, disconnecting and reconnecting to all manner of vibrations, etheric frequencies and substances.

Nadis can perform various functions. Some Nadis are **Receiver** Nadis, some are **Messenger** Nadis, whilst some are both and act as two-way receptor and transmitter Nadis. There are also what I call **Stability Anchor Nadis** which execute a more steadfast role to assist in maintaining the status quo of the existing positions of various energetic structures and anatomies, which obviously includes Chakras.

In-Body Nadis - Nadis can act as permanent energy connections, maintaining communication and ordering along a variety of energy systems. Body systems can include connections between all of the organs, or all of the glands. Different systems such as the Nervous System or the Digestive System, have their own Nadi networks. Meridians are commonly recognised form of Nadi systems. Nadis tend to have set pathways, and part of their function is to maintain these pathways.

Nadis may also perform extra-curricular activities too. Within the body itself, Nadi connections can also be between any organ, gland or Chakra to any other organ, gland or Chakra. Continually moving in a kind of researching and seeking-energy antennae-like way, they can stream out on existing lines but can also create other pathways of connection, similar to the nerve-endings and neural pathways in the brain.

Out-of-Body Nadis - Other specific Nadis can also connect externally from the body, often (and usually) from and to the Chakras. But they are not necessarily restricted to this sort of activity. In communication and interaction, these filaments of light and energy are able to connect with others.

As well as the ability to pick up light vibrations from the Sun to nurture the body systems, Nadis are also equipped to process and release unwanted vibrational energies from the foods we eat or ingest, or even put on our skin.

However, they can get blocked, gunked-up, damaged, break, weaken, dim, turn back-in on its own Chakra or even short-circuit.

When viewed by clairvoyants, the external connection Nadis can generally appear like grids, or webs of light, and can also appear as networks.

I cannot stress enough that one must treat these essential components of the subtle body very carefully and respectfully.

Interconnecting Nadis – Passing from the Main Chakras to external sources, and from energy body to energy body, interconnecting Nadis create their own gridlike or hublike patterns.

The actual composition of Nadis can vary, depending on their intended function: an Auric Nadis may tend to be more suited to the purpose of protection and containment, (the Aura having a high ratio of Stability Anchor Nadis), though it still has the ability to register energy impacts, flow and action. Compare this with a Spiritual Nadi, one which reaches into higher frequency levels and areas, and is responsible for not just energy flow, information and connection, but also the transfer of tone and Light.

Human Nadis

The Human Nadis as described above, can connect in the body and externally. Human Nadis connect organs with organs, glands with glands, systems with systems, Chakras with Chakras and so on. Other internal Human Nadis support communication, flow and functionality between the myriad of functions performed by the body. Meridian Nadis run along the meridian line itself.

The original standard Nadi system in the human body was like a split winding thread that connected the Ida Nadi and the Pingali Nadi that ran up the entire body like an intertwining rope. They evolved or intended to meet through the Sushumni Nadi, a central Nadi. However, in evolved beings, I have found it hard to trace the separated Ida or Pingali and often only find the central Nadi. There are so many Nadis that when I come to working with this delicate part of a meridian or etheric connection in the body that I do not have a name for, I just work with them wherever I find them and no longer worry about seeking their exact label. If I can see it or locate it or sense it or simply identify it *as a Nadis* (as some form of identification *is* essential for healing) together *with* its source of origin and its destination, then that is generally sufficient for me to heal, repair, clean, strengthen or reattach it.

There are many Nadis that flow not only through the normal Element Meridians – the Meridians connected to Earth, Fire, Air, Water and Metal – but also through the Extra-Ordinary Meridian Vessels.

Chakra Nadis

We mentioned Chakra Nadis. Where these emerge externally, stress or trauma can affect them, causing them to lose their direction, or tone, or to become damaged. The Nadis that emerge downwards to the ground from the Base Chakra for instance, can sometimes get tangled. There are several reasons for this, all generally caused by stress or trauma. To restore order again in these vital energy lines, first sort the issue that caused this tangling or stress. They then need to be treated very carefully physically and can be gently 'combed' and coaxed back along their correct downward path again. By holding the hand flat, and using the fingers spread far apart, the Nadis can be gently combed along its normal path. For instance, the Base Chakra Nadis can be combed in a down wards direction away from the body, taking care to go slowly, feeling one's way. If there is a knot, combing too roughly may break the Nadis. This then takes time to repair and regrow again. The Solar Plexus Nadis can also be disentangled when gently combed outwards away from the body.

The Heart Chakra can become tangled front, back or even both. Gentle combing may assist here, though addressing the causal issue as well shouldn't be discounted.

But all must be treated with great care, as working at this level it is essential to be mindful of what one is doing and also of what one is thinking, for these delicate tendrils are super-sensitive. Done safely, this technique can be applied to many if not most of the Chakras where there is tangling or a need to clear the etheric energies in this way.

Nadis can also make energetic connections with external sources too. These can become the basis of Gridding Systems in Advanced Energy Anatomy.

They can also hold one in a particular pattern when the Nadis and its energy connect from a stronger energy system into a weaker one, the stronger energy calling the tune, so to speak. When these are inappropriate connections, these need to be cleared and freed and the boundaries and energy systems that have been made vulnerable or continue to be susceptible should be enhanced, strengthened and improved to avoid further over-ride by another's energy or intent.

AURIC NADIS

The Nadis of the Aura tend to be layered over one another at the surface, but have interconnecting Nadis passing right through all of the energy bodies, connecting them and attempting to hold them in flexible equilibrium.

The Aura is basically the 'egg' shape of energy and Light that surrounds all of the energy fields on a person. The Auric Boundary

A healthy Aura has a sense of 'silk' about it, with a peaceful pulsing of life, and an ordered feel to it. This condition then allows easy and healthy interaction, allowing for disruptive waves or emanations to be dealt with simply and elegantly. A fractured Aura, or a frantic Aura will make this kind of interaction difficult and unclear. Auras can be damaged by vindictive action, thought or intent in a Sensitive, and outright conflict can affect them. Often Sensitives require space apart to recuperate and repair the effects of highly charged interactions. There is nothing wrong with these beautiful Souls, though learning to let negative energies roll through and then to clear and address repair may sometimes be required.

Surface of the Aura can be weakened by:

Stress, Shock, Trauma, Intrusions, Lack of Electrolytes, Dehydration, Entities (non-physical beings of any sort), Incompatible ElectroMagnetics.

The Auric Boundary:

- Separates the internal environment from the external environment.
- Internal structure is composed of luminescent fibres criss-crossing in every possible direction, to provide a porous, yet flexible and strong surface
- Creates boundary to allow correct regulation of appropriate pressure
- Allows release of toxins, and access to external prana or potential energy
- When weak, allows invasion by and accumulation of intrusive energies

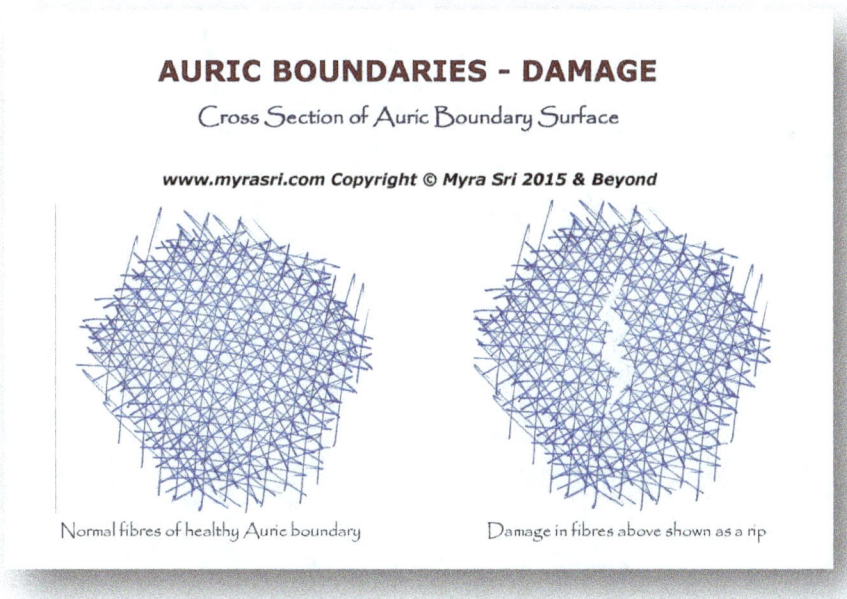

THE AURA

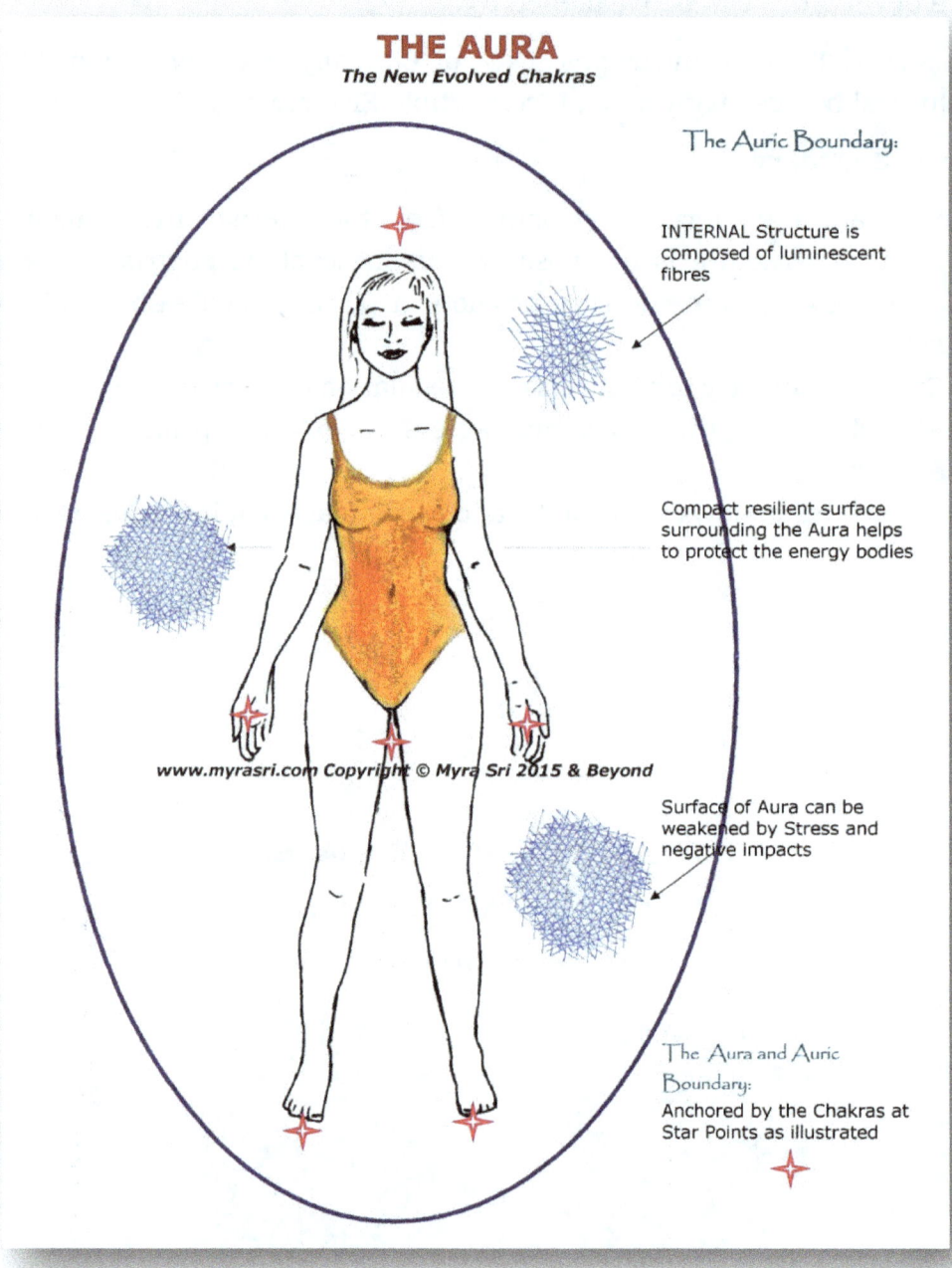

Anchored by Chakras at ✦

Planetary Nadis

The most obvious Planetary Nadis are those geographical connection lines known as Ley Lines. They tend to carry energy and connect energy points or centres. These are all natural formations of existing Nadis, whilst others can be connected by manipulation or knowledge; Stonehenge, The Pyramids, Cleopatra's Needle, Crustal Caves, buildings built in specific geometrical shapes and designs... All of these can harness unseen etheric energies, and create places of power. Yes, some places have a certain power to begin with, but as guardians and residents on the earth, we can create energetic centres ourselves. Gardens have been known to change a place's energy and to refresh it.

There are other Planetary Nadis, too. Those that go beyond the Planet's immediate surroundings. Those Nadis that connect with the Moon, and our Solar System. These are not so obvious, not so easily felt or seen. But they exist, and these become part of the Gridding Systems.

One more word on Planetary Nadis; each of us is connected to it in some way. For intrinsically in this system, we cannot avoid but being connected with this Earth we call home.

Universal Nadis

The Universal Nadis are the energy lines that run on a differing energy system and that plug into certain unseen major grids just beyond this reality of our everyday existence on the Planet. They govern or coordinate order or chaos, success or victimhood, and they can include major matrices of world systems. Our Universe has a history, and great dramas have been played out on this huge stage of life – and death. In a way, it is a dim image that reflects a similar scaffolding backdrop seen in the movie *'The Matrix'* in that it holds resonances and connecting lines of resonance that can be attracted, magnetized or programmed to certain events, situations, groups, power-plays or historic replays.

These Universal threads can experience resonances forcing similar energies to be re-experienced and relived again on planet earth; memories being reactivated as we pass Globally en masse through these possibly ancient energy fields.

The space where a planet no longer exists still holds resonances: some are memories of the life, existences and experiences of that planet together with its original creation blueprint and purpose (if any), as well as its demise and the *way* of its demise or passing. This may include shock vibrations, attack memories, or a slow death from destructive draining of resources, deterioration or burning up of its own energy systems.

Galactic Nadis

The Galactic Nadis are on another level again, and connect us to the Star Systems, to the Galaxies and to the Central Suns, creating a light filament-al type web that covers the whole of the known Galaxies, and where necessary to beyond, and to all that is yet present.

As the Universe is expanding, and Galaxies are dying and being reborn, this is an ever changing picture, and quite an immense scope energetically. As our Nadis connect with the different quadrants, sectors and slipstreams within the wormholes of time and space, as well as encountering the possibility of meeting up with past energies of ancient wounds – which can trigger any similar unresolved buried issues thus causing a fresh emerging of residual frequencies or codes for recognition and healing - we can also travel to where new codes can be accessed, and new healings or creations can be undertaken.

GRIDDING SYSTEMS

Nadis are the basic building and connecting tool for creating, maintaining and supporting the various Gridding Systems. They may also be controlled by a Key Chakra which can be vital for etheric communication between points and systems, the inner and the outer, the world and the individual.

The new evolving Gridding Systems are now more available to more Souls. They are more than the existing systems as they have been updated, upgraded, enhanced and further developed; these now require clear and optimally functional Nadis for correct and current energetic alignment at this time in the Planets evolution.

The purpose of each grid is to create a unified system whereby each relevant and associated Chakra is attached and connected to a specific sequence; these strings or waves of energy resonate and pulse specific vibrations or holographic in a series of codes and codings. The grids are highly sophisticated coordinated and cohesive structures composed of Nadis and Chakras that pulse with energy whilst maintaining a recognisable picture of stability. If you placed a floating net on the top of an expanse of water, there would be fluctuations of movement, but the net would stay functional and connected even with the up and down impulses it experienced.

Chakras on occasion can be prone to insult, damage, clouding, blockages, blow out, burn-out and tears. Nadis can be prone to breaks, thinning, tears, fuse-blow-outs, burn-out, diversions and redirection. So under normal conditions, we may sometimes require rest or active healing to repair and clear these vital energy lines for optimum function.

With the new Gridding Systems, in order to be fully aligned we may well require some form of download or upload, fine-tuning and alignment, correct and appropriate distribution or redistribution as well as frequency re-setting before the finally appropriate activation. When exploring and investigating these systems, I discovered several main systems that are of major influence. As more are discovered or revealed concerning these, this section will be revised.

So far I am aware of the following major Gridding Systems. The newest to be formed that I have recognised is the New Galactic Gridding System, and this new Grid may replace the old Cosmic Gridding System for some Souls and their Advanced Soul Body anatomy. However, both systems can still co-exist in some human energy systems, depending on the Soul's chosen purpose and their evolution.

Brain Gridding System

Heart Gridding System

Link (Chakra) Gridding System

Family Organism Gridding System

Planet/ary Gridding System

New Galactic Gridding System

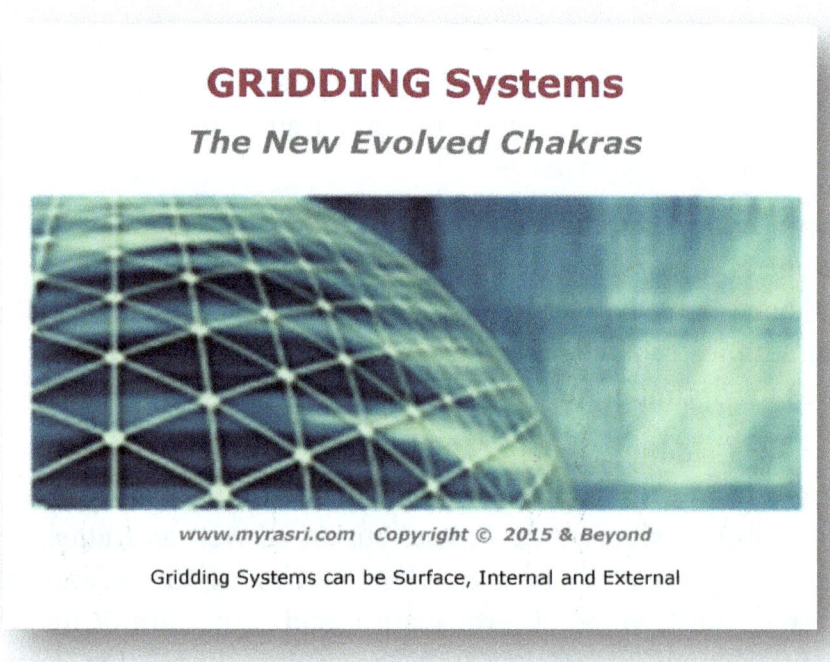

Brain Gridding System

A remarkable and respected colleague of mine, Leonie A David, discovered the presence of this grid after I shared what I knew of the other Gridding Systems with her. Upon further investigation, I found the Brain Gridding System to be associated with the following:

- The Psychic Chakras and The Psychic Centres in the Brain
- The Nervous System
- The Heart – as an Organ, a Gland and a Feeling Centre
- Certain aspects of The Mind
- Certain aspects of the Minds of Others Who Are of Influence
- Codes and Programs from a variety of sources

The Brain is usually seen as a physical collection and formation of soft tissue and motor control centres. Some think that The Mind lives there. It doesn't. The Mind is connected to the Brain in certain respects, and memories can certainly be stored in the Brain. But The Mind exists throughout the body and energy systems and has its own identity and capabilities. Consider the passing on of some of the preferences of organ donors being adopted or experienced by their recipients.

When the Brain has been somewhat deactivated during anaesthetic, numerous reports have proven the possibility of not only viewing externally from the body, and travelling out of the body, but also of remembering these experiences in an accurate fashion.

The Brain is a Central Control Centre for a variety of functions. It can contain codes and programs, some of which are passed on by family or during childhood, to name a couple of sources. On an energetic level, it can be overshadowed by the Mind of another if the brain of this other is stronger, toxic, insidious or controlling. Programs from another source can be introduced to it, creating some confusion in the body as well as Thought Processes.

Clearing the Nadis of the Brain Gridding System from the influences etc of others can make for a better cohesive experience and understanding.

Heart Gridding System

Many of us are familiar with the Heart and its capacity to love, accept and welcome another into its space. There are many philosophies that preach this concept, and label it as being a Spiritual concept. This is useful and illuminative in particular to those who have closed hearts to start with, or who come from very heart-closed or traumatised families. Indeed, romantic and familial love often involves opening the heart. And this is right and as it should be. This welcoming and accepting is truly wonderful and supportive when those that connect with us on a heart level also have our best interests at heart. There are many that encourage the Heart and the Heart Chakra to open – and not only just to open, but to open to All (and all – the populace at large).

When one already has a soft and tender heart, and a sensitive disposition and yet meets with those that are devious, destructive, vindictive and harmful, then the open heart can not only take a beating, but may require some time to recover. We all have to learn to take care of our hearts and to be personally responsible for its health and well-being. And of whom we open to.

When one naturally has an open heart, and is willing to embrace all on a spiritual and heart level, unless their path has no dark hearts along the way, they will always be rewarded back in kind. However, when another untrustworthy or disrespectful heart has connected to the open and sensitive heart and they do not take care of it, then there is another aspect to be considered regarding this; for often certain energetic and protection practices may well be required, and most Sensitives will know what I mean by this. Dark hearts may arrive not because of anything that we have personally done ourself. We may be still heart-open, but energetically, this can also leave us energetically open.

I stumbled across this discovery as I was seeking to resolve a personal issue. To recognise that those that we have loved and cared for have attached themselves to our Heart Gridding System, not necessarily in order to love us back, but in order to take from us or to control us, is a rude awakening. Opening one's heart to those we love can leave us vulnerable. If one is a Sensitive, one may well find it difficult to monitor one's boundaries of the heart, that is assuming that they have maintained any boundaries. Many glib and supposedly 'spiritual' quotations still give misinformation when they talk about 'opening the heart' in order to be evolved or 'spiritual'.

The message may be correct in some quarters and for some Souls, but in the same message there is no differentiation between those with already open (and wounded) hearts and those who have closed their hearts because they do not wish to care, to share, to truly love or to be honest with life.

The Heart Gridding System contains connections via its Nadis to all of the relationships we have had that we have not yet let go of. Or, possibly more importantly, that have not let go of us. And this is the important part. People in your past who treated you badly, or whose spiritual or heart path greatly diverged from yours, or who wanted to own a part of you at some stage, or who are jealous or resentful in some way, may still be locked into your own personal Heart Grid.

The Heart Grid needs to be kept clear, loved and current to be able to function at its highest potential frequency. Nurturing and loving the self can involve clearing not only past hurts and relationships, but also past 'hanger-on-ers'.

So it is important to trace and track and remove any unnecessary connections; any unsupportive ties; any past sycophant, associate or follower; any past bully or controller; or anyone who no longer deserves to be involved in your heart and your progress. This can also include past projects based on the heart's desires started and then aborted; and preferred pathways that you were unable to complete; any dreams that you now realise are no longer a part of your life, future or reality. This then frees up your Heart Grid to embrace more relevant possibilities.

Be aware of when someone has created several connections that have become a thick cord, and clear this and any hook attaching it to your grid system, sending it back to its origin. Purify and cleanse where this connection has been, and lovingly clear and filter all of the Nadis involved in your Heart Grid. You may also wish to reconfirm all those that you wish to be a part of your journey from this point on.

You would be wise to reciprocate with all those whose lives you were a part of too. Let them go, and filter and recall your own personal Heart Strings (Heart Grid Nadis) back to yourself, with self compassion, love and gratitude for the time you had with them, ackowledging that this time is now past.

This also allows one to be ready for *new* connections, new and more positive possibilities, one's that reflect the new you; the you that has grown, learned and developed and that is the you that are now.

The Heart Gridding System is centred at the heart and runs through and around the heart area and chest through several dimensions. From here, it progresses through the energy bodies into the Spiritual Body and the Soul Body. Importantly. it also connects with the 11th Earthing Chakra in advanced beings.

Nadis from here that are destined or allowed to connect with the Heart Strings or the Heart Nadis of another have the opportunity to grow in strength or in dependency. Along this connection line, there will usually also develop a Chakra that is the **Relational Chakra** that governs or mirrors that relationship. How this Chakra is placed and managed can impact on either of the people involved, for good or not for good. Managing this Chakra can become a key to maintaining equity or order or toward supporting a good relationship. See the section on *Relational Chakras*.

The Heart Gridding System is Internal and External.
The connections and Nadis can originate *from* the Heart or *to* the Heart.
The Gridding System includes all current (and if not cleared, past) relationships.
Illustration indicates that other Hearts can be held, or hide in or hold onto the Heart.

Link (Chakra) Gridding System

The Link Chakra is a Key Chakra. It is also a Gateway. Its usual colours are Silvery Icy Blue, Crystalline or Etheric Silvery Pearl though it may also run to Red-Maroon.

The Link Chakra is as its name implies – a major Link between many Chakras and Chakra Systems and connects to the Advanced Soul Body.

Located just above the knees and between the knees, it must be handled with great care. I experienced a very bad occurrence when someone I had previously trusted worked on this Chakra energetically; and it took me many years to recover from this mistreatment. Please only ever handle this area gently and with respect. I classify this as an Advanced Evolved Chakra and will write about this publically when more Souls require this information.

It is sufficient for most people at the present time to know that the Link Chakra Gridding System is a comprehensive system that encompasses many areas and dimensions. Connections regarding this system can be approached by ascertaining if the intended connection is in the highest good and in alignment with the person's Soul Purpose and Destiny – if it is not, then ask the Soul of the person to disconnect from it. If it is in the highest good and in alignment with the Soul Purpose, and it is not connected, then work with asking that the Soul of the person themself connects it. This way, you will not be interfering (nor placing yourself in the way of karmic rebound) and you will be facilitating for the Soul to heal itself.

I ask that if this issue / connection is in alignment with this Soul's Purpose and Destiny then this Soul now makes the correct and appropriate connection safely and harmoniously, with harm to no-one. So be it, so be it, so be it.

I ask that if this issue / connection is NOT in alignment with this Soul's Purpose and Destiny then this Soul now makes the correct and appropriate DIS-connection in safety and harmony, with harm to no-one. So be it, so be it, so be it.

Should you wish to know more about this now or feel you have a problem here, you are welcome to contact me personally; admin@myrasri.com.

Family Organism Gridding System

This is similar to the Heart Gridding System in that it involves relationships. However, these are more specialised. This grid incorporates all of the aspects of family; one's family of origin, one's adoptive family if there is/was one, one's own offspring and their future progeny and all of the relevant DNA and stored information, experiences, capabilities and possibilities. It also holds one's Relational Chakras and their connections.

It includes areas of health, attitude, beliefs, and destiny.

This grid projects into the future as well as way back into the past. It contains all of the hopes and dreams of one's parents, ancestors and blood line. And also the curses and blessings placed against or for the generations involved.

The Nadis in this grid, like most Gridding Systems, are inter-dimensional.

Families: or Types of Families

- Human family
- Species Family
- Cosmic, StarSeed or Planet of Origin Family
- Soul Family

Inherited legacies, potentialities, opportunities and possibilities as well as health legacies, financial prospects and benefits are all part of this Gridding System, no matter where they lie in the energy bodies or Chakras. The DNA of ancestors, the past experiences through the generations, the hopes and aspirations for the future, these are all connection points on this Gridding System. This grid connects and operates inter-dimensionally and through time and space.

Ensuring that one's Family Organism Gridding System has not been penetrated by a usurper, or drained off by an energy vampire, can make a difference to the optimal functioning of this – not just in the present, but for the future.

Planet/ary Gridding System

The planet has her own Gridding System. Within this is held all of the records of not only the history of Planet Earth, but of all of the Consciousness of this planet in all of her past incarnations. This includes her attempts to overcome the raping and pillaging that she has suffered. Some believe that the planet has been quarantined from the wider Cosmos community in order for her to solve this dilemma – that of providing a home to humanity as she has contracted to do, whilst living to tell the tale at a later date.

The history of our Earth so far has included the ripping out of her various metals, minerals, fossil fuels and natural constituents, whilst tearing down her forests, polluting her waters, and further dissing her with unchecked downpours of chemtrails, environmental oil pollution, nuclear fall-out and various weapons test effects together with a general disregard with whatever activity the greed of man decides to visit on her.

The space race for some is the only way that they can think of to solve the problem – that of escape from life on a world that has been trashed totally by mankind. The lack of responsibility, respect and recompense to this planet by certain individuals has greatly weakened the planetary grid, and it is often the more aware and enlightened consciousness of the same species that is supporting her and aiding in giving her 'heart'.

The powers of darkness driving the greed of some men do not care that with each ripping off of her natural resources, they have been weakening her. Gold, ore, coal, oil, minerals; these are her blood, arteries, nerves, resources.

Some of the Planet's Nadis, supported or aligned to certain minerals, metals and substances underground, have been damaged, yet she still continues... The energy networks weave through her EMF, sub-strata, meridians, tectonic plates and also her atmosphere and stratospheres.

However, on the etheric level she has had great support through the Grids that also stretch out to her unseen Helpers.

We are each connected to the Planetary Gridding System. The degree to which each of us are connected depends on our relationship with her, and our relationship with our self. Feedback with this Gridding System is a two-way street, and she benefits from every positive and appreciative thought about her.

There is a level of consciousness which is not co-dependent on her, nor she on us, but which is mutually admirable, respectful, and sustaining.

The following image is intended to illustrate some of the gridding possibilities. Grids can be linked into Places (City etc), Geography, Time Zone, Ground Level (below, surface or above) and ElectroMagnetic frequency to name a few.

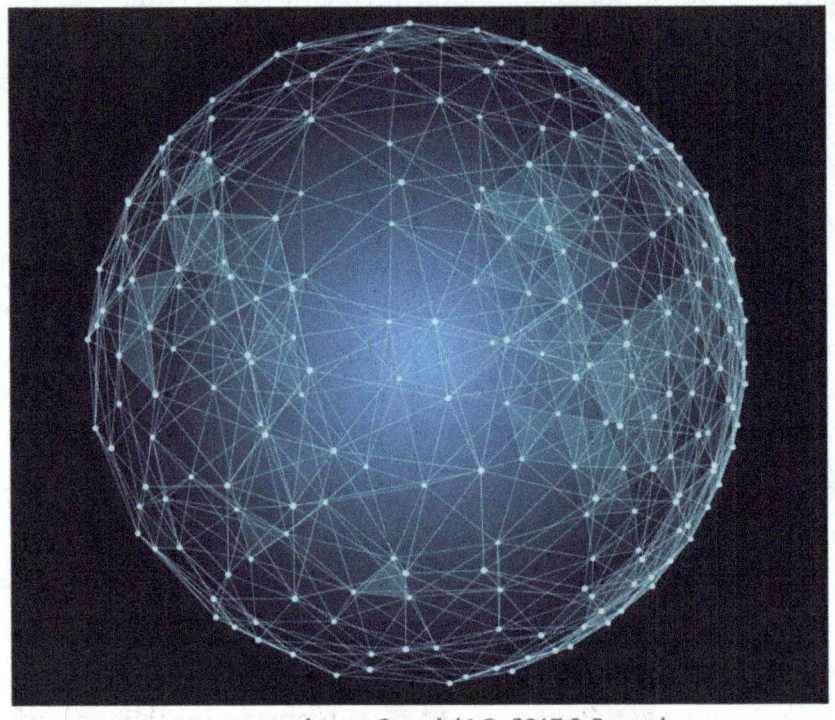

New Galactic Gridding System

This Gridding System is a key step that depends not only on the individual's consciousness and the raising of global consciousness, but also on the correct connections to the most supportive stations and locations (time-space-dimension) in the Galaxy and the Cosmos.

As Humanity takes up the challenge to overcome its past tendencies (Self-Destructive and Other-Destructive) and nurtures its potential ability to raise its consciousness sufficiently to join the greater galactic community, the opportunity to enter into wider alliances is presented through this grid. It is already present, and some are already aligned to it, whilst others are holding some of the threads together with the aid of invisible Helpers. As we evolve our anatomy sufficiently to be both connected with and anchored correctly to this grid, the number of Nadi connections grows accordingly, raising the 'tipping-point' threshold for our next global upgrade and the step is achieved.

The New Galactic Gridding System is connected with and requires correct alignment to;

- 5th and 8th Earthing Chakras
- Link Chakra
- New Galactic Grid that is being constructed in the Galaxy
- One's True Soul and Spirit Blueprint
- One's own True Purpose and Destiny
- One's Soul and Spirit Birthright
- One's own Star Birthright

All these connection points are necessary to consider and confirm for one to be correctly positioned on this particular Grid.

EXTRA-ORDINARY CHAKRAS

Link Chakra

The Link Chakra is a relatively new Chakra and its functions are many and varied. It is a *major* Integration Point and has its own Gridding System. Great care should be exercised in the handling of this Chakra and its connections, and because of its sensitivity and vulnerable nature I generally only share more about this Chakra in workshops with those ready for the information.

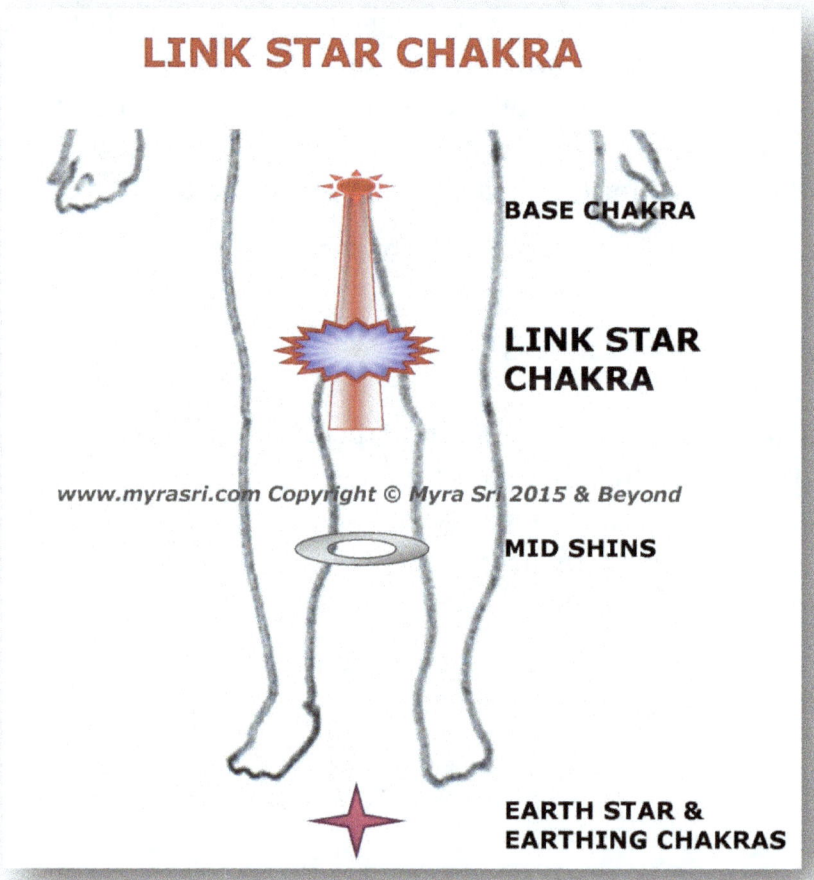

Further Advanced information will be available in due course.

The Link Gridding System has been mentioned because of its relevance in the currently evolving greater energy systems.

Relational Chakras

These are Out-Of-Body Chakras.

Each significant relationship has a Relational Chakra that supports, records, governs or controls the relationship and its conduct.

In a healthy relationship, the Chakra is located along a series of Nadis connecting the two people, and is positioned approximately half-way between each person. This generally shows a reasonably equal input and control between each person. Neither one is giving too much or taking too much. Again, at this point, these are only generalisations.

When the Positioning of the Chakra is closer to one person than another, particularly when it is quite close, this indicates the person it is closest to is doing the most work or input, or who is the most affected by the relationship. It can also indicate a dependent or needy relationship.

When it is far away from one of the partners, it can indicate diminished care or lack of genuine love, or even that this person does not want to be in relationship but is only connected (and impacted if Sensitive) by the desire of the other party.

The Relational Chakra itself can be entwined, overlaid or interfered with by another Relational Chakra. This usually happens in three-way dramas, when a third person is forever attempting to influence what goes on between two people. They may be invited in (generally unknowingly) by one of the two, or they may have inveigled themselves between them.

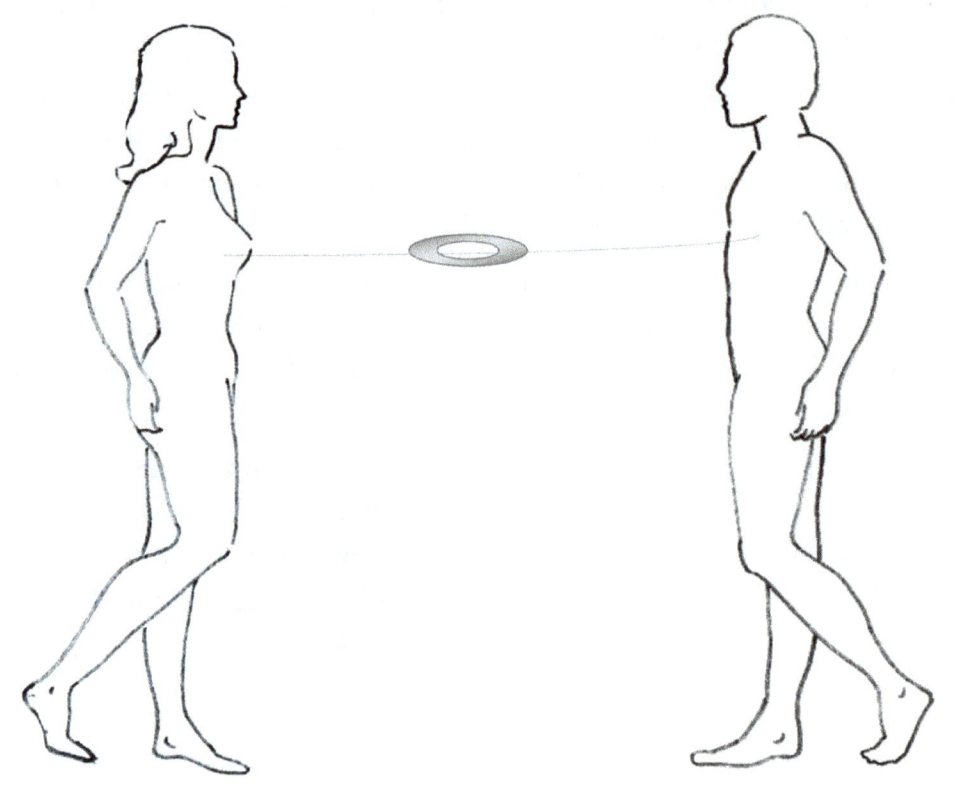

A further series of Guided Meditations including for these Chakras is being developed for your convenience and support.

Preparing to Work with the New Chakras

In each section of the New Chakras, there are recommended procedures for healing and balancing the Chakras. There is also a section on **Balancing Techniques and Tools,** at the beginning of the section on the New Chakras.

To work effectively with the new evolved subtle body energy systems, and with their related Nadis, one needs to have clear channels to intake and utilise the available positive Solar, pranic and healing energies necessary.

As part of preparation of your healing and alignment process, it will greatly assist to clear your light channels and to ensure appropriate connection to your true Divine Source. This same process can also enhance your client's energy systems for a greater intake of energy and connectedness – if they are willing and it is appropriate for them at this stage in their development and awareness. Another benefit of this alignment process is that any previously unseen or unacknowledged parasitic, controlling or dark energy is arrested and removed. This benefits not only the healing but all aspects of one's human experience.

There are usually two different energetic types of light channels in the head and this is usually simply dependent on the Soul's own journey, growth and experience. There is no right or wrong, simply *different*, and the two channel methods are illustrated below.

There may also be filters along the channels, which are part of their protective and supporting mechanism. These filters need to be consciously cleansed and instructions are also given for this.

After your preparations and processes, after your healing session, it is recommended that one ensures that the healing has been registered with the Soul Star above the head as mentioned previously.

Light Channels, Filters, Blocks

Most people are only aware of the link to the Crown Chakra through the head from the Third Eye Chakra and the other Main Chakras.

There are other links to the Crown Chakra, and subsequently through to the Soul Star (Individuation Point) above the head, and from thence to the Upper or Higher Chakras; and to one's own personal Divine Source. Connecting these links correctly allows clearer, purer and higher vibrational energy to be received or rather, to be interpreted correctly, for appropriate use in the being.

The Light Channels in the head seem to enable a swifter connection to the Higher Chakras and to one's Source connection because they also pass through some of the Psychic channels and centres in the head (or brain if you prefer). Within the brain and on a physical level of course, are the hormonal regulators and major neurological and glandular centres. Co-existing in the same space is a variety of energy systems and centres; Third Eye and Crown Chakras and the Central Channel that connects them throughout the Main Chakra System. Alongside these and on a different energetic layer or dimension, are the psychic centres in the brain that correlate with the Psychic Body Chakras and anatomy.

Ensuring clear pathways along the Light Channel in the head will also assist in clearing and recharging these energy centres.

AFTER clearing the **Hara Line** and its components, one is ready to clear this channel for connection to one's Divine Source.

TO CLEAR: First, focus on centring and calming the body and mind, then focus on the philtrum: this is located on the vertical centre line for the main control or Governing Meridian.

It is positioned directly under the nose and above the top lip. It is a Gateway Channel and an access point for Light.

Breathing consciously, allow each breath to draw in Light along this channel, and into the head.

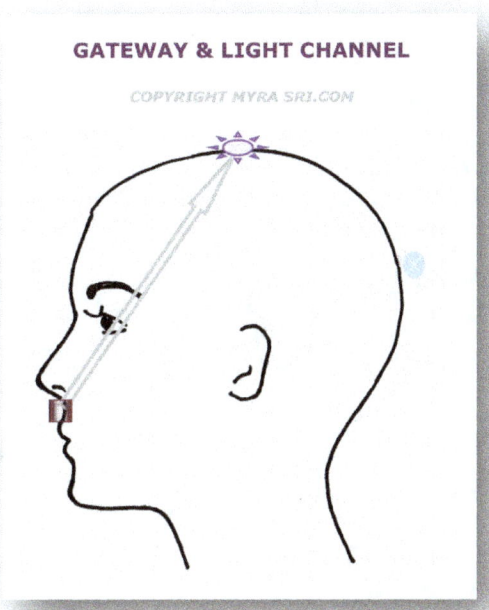

Instruct that the Light is to be drawn along to the Crown Point, clearing and filling the channel with light as it goes. The Light will want to follow its true individual anatomical pathway, which may be directly up to the Crown at a slight angle, or directly to the back of the head (in a line that hits the protruding part or Parietal aspect) at an approximate 45 degree angle. From here it will want to perform a mirrored 45 degree angle to the Crown, creating a kind of stairway similar to the one in the pyramids. It doesn't really matter which of these two ways it chooses to go as both are valid and just denote different Soul experience and history.

When we compare these with the Psychic Centres in the Brain, a pathway may become more obvious.

If one encounters a blockage, simply keep on breathing and clearing through the blockage, intending that the Light itself melts away all opposing obstructions or darkness. Continue breathing in Light consciously in this way, until one feels or senses that the flow is easy and the passageway is free and clear.

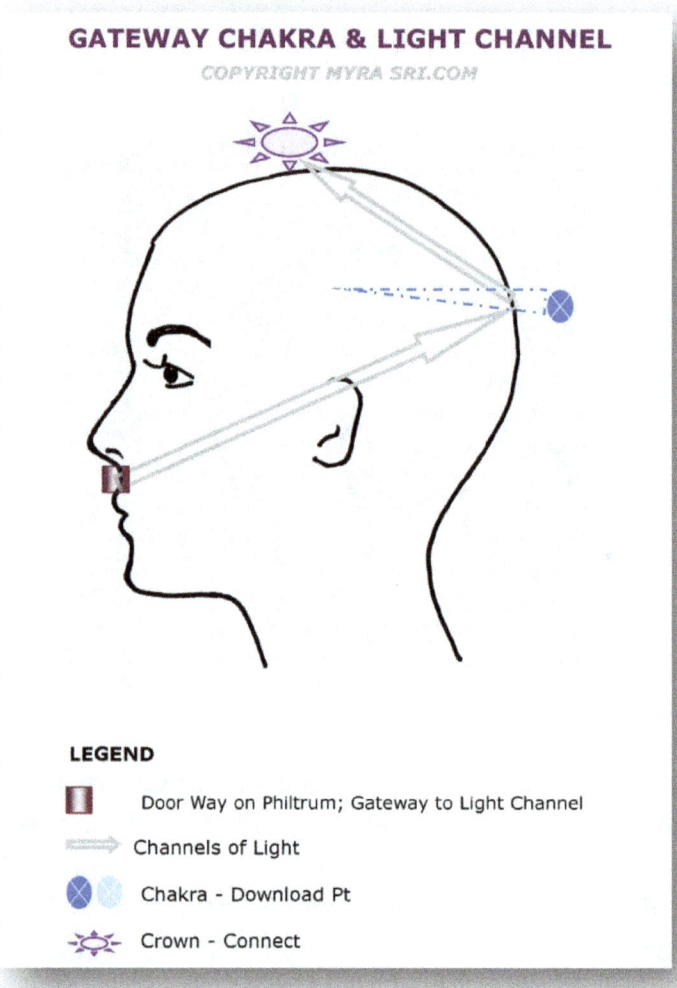

With the stepped stairway Channel of Light, one can see that it connects with the rear Download Point or Causal Chakra, located near and sometimes parallel to the Bindu Chakra. The Bindu can mark the mid-Point in this stepped stairway Light Channel

This configuration may sometimes be more prone to interference and usually has a system of filters to protect the delicate sensory and etheric anatomy here.

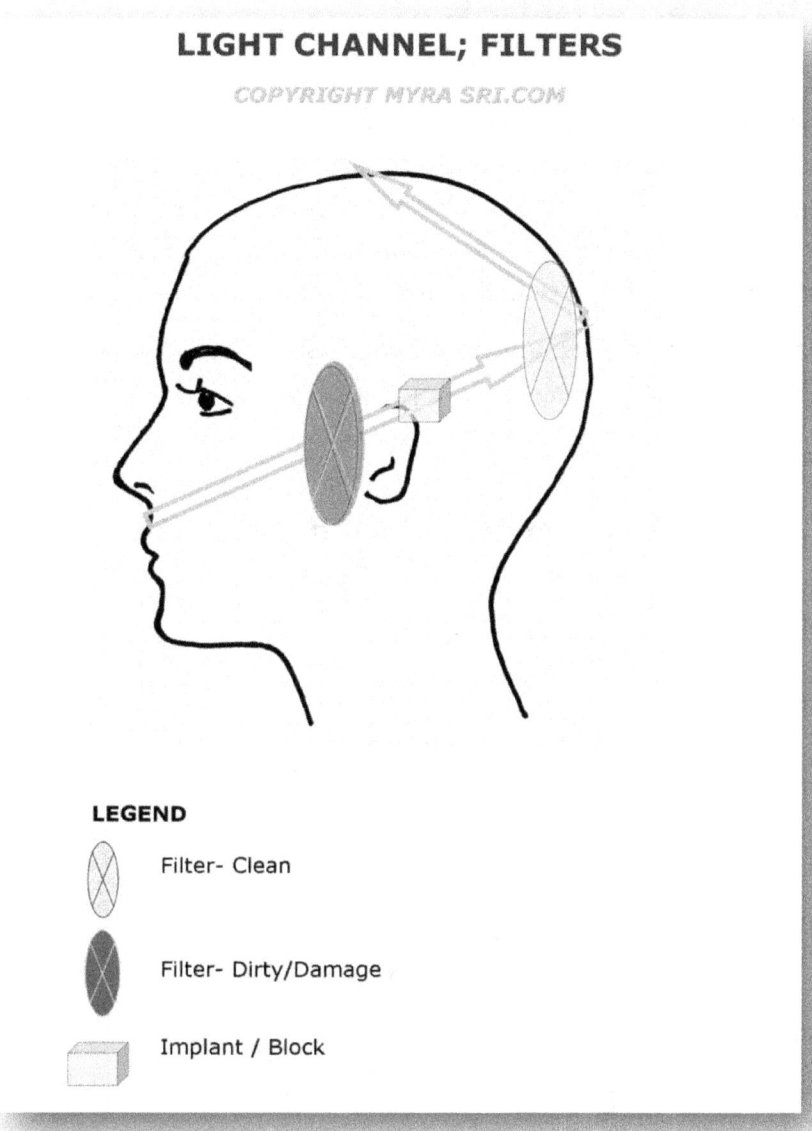

Breathing in, infill with Light and clear any blockages or implants as you go.

CLEARING BLOCKS AND FILTERS

BLOCKS:

Blocks along the Light Channel can be through a variety of things. Some of these include: interference from others along life's path; trauma through accident or injury; betrayal or abandonment causing one to doubt self, life or one's Divine Source; and negative attack or bullying by others. Blocks can also be located by any of the Psychic Centres in the head.

Blocks can be cleared by focused breathing, using the incoming Light to push through and disintegrate the block as it goes.

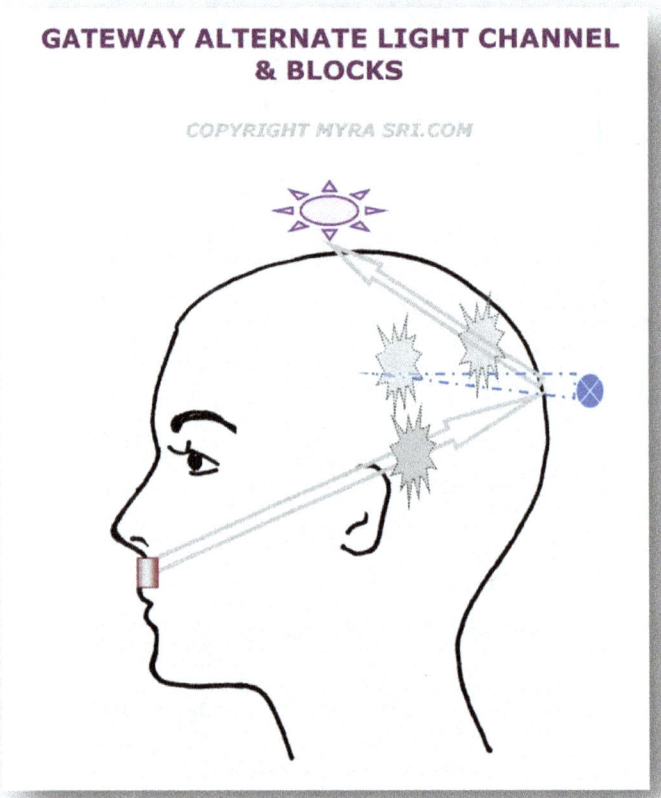

There are rare occasions when its actual cause needs to be identified in order to clear it away, so counting back down through the years to locate the time of the block can assist in this, as an associated picture may well reveal itself for release and resolution.

Implants:

Implants are a form of coded construct that intended to control in some way. There is the possibility of positive Implants, whereby someone has agreed to support a certain mission and has accepted the Implant willingly, whether knowingly or not. However, Implants are usually categorised as not appropriate for the Soul walking and being responsible for their own path and choices.

Implants need to be removed completely and all agreements or hypnotic subscriptions associated with them must also be dissolved, deleted, destroyed and voided so that there is no resonance for a future Implant to be embedded again.

Filters:

Filters are often necessary protective mechanisms, particularly for the empathic and the Sensitive. These filter out harmful or toxic frequencies and projections so that the associated energy channel or centre is kept clear and safe.

They are usually of a fine resilient etheric filamental construction, and for a visual idea of their appearance and function, they can be compared to the filter in a washing machine.

Filters can become overloaded over time, especially when greeted with lots of other people's overwhelm or issues. If one has not had the time or the support to unload, debrief or to deal with the residual or fragmented energies from other's dilemmas or traumas still attached to oneself, they may find that the filters can gunk up with a kind of etheric phlegm. This slows down their efficiency and prevents proper protection where it is needed most. They can also be damaged or torn by trauma or negative attack from another person or, in rare cases, from another dimension or quadrant.

Repairing the filter as well as clearing it is a unique exercise and must be done carefully, gently, respectfully and correctly.

AFFIRMATIONS:

Here you will find some of the Affirmations shared earlier with some other Affirmation ideas together in one section for your added ease of reference.

SOUL HEALING REGISTRATION

The Soul requires recognition and consideration in all healing processes, and it is necessary that the Soul accepts and is party to the positive changes therein. It is vital that the Soul registers the changes. This can be done as the important 'LOCK-IN' procedure for the end of EVERY session or healing, to ensure full and accepted benefit by balancing the following;

My Soul, body and being now 100% accepts this balance and healing, easily and safely

I now 100% integrate and retain ALL of the benefits of this balance for my Highest Good and in alignment with my own True Soul Purpose and Destiny

GENERAL AFFIRMATION IDEAS

It is safe to ...

It is easy to ...

It is fun to ...

I am ready to ...

I give myself permission to ...

...Learn from the past, to live in the present, and to plan for the future

GENERAL EARTHING CHAKRA STATEMENTS

This ... Chakra is now 100% Clear and Whole

This ... Chakra is now 100% ready for initiation and activation

This ... Chakra is now 100% initiated and activated

PSYCHIC AFFIRMATIONS

This ... Chakra is now 100% clear

This ... Chakra is now 100% clear and ready for integration with my Psychic Body

This ... Chakra is now 100% aligned to the New Incoming frequencies

I now safely use my Psychic Chakras in integrity and without harm to others

My Psychic Chakras are now 100% free from the ... of others

SHOCK AFFIRMATIONS

It is now 100% safe for me to acknowledge that there is shock still held in my body or being at some level

It is now 100% safe for me to release any shock that is held in my body and being

I am 100% ready to begin to heal any shock that is held in my body and being

It is now 100% safe to deal with old hurts, old traumas, old crises in a positive manner

I am now 100% ready to deal with old hurts, old traumas, old crises in a positive manner

I am ready, willing and able to recover from past hurts and alerts

I am 100% ready, willing and able to recover from past hurts and alerts

SIGNAL AFFIRMATIONS

It is now 100% safe for me to acknowledge that there is shock still held in my body or being at some level

It is now 100% safe for me to release any shock that is held in my body and being

I am 100% ready to begin to heal any shock that is held in my body and being

It is now 100% safe to deal with old hurts, old traumas, old crises in a positive manner

I am now 100% ready to deal with old hurts, old traumas, old crises in a positive manner

I am ready, willing and able to recover from past hurts and alerts

I am 100% ready, willing and able to recover from past hurts and alerts

Summary — Evolution or Enlightenment

As is obvious by now, our evolving subtle body anatomy has undergone quite some changes over the years.

We appear to be in the midst of further changes still, as we hold our ground and hold the light. There are still some challenges to be had and some tests to be passed or overcome. For some, this is part of the Soul purpose and journey and part of the mission here. It hasn't been easy and we may not fully reap of the rewards, but we are at the Coal-face, if you like, actually being part of the shifts and changes and in the long run, this is something that cannot be experienced or understood any other way than by full and complete participation.

Working with the New Evolved Chakras assists our own evolution, and it helps us house and hold more higher vibrationary light. This is essential, as going Out-There to change the world does not necessarily automatically mean that we are changing or holding the light within. For we can get caught up with the agenda of things, or allow too much energy of others to interfere. Finding the balance is so important, for we may find that without it, we also run the risk of an enlarged or out of control ego.

Having seen others do certain supposed spiritual processes and then claiming to be enlightened does not convince me that they have actually attained that position. Reaching enlightenment on certain points of understanding doesn't mean full enlightenment. And claiming to personally be an Enlightened One certainly gives me cause to doubt the truth of the statement. I don't think a really Enlightened Being needs to state that that is who or what they are. The term Evolving sits more readily with me, as it is a process, and from here I cannot fully yet see what I am evolving into, though I may dare to hazard a guess or two. Keeping the highest and purest intent is the only way to evolve correctly, or the ego can turn it into a *de*volving.

I feel this current anatomy will serve us well for quite some years, and may actually be all we need to know for some time about the new energy anatomy and Chakras. Be assured I will keep my ears to the wind for further updates. In the words of techno-speak, we now have upgrades for the next Generation.

SPIRITUAL POWER, NOT FORCE

Here are some of my thoughts on the subject.

To achieve the best results with the information in this book, it is always best to by-pass the astral, the spirits, the etheric, the pseudo-psychic, power-hungering and –mongering and only seek the highest Divine that you possibly can. In the Divine there can be seen darkness – one only has to read the bible to know that there is an angry and a jealous God out there – but in the True Divine there is no Darkness. Rather than seek personalities, power-beings, 'Masters' or 'Gurus', seek to embrace your inner knowing and Higher Self and reach to your Highest and Purest Light manifestation and access. This will guarantee you no karma from using any psychic talents for spiritual ends.

I have seen Masters of psychic powers, manipulators of laws and energy, who channel in the dark without realizing it, and this taints not only their work and their 'patients' but also their karma. In healing we must break away from the old model of using psychism for power or gain and engage in the right use of it – for good, the benefit of all.

To be Spiritual is so much more important than to have flashy psychic gifts or to know all the correct language and quotes, or to be able to spew forth the latest spiritual 'buzz' words on command.

I will also issue a warning here, one that I usually teach in the Spiritual-Protection-HygienEthics class; Do not go checking psychically into another person's business or affairs without *invitation*, or unless they are negatively impacting on you directly. It is none of your business. Just as the act of them checking into you, into your mind, into your thoughts or into what you are doing is none of their business. If they are playing with or holding any aspect of dark, or going through difficult times, or are of an inharmonious vibration, or if they have a negative entity on them, you will soon enough know about it because it will knock your own Psychic Body and system around, and create problems for you. So clear these off and out and keep your affairs separate. If you are in the habit of letting your mind wander into the affairs of others, this will leave you open to others wandering into your personal business.

So unless requested to do so or for your own personal protection, don't open up to another's personal business for there is also a possibility that you will also be opening portals to whatever it is that they are dealing with or doing.

Don't.Do.It!

Make sure that when you think of someone that when you cease thinking about them, you *close* down that space and that opening.

Practice Spiritual-Cleansing (or Protection-HygienEthics) if you get hit this way. There are some ideas for this in my book '*Secrets Behind Energy Fields*'.

Also another reminder here.

Most of us possess these unique aspects of the new Psychic Chakras and their subtle body connections and functions or most of us will possess them eventually. But their presence or the possibility for full activation and function may also depend on the Soul identity, essence, character, journey and mission for each being or person. The spiritual calibre so to speak.

Our job, if you like, should we be called to energy work, is to assist the presenting Soul with the technology and knowhow to help them activate these centres appropriately, whilst being also aware that the results may be dependent on the Soul's present capacity for these new Chakras and connections. This does not necessarily mean that if a Chakra is not showing right now, that it won't show up at all. It just may be a matter of time, or of further processing, or even simply more new energy light frequencies emerging that give them the extra oomph or boost to their next stage. Meanwhile, you are now equipped and have knowledge and an understanding in this area. Congratulations!

It has been a pleasure to share with you and journey with you. I wish you well in your explorations.

PUTTING IT ALL TOGETHER

I trust that by now you are beginning to gain some understanding of the benefits and the functions of these new or re-accessible Chakras, and of how they can enhance and assist with our progress in the new Era.

We have looked at the original Human Chakra system; that is, the Main Chakra anatomy for humanity. Building on these we have explored the New Extra-Ordinary Chakras and Systems that make up the Evolved Energy Systems for these current times. These new systems have included the new Earthing Chakras, the Psychic Body and its Chakras, the Signal Chakras and its anatomy, and we have referred to where these new Chakras and Connection Points fit in with or relate to the Higher Chakras, the Advanced Soul Body, the new Extra-Ordinary Chakras and the new emerging Gridding Systems.

We have had the opportunity to align with some of these as we have progressed through the pages. At certain points there have been references to specific ways of working with and balancing some of these Chakras. We have also become familiar with the general guide of *Balancing Techniques and Tools* for the therapist or self-journeyer to utilise.

We have covered the requirements of extra energetic preparation for starting off any accurate energetic work with the new Chakra systems that I doubt have been covered anywhere else (I could be wrong, but I personally have not yet read of these anywhere else). This has included illustrations of the clearing required for the Light Channel in the head, the Central Core Channel and for the clearing of Filters and Blocks.

Affirmations have assisted us to trigger and navigate through various histories, stories and consciousnesses of a Chakra, whilst understanding of the Nadis have also been explored and shared.

Colour infusion has assisted in correcting shock or erroneous vibrational frequencies.

Recalibration and anchoring processes have been outlined for increased energetic and evolutionary benefit and for enhanced and correct energetic alignment to the new incoming frequencies.

Changes and shifts have begun or have been concluded along the way.

In short, I trust that *now* you are not quite the same person that *began* reading this book, but a more balanced, supported and confident spiritual Human being.

It has been my privilege to share this new information with you.

For assisting the reader with energy balancing, colour images and charts are available for the genuine print book-buyer upon request. The New Evolved Chakras Workbooks with full colour images will also be ready soon. Email me at admin@myrasri.com for more information.

Be Well, Stay Well,

Myra Sri

FAQ's

I heard that there are many more Chakras above the head than the ones you mention — how come this is so?

Higher Chakra Numbering

Over time, I have had lots of opportunity to work with the Higher Chakra systems, and surprisingly to me at certain times they have numbered from over 60 and ranged up to over 100. I found this hard to understand initially as I had only been aware of up to four other Chakras above the Crown Chakra. But this did become clearer after some time.

This particular Chakra numbering system began above the head or crown by approximately 18 to 24 inches or 45 to 60 cms. There appeared to be Sets or collections / groupings of Levels of Chakras. There also may have been some specific connections when they ended with say a '3' or a '1', i.e. 33, or 63. Though the 29th chakra appeared to be a sort of ceiling for a while. These higher chakras have been slowly increasing in accessibility, and over several years ago we were able to access and balance up to 101. Though I also worked with someone whose 111th higher chakra was indicating its presence and need for balance. Again, as we emerged into the current energy streams, things shifted again.

To clarify the possible systems of higher chakras, let me say that I found there to be several models to work with. Some models use 4 – 5 Higher Chakras, others use the ones I have just described. They do not contradict each other, as there are degrees within the latter system which allows for groups of chakras (each serving different purposes) and in some of these fewer chakras, I have found that they may contain as many as 10 or even 20 chakras. If we look at the Astral levels, we can see a similar occurrence here: there being 7 main levels of the astral fields, with a further breakdown of these into 7 levels again; making a total of 49 astral levels. Whilst some of these levels are not pleasant to be involved with, or have risky sides to them, nevertheless, simply addressing the Astral level or issues around the Astral as a group is feasible and healable without going into the exact level unless being guided or led (safely) to do so.

Not long after my working with these high levels or numbered Chakras, things seemed to shift and it settled down again to a handful of major Higher Chakras, kind of defaulting back to the 8TH Upper to the 11th (or in some cases 12th) Upper Chakras, so it occurred to me that they had sorted themselves out and had incorporated themselves into groupings of minor level higher Chakras to become the Major Higher Chakras.

Another possibility for these high numbers or levels of Chakras is that a certain kind of rebalancing was occurring, both with the individual and with the planetary energies, and possibly for a certain StarSeed line, for of late I have not come across these high numbers since. It is also possible that this coincided with the revelations regarding the new Earthing Chakra system, which supersedes the Earth Star Chakra.

I do not have an absolute opinion on any Higher Chakra system, I can only observe and list my findings and furnish you with the system that seems to work best for me at present. And in all honesty, should a client present to me specifically requesting to work with a particular Chakra model that is familiar and unacceptable to them, then I will do my best to assist them in this, for it is their session after all. However, I would also place myself in neutral space in order to ascertain if this is in fact appropriate and correct for them and facilitate if so.

Will there be a further increase in the number of Higher Chakras?

It's All Light

It is possible that the numbers of any of the energy systems or Chakras may continue to rise, though not all that likely, as we were pretty much set when we entered the 2012 new energy codes. The exception I currently see is Chakra Thirteen in the New Earthing Chakras, as previously mentioned.

The unarguable result is that we are now able to access and assimilate more light codes and frequencies, as more frequencies of a higher vibration are emitted into our solar system.

We live in grids of energy, and some of these grids can be independent of each other, and can connect to specific vibratory ranges which can trigger those frequencies housed by certain individuals or humans. As the Planet is passing further through the Photon Belt towards the Galactic and Milky Way Equator, there will continually be an upgrading of energies and light codes, which can also cause further separation of and from the lower energies.

As more light comes in, more of the 'held' and old darkness is disrupted and stirred up for release. We are being challenged to plough through and release these old energies. This will continue until we can clear – render up and surrender to the light – to e-merge fully into our full light.

(Though the fall-out can be somewhat uncomfortable at times, the benefits will certainly outweigh them when we have ridden through the waves.)

There is a general consensus however, in the healing community that there are several Higher Chakras of account. With different systems, as I have mentioned earlier, there have been different interpretations, different names, differing functions and different positions. On the whole, however, they all relate to Higher Function and are generally for the purpose of enlightenment, ascension, growth or evolution.

When we look at the different systems, and at the different possibilities and combinations, depending on the Soul's origin, its purpose, its history, its current position and capabilities, we have a whole sea of possibilities to call upon.

GLOSSARY

ANTENNAE: Erections, structures or devices to receive and monitor incoming information or broadcasts. Usually extends some distance from the host or base in order to pick-up or collect transmissions, recordings **CODINGS:** Information or data that can instruct or control depending on its content; a series of codes or code settings.

DESTINY LINES: May be found in the Soul Star Chakra (Soul I.D. Point). These are intentions from others and plans from others and **must** be removed for the Soul to experience its own autonomy and function.

EMF; ElectroMagnetic Field. The balance between incoming and outgoing, receiving and broadcasting, positive and negative polarity or electrical energies. Varying EMF's may run at varying Hertz (frequencies).

EXTRA-ORDINARY CHAKRAS: The Extra-Ordinary Chakras are those Chakras that are not part of the Ordinary or recognised system – I classify the Main Chakras and the Minor Chakras as Ordinary. The Higher Chakras, Earthing Chakras, Psychic Chakras and Signal Chakras are classified as Extra-Ordinary for the purposes of this book.

FILTER: Device, structure, plate or substance that allows passing of plasma, gas or particles through it, but holds back any unwanted substances or particles. Usually set to only allow appropriate and useful particles through. Requires periodic maintenance, or attention when mass traffic of communication or substance.

FREQUENCY: Any of these: Vibration, Wavelength, Resonance, Electromagnetic Wave, Bandwidth, Reverberation, Harmonic, Overtone, Waves.

GATEWAY CHAKRAS: Master Chakras that govern and control.

HSP: Higher Sense Perception. Sensing on a higher, more advanced or more capable level.

HUMAN SEED: A Soul whose first incarnation was as a Human or as a Human-type born on a current or past version or incarnation of Earth.

I AM CENTRE: The 'I Am' Spirit Centre is usually the Soul Star Chakra above the head.

LINK CHAKRA: An important and relatively new Chakra. Positioned between the knees and above them.

LOCK-IN: To 'Lock-in' a Chakra, is to command and intend that it takes on its new configuration and that this is its desired state from now on. It is a form of 'seal'-ing or fixing a status.

MATRIX: Matrix used in this book refers to the whole of the energy components of a particular system. This will include any Chakras, Nadis, Connection Points, origin source, and whatever elements, minerals and matter it consists of.

MERKABA: Mer-Ka-Ba; An enhanced energy body vehicle that envelopes the Aura. Co-Responsible for enhancing space-time location, stabilisation and navigation. Refer to Drunvalo Melchizedeck's work on *'Flower of Life'*.

NADI COLUMN: A collection of Nadis that create a super strong link from one component or aspect to another.

NEW COSMIC GRIDDING SYSTEM: This has been superseded and replaced by the New Golden Galactic Gridding System.

NEW GOLDEN GALACTIC GRIDDING SYSTEM: See chapter on Gridding Systems.

PHENOMENA: A remarkable or unusual happening, event or occurrence, whether natural or otherwise.

PRIORITY PRIORITY: The most important issue that is considered by the being, as a whole or in total, at this point in time; The issue to address that when cleared can affect the most change and benefit right now.

PROGRAMS: Usually an action, control or process based on a set of codings or understandings installed (usually) without prior consent or conscious knowledge.

PSYCHIC TONER EXERCISE: The strengthening of the basic anatomy to support a healthy Psychic Sensory anatomy for correct navigation and interpretation of current incoming energies.

REGULATOR CHAKRAS: These are Chakras that regulate the interpretation and flow of energies and govern their absorption rates; Chakras that govern the overall optimal maintenance and functionality of a given system.

REGULATOR: A device, authority or control to organize and manage the flow, rate or speed of a process.

SEALING / SEAL: Process of preventing inappropriate access or leakage at a particular place or junction. Assists in protection from escaping energy or particles (or Soul in case of 4½ Chakra).

SOUL NADI LINE: This is that part of the Hara Line that emerges from above the Soul Star to connect to the Soul's own personal Divine Source.

SOUL REGISTRATION: The process of aligning the healing on the various energetic levels with the Soul and Soul Body, in order for full integration in the total-ity of the being. This allows for healing to be fully 'anchored-in'.

SUPPORT: Any substance or method that assists to support the healing process or the clearing process in a way that causes no harm or further stress.

TESTED: When the word 'tested' appears, this is an indication or suggestion to use a pendulum, a muscle-testing technique (kinesiology) or some other form of identification and verification.

THE VOID: Usually the absence of Matter, though it can also be the pre-cursor to creation. It is a place of possibility and potential, for Light as well as for Dark.

TRACKED / TRACKING: This indicates that one is following the path of the issue along its timeline. Locating back to its original cause is essential to fully clear an issue, though there may also be other priority events along the timeline that may require some attention as well. An experienced and well-trained practitioner, kinesiologist or therapist should be able to handle this correctly and effectively.

TRANSDUCER: Device or structure that steps down incoming energies or frequencies into a useable form. May also act as storage unit for slower feed-through of this incoming energy. May be in the form of information, electrical charge, codes, broadcasts, waveforms, and a variety of other transmissions.

TROJAN: A set of detrimental codes or a devious offering that is hidden within or disguised by something acceptable, attractive or desirable.

Further Information

Questions and Contact Information

Please feel free to write to the Author with your success stories. Your questions are welcomed and every endeavour will be made to answer each one. This book has been compiled through long and personal journeying, personal experience whilst researching, and through teaching and practicing in consultancy. It also attempts to answer the needs of clients and energy workers. If there is anything more you wish to know about, then you are invited to contact me with your most burning questions as to the subject of this book or regarding energy, life, relationships, depression or self help, self individuation, self-identity, development or responsibility.

In return, your questions will be answered and when there are enough questions, a free copy of any resulting new book will be sent to you as a 'Thank You'!

To send your question or comments, email:

admin@myrasri.com

If you would like more information about this or any other book or meditation or to be kept informed on any further publications, you can email her direct, or register your email for newsletters at www.myrasri.com

Or follow Myra at her Amazon Author page:

http://www.amazon.com/author/myrasri

About the Author

Myra Sri was born in England and moved to Australia in her twenties with her then husband and two children. As a sensitive person, she maintained a spiritual leaning.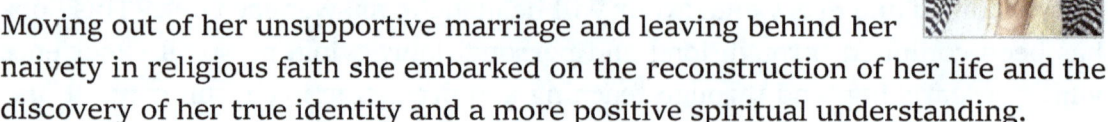

Moving out of her unsupportive marriage and leaving behind her naivety in religious faith she embarked on the reconstruction of her life and the discovery of her true identity and a more positive spiritual understanding.

Continuing to work in mainstream business, accounting and media industries, she found that connecting with other people further inspired her on her own self development journey. Assisting others on their journey led her to naturally gravitate towards the healing professions.

Undertaking extensive training and study she became an energy healing practitioner and Kinesiologist. Qualifying as an instructor in several modalities, she subsequently discovered where there was a lack of teaching and understanding and set out on her own research and discovery, resulting in unique advanced workshops which have been taught around Australia since the early 1990's. These continuing experiences encouraged her to develop her own innate skills and supported her in re-membering her healing skills and psychic abilities.

Running her own private practice since the late 80's, Myra remains an avid explorer and student of evolving ways to heal and support the Soul and spirit.

She wrote her first book in 2006. Myra continued taking trips to the UK for family connections until both her parents died. After further teaching in 2011, Myra returned to Australia, whereupon she was inspired and encouraged to document and write about her learn-ings and her discoveries of the new Chakras, including the energy shifts with oils and crystal healing.

She embarked on the *Energy Healing Secrets Series* in 2012 which fulfils part of her role as a Transformation Agent. The *Energy Healing Secrets Series* is presented to assist in self help, self healing and spiritual mastery.

With the advent of the New Era Energies and her discovery of the new Evolved Chakra systems, she has written and developed the *New Evolved Chakras Workshop series* which includes the new Earthing Chakras, the Psychic Body Chakras and the Signal-Survival Chakras.

The discovery of these extraordinary Chakras together with the clear indication of their relevance right now has been instrumental in Myra making the information available for release to general publication.

Myra provides a safe and attentive healing space for her clients and students, and works multi-dimensionally, enabling major energy and spiritual shifts. Her focus is on the Soul and spirit, and healing the Soul of trauma is a major mission.

Considered as a dependable resource for difficult or complicated situations, she has often been referred to as 'the Healer's Healer'.

Labelled by colleagues and peers as a Metaphysical Kinesiologist and a Transformation Agent, she is also gifted with an ability to work inter-dimensionally, thus enabling major personal energetic and spiritual shifts.

About Myra's Workshops

Some of Myra's workshops include:

> Past Life Training – Navigating Soul Journey and Genetic Issues and Karma Safely
>
> Spiritual Protection; HygienEthics[1] Series –Working With Energy, Living With Energy, Being Energy, Protection HygienEthics, HygienEthics for Therapists, Advanced HygienEthics
>
> Navigating Life in a Changing World
>
> Muscle Testing Basics
>
> Neuro Linguistic Kinesiology
>
> Crystal Workshops
>
> New Evolved Chakra Series - New Earthing Chakras, New Psychic Body and Chakras, New Signal-Survival Chakras

---

[1] *HygienEthics; The Ethics and Practices of Energetic and Spiritual Hygiene*

ENERGY HEALING SECRETS SERIES

Other Books available on Amazon. Some also available in paperback.

SECRETS BEYOND AROMATHERAPY

The beauty and power of Essential Oils has been known to us for thousands of years, from Ancient Indian healers to current day aromatherapists.

Few were aware of etheric Colour Codes of Essential Oils.

Until now!

Essential Oils, like the Chakra systems, have evolved and Come of Age.

Their abilities have expanded and they are now poised ready to assist us all as we work with and move fully into the new energies of this new Era.

Come on a journey into the astounding colours of oils; see how they interact with human senses and subtle body anatomy. Learn their impacts and the unseen implications with the Soul and incarnational aspects. Discover which Chakras respond best, and which energy system is most enhanced by their actions. You may be pleasantly surprised!

The basic etheric body colours of the human energy systems appeared to have undergone change. Even the Main Chakras are responding differently to colour and vibration. It would seem that no longer do most of us reflect (and often poorly at that) the basic opaque paint-box-type colours previously associated with the seven basic colours of the rainbow – some of us are now able to reflect more glorious and colourful hues and iridescences from and through the auric layers and chakras when balanced correctly.

Living in cities can prevent some of these new hues and their tints from shining within and without, as the electromagnetic smog and pollution can lower the frequencies to a paler and poorer version. In these times it is becoming more important to reconnect back to nature, the land or the sea, purer energies, higher vibrations and natural remedies whenever and wherever possible to sustain us. And the essential oils is are part of this remedy.

The humble oil along with knowledge of its inherent etheric colour codes and abilities will further enhance everyone's experience of the nature and the knowing that is held within each loving oil and hidden within the etheric world itself, and will further enhance and amplify all of your current benefits when used with the increased awareness.

Recognize the New Roles that these amazing gifts from our Planet are playing right now.

Explore the Etheric Colours of over Thirty Essential Oils. Learn their Secrets.

Find new and powerful ways of working with them.

Spend time with them. Let your choice of Oil reveal to you further hidden information to assist you with your client or with your own personal transformation.

Work with Essential Oils in ways you've never done before!

Amazon Reviews:

A treasure of energetic information

Thrilled with the content of this book and I have read almost every aromatherapy book there is

I wonder why this book is not used as a textbook

SECRETS BEHIND ENERGY FIELDS

When we have good health, we really do have a huge asset at the ready – there is no price to be placed on it as from our good health so many positive things can arise. When we are exhausted and tired through dealing with other peoples issues, emotions and energies, we are cheating ourselves of our true destiny and life journey.

Nobody lives as an entire isolated and energetic island to themselves. We are all social beings and part of life is social interaction of some kind or another. Which also means energetic interaction - the contact that takes place on those unseen levels, yet we can still feel their action and their impact.

When we don't know where our energy goes, when we work with others closely, when we are faced with emotional or traumatic scenes, when others think it is ok and acceptable to explode around us, when we think there must be something wrong with us because of what we continually encounter in our life, we need answers to what is happening, and what we can do about it!

Learning to navigate through life in energies that are less than positive or harmonious sometimes requires outside information or help. And all you really need to invest is some of your time and energy to become your own energy guru and healer.

Here is a collection of techniques, exercises and tools that are proven energy strengtheners. Selected from the many workshops I have taught on this topic are easy, effective solutions and understandings for anybody who is involved with other people and not coping as well as they could.

You can begin to reclaim your own identity and autonomy again, and easily recognise who and what has been affecting you with the easy to follow instructions and ideas.

Be successful and happy, protect your energy and let good health and good energy be your positive foundation.

Amazon Reviews

"Thanks to this eBook, I am teaching myself to rise above the conflict at work... these life skills are priceless!"

"This is an excellent, practical, down to earth book that is filled with simple techniques to get in touch with yourself, your own energy, what is affecting it and then how to do something about it."

"I found this book very informative and the techniques were simple and easy to follow. I would recommend it to anyone who does energy work."

SECRET TRUTHS – HEALTH and WELL-BEING

If you are doing everything "right" and yet there is something that cannot be explained that compromises your experience of life and vitality, you may well need to look deeper… look past symptoms, past the apparent, past expecting a pill to fix what you can do for yourself.

Exhaustion and tiredness can have several causes. Compromised health can often find us resorting to the local doctor or our health food store. Energetic and emotional impacts, toxicity or damage from others may need to be addressed and resolved separately ("*Secrets Behind Energy Fields*"). We are not just our body, we are not just our mind, we are not just our emotions. We are an amazing combination of all of these and more. The being is an amazing orchestration of matter and that unseen life-force; spirit. When one part is hurt, the other parts are affected.

Here in this book we look at important and often hidden contributors to compromised health and equilibrium as well as very real yet often hidden aspects of tiredness, exhaustion and depletion of energy. Many are not aware of simple things that one can fix for oneself. Nor how easy it can be to make a few mental or verbal changes for oneself that creates a positive impact on health outcomes.

If the nervous system is compromised by amalgam fillings, or lack of hydration, or unresolved issues, then results will be way short of what is possible. If the mind is blocked through lack of simple yet essential nutrients, and is not even aware of essential requirements for health, if a person cannot recognise when they have adrenal exhaustion and how their thoughts can feed into this, what chance does one have of full recovery?

If inflammation is causing pain in the body, what can one do about it?Here is a mix of experiential physical advice and of energetic and spiritual tips from a long-standing expert on body-mind-spirit issues, written to help those who wish to find answers to their problems or symptoms on the *physical level* themselves.

The NEW CRYSTAL CODES

Since the huge energy shifts of recent years, frequencies have been updated in many areas. The discovery of the new Evolved Chakras has demonstrated that we are all in a process of upgrade and re-alignment. This includes not only the human subtle bodies but also the energetic frequencies of oils and crystals.

This book contains clear instructions on How to Align your Evolved Crystal to the New Incoming Energies.

The author shares her knowledge on the new Crystal Codes and Ciphers, as well as how to read where your crystals energies are at and how to align them with the new Era frequencies.

You will not find this knowledge anywhere else.

This little book also has everything you need to identify the different functions and powers of Quartz Crystals and much, much more.

You will learn about how to connect to your crystal, how to care for it, code and program it and how to use it wisely.

You will find in these pages ideas that will inspire you to love and journey with your chosen gem.

You will also learn how to identify various types of crystals, some metaphysical properties, sets of crystals and learn the difference between an Isis crystal, a Record-Keeper, a Lemurian and much more...

Make the most of your willing crystal and harness its energies for the new energy shifts right now!

This is cutting edge information and the time is ripe to re-energise your crystal.

SECRETS TO SERENE SPACE

A new look at the Art of Space Clearing. Clear Negative Energies and Use Metaphysics to Change Your Space and Life. Become your own Guru. Learn the Art of Creating Sanctuary, within and without…

A home is a place to return to for safety, nurturing, rejuvenation and love. Does your home sanctuary nurture and support you? Does it fill you with pleasure and enjoyment?

Take a moment to look around your home… how does it reflect you? How does it feel to you? Are you able to revitalise and rejuvenate there whenever you need to? Does your home welcome you? If the answer is "No" and you are aware that you need to do something to change your space, and possibly yourself, then you will find lots of ideas and help in this book.

If you want to go deeper than just shifting surface stuff around, if you feel that there could be some old "nasties" lying around somewhere that you would like to shift, if you feel that you would like to get clearer within yourself as well as within your living space, then this is the book for you!

Decluttering may be needed. Or it could be that there are some old or negative energies to clear. What about the sense of being "spied" on? Learn about how to remove not only "nasties" but also learn what a Portal is and how to clear these, as well as Orbs and Thoughtforms. Discover not only how to Clear your place and enhance your home and life, but the crucial and essential step that must follow for true and lasting success in your Clearing.

Here in an easy to read book you will find how to create Sanctuary in your own personal space with time-proven tools. Decluttering is made easy. Imprints are explained and removal instructions are included together with further powerful techniques to incorporate into your ritual or chosen exercise to bring healing into the home.

This is a true self help book!

www.ingramcontent.com/pod-product-compliance
Lightning Source LLC
Chambersburg PA
CBHW060454300426
44113CB00016B/2587